CHARLES DICKENS:
LINGUISTIC INNOVATOR

Knud Sørensen

Charles Dickens:
Linguistic Innovator

Acta Jutlandica LXI
Humanistisk serie 58

ARKONA
Aarhus 1985

© 1985 by
ACTA JUTLANDICA
Det lærde Selskab
Aarhus Universitet
DK 8000 Aarhus C
Denmark

ISBN 87 7244 009 0

Tryk: Kannike Tryk, Århus

CONTENTS

1. Dickens's nineteenth-century reputation. 2. 'Shockingly revolutionary'. 3. Archaisms. 4. Nineteenth-century criticism. 5. The criticism partly warranted. 6. Dickens's world view. 7. Dickens on language. 8. Sustained linguistic comment. 9. Grammar and dictionary. 10. The textual problem.

1. Most neologisms unspectacular. 2. The *OED*. 3. Chronology. 4. The Supplement. 5. Admission and omission. 6. Striking omissions. 7. Dickensian archaisms. 8. Words last used by Dickens. 9. Contemporary writers' neologisms. 10. Dated and current words. 11. Arrangement of the material. 12. Idioms. 13. Colloquialisms, slang, and humorous terms. 14. Conversion. 15. Phrasal verbs. 16. Nominalizations. 17. Nouns in *-er*. 18. Nouns in *-ment*. 19. Nouns in *-ness*. 20. Adjectives in *-ed*: type *thief-dreaded*. 21. Adjectives in *-ed*: type *sedentary-pursuited*. 22. Adjectives in *-ing*: type *promise-breaking*. 23. Adjectives in *-ish*. 24. Adjectives in *-less*. 25. Adjectives in *-ous*. 26. Adjectives in *-y*. 27. The prefix *un-*. 28. Verbs in new constructions. 29. Adverbs. 30. Prepositions. 31. Interjections. 32. Latinisms. 33. Gallicisms. 34. Americanisms. 35.Theatre and circus terms. 36. Dickensian institutions. 37. Changed collocational range. 38. Pregnant senses. 39. Euphemism. 40. Beyond conventional semantics. 41. Animals, things, and people. 42. Animation. 43. From physical to non-physical. 44. Rare words and nonce-words. 45. Fanciful words. 46. Private and occasional. 47. Dickens's contribution assessed.

1. Existing patterns exploited. 2. Archaisms. 3. Premodification. 4. String-compounds. 5. Second mention condensed. 6. Articles and

determiners. 7. Countable and uncountable nouns. 8. Collective nouns. 9. *Person* and related matters. 10. *Every gum*. 11. *We* and *our*. 12. Non-pronominalization. 13. Adjectives reclassified. 14. The use of the present tense. 15. Finite verbs dispensed with. 16. The passive of phrasal verbs. 17. Inversion. 18. Emphasis. 19. Superlatives. 20. Keywords, variation, and tautology. 21. Syntactic support. 22. Doublets and triplets. 23. Sound effects. 24. Imagery. 25. Extended metaphor. 26. Contextual pressure. 27. Idioms varied. 28. Punning. 29. Textures of discord. 30. Common-sense expectations disappointed. 31. Some other unequal yokefellows. 32. Syllepsis. 33. Animism and automatism. 34. Articles of clothing. 35. Parts of the body. 36. Oblique subject. 37. The status of human beings reduced. 38. Summing up.

1. Realism vs. conventions. 2. Narrative modes. 3. The conventions. 4. Report. 5. Borrowing. 6. Direct speech and free direct speech. 7. Indirect speech. 8. Free indirect speech. 9. Alternation between narrative modes.

PREFACE

No apology should be needed for the approach adopted in this book if it is accepted that 'the art of the novel is linguistic, and [that] the language of fiction is as proper a study as the language of poetry' (Rachel Tricket in *The Modern Novel*, edited by G. Josipovici, 1976, p. 37). One of my aims has been to show that provided forbidding jargon is avoided, there need be no divorce between linguistics and the study of literature. I may perhaps be permitted to add that many of my students when exposed to a linguistic and stylistic analysis of Dickens's prose have told me that they found this approach refreshing and rewarding. But let the reader judge for himself.

I am very grateful to Professor K.J. Fielding for encouraging me to undertake this study and for giving me sound advice as the work progressed. I also wish to express my gratitude to the Danish Research Council for the financial support of this publication.

ABBREVIATIONS

Most of the quotations are taken from *The Oxford Illustrated Dickens* (21 volumes, 1947-1958); obvious misprints have been corrected (see I. 10). In order to save time for the reader who wants to check quotations, both chapter and page references are given. The following abbreviations are used:

AN	*American Notes* (1842)
BH	*Bleak House* (1852-1853)
BR	*Barnaby Rudge* (1841)
CB	*Christmas Books* (*A Christmas Carol*, 1843; *The Chimes*, 1844; *The Cricket on the Hearth*, 1845; *The Battle of Life*, 1846; *The Haunted Man*, 1848)
CS	*Christmas Stories* (1850-)
DC	*David Copperfield* (1849-1850)
DS	*Dombey and Son* (1847-1848)
ED	*The Mystery of Edwin Drood* (1870)
GE	*Great Expectations* (1860-1861)
HT	*Hard Times* (1854)
LD	*Little Dorrit* (1855-1857)
MC	*Martin Chuzzlewit* (1843-1844)
MH	*Master Humphrey's Clock* (1840-1841)
NN	*Nicholas Nickleby* (1838-1839)
OCS	*The Old Curiosity Shop* (1840-1841)
OMF	*Our Mutual Friend* (1864-1865)
OT	*Oliver Twist* (1837-1839)
PI	*Pictures from Italy* (1846)
PP	*Pickwick Papers* (1836-1837)
SB	*Sketches by Boz* (1833-1836)
TC	*A Tale of Two Cities* (1859)
UT	*The Uncommercial Traveller and Reprinted Pieces* (this volume contains works spanning the greater part of Dickens's career; where material, dates are given)

Other abbreviations used are

Fielding	*The Speeches of Charles Dickens*, edited by K.J. Fielding, Oxford 1960

HW	*The Uncollected Writings of CHARLES DICKENS. Household Words 1850-1859,* edited by Harry Stone, The Penguin Press 1969, I - II
MEG	O. Jespersen, *A Modern English Grammar* I - VII, 1909-1949
OED	*The Oxford English Dictionary* and its Supplement
Pilgr.	*The Pilgrim Edition of the Letters of Charles Dickens,* Volumes 1 - 5, 1965-1981
Visser	F. Th. Visser, *An Historical Syntax of the English Language* I - III, 1963-1973

Other sources that are drawn on occasionally are given with their full titles or with the abbreviations used in the *OED*.

CHAPTER I: INTRODUCTION

1. Dickens's nineteenth-century reputation. In the popular estimation Dickens's career is a brilliant success story: with the publication of *Pickwick Papers* he rose to meteoric fame, and ever since then he went from strength to strength, acclaimed by everybody. That is of course only a qualified truth; for while many of his readers found him delightful, there were not a few whom he offended. In Mrs Gaskell's *Cranford* (1853) we are given an amusing illustration of these different attitudes. The small town of Cranford is dominated by genteel ladies. When a newcomer, the 'brazen' Captain Brown, praises *Pickwick* to the skies, Miss Jenkyns, who is the local arbiter of literary taste, reacts by sending for Dr Johnson's *Rasselas*. To Captain Brown, Dr Johnson is 'pompous', to Miss Jenkyns, Mr Boz is 'vulgar', and the latter epithet should probably be taken to refer both to manner and to matter: Dickens describes lower-class people, and he does it in language that abounds in colloquialisms and slangy expressions.

When nineteenth-century critics read Dickens, they were not mainly concerned with his language. They focussed on other aspects of his fiction: plot, character-delineation, and his moral and social message. Those of his critics who did make pronouncements on Dickens's style tended to disagree, the majority of them being hostile.[1] One of his harshest critics was Anthony Trollope: 'Of Dickens's style it is impossible to speak in praise. It is jerky, ungrammatical, and created by himself in defiance of rules...'[2] From among the positive critics we may select an anonymous writer who stated in 1870, just after Dickens had died:

As to his literary style, that was his own - striking, brilliant, not seldom odd, sometimes awkward, yet even then with its own sort of tact. He was artful and skilful, but never attained, and never seems to have sought to attain, the kind of art which conceals itself; a certain care and elaboration were never absent; he took his aim carefully (he was in dress and in every other respect the opposite of a negligent man) and usually hit the mark. (*Fraser's Magazine,* July 1870; quoted from *DICKENS. The Critical Heritage,* edited by Philip Collins, London 1971, pp. 527f.).

Here we have two very different verdicts which agree, however, in stressing that Dickens's style was his own. Such statements show that some of his readers were alive to his stylistic unconventionality though they did not usually go into much detail about it.

2. *'Shockingly revolutionary'.* Some twentieth-century scholars have maintained that Dickens was linguistically ahead of his time. This is done very emphatically by George H. Ford: 'What we have lost is a sense of how shockingly revolutionary Dickens' prose seemed to his contemporaries.'[3] And Harry Stone makes the following statement in an article dealing with Dickens and interior monologue: 'It is only after reading Dickens's contemporaries that one is able to understand how fresh and impressive his experiments were.'[4] I subscribe to such statements, and I believe that there is a case for maintaining that Dickens was linguistically ahead of his day. Up till now there has been limited documentation of the innovative aspects of Dickens's prose.[5] This book presents the evidence I have found.

It is perhaps not so strange that Dickens's innovations in language should until recently have gone comparatively unnoticed, for in fact many — if not most — of the constructions, idioms, lexical items, and special uses of words that he introduced are current today, and hence unobtrusive. If we want to form an idea of the areas in which Dickens's nineteenth-century readers found his language 'shockingly revolutionary', we must make use of a 'reconstructive stylistics':[6] we must try to ascertain the state of the language before Dickens made his contribution and then note the areas in which he was an innovator. The ideal reconstruction would be a formidable task that a single person could hardly cope with; it would rest on a thorough familiarity with the style of all Dickens's predecessors and contemporaries. There are, however, other approaches that can yield some results: we can consult historical grammars like those of Jespersen and Visser; we can draw on the wealth of information available in the *OED* (I have not worked my way systematically through it, but have followed up hunches and have been much helped by serendipity); we can examine the pronouncements on Dickens's style that were made by nineteenth-century critics, particularly the hostile dicta, taking them as useful pointers to what was disapproved of; and finally we have Dickens's own comments on language. The *OED* will come up for discussion in Chapter II, and Chapter III will contain a number of references to historical grammars. In sections 4 and 5 of the present chapter we shall glance at the criticisms made by some nineteenth-century reviewers, and sections 7 - 9 will discuss Dickens's metalinguistic comments.

3. *Archaisms.* As was pointed out above, many of Dickens's neologisms are unspectacular since they have become part and parcel of contemporary English. There are, however, some linguistic features of Dickens's prose that appear odd to twentieth-century readers, namely his archaisms. If our aim is to reconstruct the English language as it was

when Dickens began to write, it becomes part of our task to pinpoint these archaisms. Now we may speak of 'archaism' from the point of view of twentieth-century English, but here a distinction has to be made: on the one hand we note in Dickens's language some elements that were archaic even in his own day; they will be discussed in II.7 and III.2. On the other hand there occurs language that was not archaic in Dickens's day, but which has become so since then. It must be emphasized that although this stratum of language strikes twentieth-century readers as being outdated, it was current nineteenth-century usage and would therefore not have surprised Dickens's contemporaries. Let us glance briefly at some representative examples.

As far as **spelling** is concerned, there are only minor deviations from the contemporary standard; Dickens occasionally writes *controul, secresy, villanous,* and *expence* (alternating with *expense*).

Among **morphological** peculiarities it may be noted that some words have negative *un-* where modern English has *in-*: *unfrequently* (e.g. *NN* 7 81), *unpolite* (e.g. *PP* 3 42), *undefinable* (e.g. *BH* 31 429), and preterit forms like *rung* (e.g. *SB* 225), *shrunk* (e.g. *SB* 127), *spake* (e.g. *OMF* III 2 433), and *sung* (e.g. *SB* 253).

In **syntax** there are a number of points that call for comment. The definite article may appear before a transitive gerund, as in 'the inducing Mr. Swiveller to declare himself' (*OCS* 8 65). The pronoun *neither* sometimes refers to three: 'neither of the three' (*BR* 56 426). The sequence *they who* may correspond to modern *those who*: 'They who knew the Maypole story...' (*BR* 5 41). A personal pronoun may be used with a qualifying prepositional phrase: 'both ... regarded him of the flapped hat no less attentively' (*BR* 1 5). A personal pronoun may be found after the imperative *do*: 'Do you stay here' (*BR* 5 42). When a noun is qualified by two adjectives, the second adjective may be postposed without the prop-word *one*: 'Wegg was a knotty man, and a close-grained' (*OMF* I 5 45).

In verbal syntax it is noteworthy that the perfect tense of intransitive verbs is sometimes formed with *be* as an auxiliary: 'She is come at last' (*NN* 49 648), and that *do* as an auxiliary is occasionally dispensed with where it would be obligatory today: 'How came it there?' (*BR* 3 27); 'She saw it not' (*DS* 45 626). The subjunctive occurs with much greater frequency in nineteenth-century English than today and is particularly striking in main clauses: 'It were too much to pretend that...' (*OMF* III 8 504) and in subordinate concessive and conditional clauses: 'a wall, that never will be brown, though it bake for centuries' (*PI* 272); 'If he ever steal forth...' (*BH* 10 127). There is sometimes inversion in sentence-types where it is ruled out today: 'Here, too, would they tell old legends...' (*SB* 65).

Dickens employs a few **idioms** that are no longer current, for instance: 'they ... cannot *by possibility* be anything else' (*BR* 1 10); 'I found the white down falling *fast and thick*' (*CS* 100; today it is normally *thick and fast*, which also occurs in Dickens). We use the preposition *from* in the set phrase 'from a — point of view', but Dickens has *in*: 'in a worldly point of view' (*OMF* IV 5 676).

In **lexis** we may note *abroad* for 'outside': 'Mr. Willet ... looked abroad' (*BR* 1 3); *combination* for 'conspiracy' (e.g. *NN* 2 14); *counting-house* for 'office' (e.g. *OMF* II 5 276); *(foot-)passenger* for 'pedestrian' (e.g. *MC* 46 702); *mother-in-law* for 'stepmother' (e.g. *PP* 33 454); *warehouse* for 'shop' (e.g. *MC* 46 698); and *carry* for 'conduct' or 'escort' as in 'I was carried thither by an official gentleman' (*AN* 8 123).

4. Nineteenth-century criticism. In 1846 the Professor of Rhetoric and Belles Lettres at Edinburgh, W.E. Aytoun, published an article, 'Advice to an Intending Serialist'[7], addressed to a fictitious author, Smith, but in actual fact a satirical outburst against Dickens. About grammar and syntax he had this to say:

You have, and I think most wisely, undertaken to frame a new code of grammar and of construction for yourself; and the light and airy effect of this happy innovation is conspicuous not only in every page but in almost every sentence of your work. There is no slipslop here — only a fine, manly disregard of syntax.

Aytoun does not specify his criticism, nor do most other nineteenth-century critics. A number of them voice general dissatisfaction with Dickens's imagery; one speaks of 'strained, and whimsical, and far-fetched images and comparisons'[8]; another employs very similar epithets: 'the most exaggerated similes and far-fetched metaphors'.[9] Critics agree in finding Dickens's style striking owing to his tendency to bestow elaborate description on commonplace things and incidents, and this tendency may be either positively or negatively assessed:

Mr Dickens' style is especially the graphic and humorous, by means of which he continually exhibits the most trifling and commonplace things in a new and amusing light. (R.H. Horne in *The New Spirit of the Age*, 1844; quoted from *The Critical Heritage*, p. 201).

Mr. Dickens's writings are the apotheosis of what has been called newspaper English. He makes points everywhere, gives unfamiliar names to the commonest objects, and lavishes a marvellous quantity of language on the most ordinary incidents. (Unsigned article in the *Saturday Review*, 1858; quoted from *The Critical Heritage*, p. 385).

14

But if Dickens is charged with raising trivia to an august level, this is half way to accusing him of having a tendency to lose himself in mere verbiage, and this is the point that is made in the following quotation:

in Mr Dickens's sentences there is a leafiness, a tendency to words and images, for their own sake... (David Masson in the *North British Review*, 1851; quoted from *The Critical Heritage,* p. 250).

Occasionally, specific criticisms are voiced. Thus one reviewer charges Dickens with offending 'the shade of Lindley Murray with such barbarisms as "it had not been painted or papered, hadn't Todgers's", and he also expresses disapproval of Dickensian collocations like '*impracticable* nightcaps, *impossible* tables, and *exploded* chests of drawers, *mad* closets, *inscrutable* harpsichords, *undeniable* chins...'[10] Another reviewer criticizes the use of *mutual* in 'mutual friend'.[11]

In 1843 Dickens's friend Cornelius C. Felton published a lengthy article in the *North American Review*,[12] ostensibly a notice of *American Notes for General Circulation*, but actually an assessment of the works Dickens had published till then. High praise is bestowed on both content and form. Dickens's style has 'great originality and power' (p. 222), and 'His command over the English language, in its most native and idiomatic parts, is really marvellous' (p. 223). Felton adds, however, that Dickens's style is marred by 'several solecisms', though they do not 'detract materially from its singular purity and grace' (p. 224). Only two concrete solecisms are adduced. The first is the use of *directly* in the sense of 'as soon as', which is said to appear over a thousand times in Dickens's works. The *OED* informs us that this use of *directly* dates back to 1795, and labels it 'colloquial'. Felton's second grievance concerns 'the new-fangled and most uncouth solecism, "is being done", for the good old English idiomatic expression "is doing"' [as in 'while some pretty severe bruises ... were being rubbed with oil' — *NN* 33 420]. This progressive passive construction is not all that new-fangled, however: it began to be common in colloquial use towards the end of the eighteenth century, but many people objected to it, and it took about a hundred years for it to become fully established.[13] In hindsight Felton's criticisms appear to be the strictures of a linguistically conservative reader — Felton was a classical scholar — since his only specific grievances concern usage that was not new when Dickens began to write.

5. The criticism partly warranted. The samples of criticism quoted above are thus levelled against faulty syntax, exaggerated imagery, odd collocations, and lapses into verbiage. To some extent this criticism is understandable if we try to reconstruct the pre-Dickensian state of English. It is easiest to do this for the vocabulary of English. Dickens introduced more than a thousand neologisms, and some of them, particularly the unorthodox ones, were bound to offend conservative readers. As to syntax, he was not an innovator in the same sense as for vocabulary, but in several respects he was highly unconventional, stretching existing syntactic patterns to bursting-point; see, for instance, Chapter III for a discussion of his reclassification of nouns and adjectives, his packed premodified constructions, and his striking use of the tenses. He undoubtedly had a penchant for exaggerated imagery and odd collocations which was partly due to the special way in which he viewed the world; on this see the following section. And Dickens cannot wholly be absolved from the charge of occasionally lapsing into verbiage. There do occur passages in which it is 'a tendency to words and images, for their own sake' that appears to determine his choice of words. It is relevant in this connexion to mention a number of points: his intensive style, which sometimes makes use of synonyms that seem to have no other function than a rhetorical one; his cultivation of the phonetic aspect of language, often manifested in his poorer jokes and puns; and those many cases in which his choice of words appears to be dictated by contextual pressure.

6. Dickens's world view. It is generally recognized today that Dickens's characteristic style is a reflection of his artistic vision of the world, a vision that entails the flouting of linguistic conventions. This was realized — or at least glimpsed — by some critics during his lifetime, but it was perhaps only after his death that it was fully understood. One critic said:

He saw all from a child's point of view — strange, odd, queer, puzzling. He confused men and things, animated scenery and furniture with human souls... (Robert Buchanan in *St Paul's Magazine*, 1872; quoted from *The Critical Heritage*, p. 579).

Today we would hardly find it fair to Dickens to speak of his 'confusing' men and things. The same basic point has been given more precise and adequate definition by Dorothy Van Ghent:

The course of things demonically possessed is to imitate the human, while the course of human possession is to imitate the inhuman. This transposition of attributes, producing a world like that of ballet, is the principle of relationship between things and people in the novels of Dickens. The masks, the stances, and the shock-tempo are comic. The style which they have for their perspective is the style of a world undergoing spiritual transformation. ('The Dickens World: A View from Todgers's'; originally in *The Sewanee Review*, 1950, pp. 419-438; reprinted in *DICKENS. A Collection of Critical Essays*, edited by M. Price, 1967, p. 24).

Examples of this 'transposition of attributes' will be given in II. 40ff. and in III. 33ff.

7. Dickens on language. Dickens is a very language-conscious writer who most of the time knows precisely what he is doing with his medium. Scattered all over his works there are a great many comments that draw our attention to words and expressions used by himself and by his characters. This is something that will come up for repeated discussion in the following chapters, but we may touch briefly on it here.

Sometimes Dickens's minute attention to descriptive detail makes him add a comment that is intended to prevent misunderstanding; in *Great Expectations* we hear of 'a house with a wooden front and three stories of bow-window (not bay-window, which is another thing)' (46 354). If he makes use of a slang expression, we find him putting it in inverted commas and appending an apologetic remark:

Sticky old Saints, with ... such coats of varnish that every holy personage served for a fly-trap, and became what is now called in the vulgar tongue a 'catch-'em-alive-o'. (*LD* I 16 193).

Yet it 'crops up' — as our slang goes — rather frequently ... (*OMF* II 9 327).

The introduction of colloquial neologisms lends zest and authenticity to the narrative, but from time to time Dickens must have realized that the price to be paid for the use of such words was the addition of a familiar paraphrase, as we see below:

'Too much crumb, you know,' said Mr. Bailey; 'too fat, Poll.' (*MC* 29 460).

'My misfortunes all began in wagging, Sir; but what could I do, exceptin' wag? ' — 'Excepting what? ' said Mr. Carker. — 'Wag, Sir. Wagging from school.' — 'Do you mean pretending to go there, and not going? ' said Mr. Carker. — 'Yes, Sir, that's wagging, Sir.' (*DS* 22 305).

Inverted commas may also be used when a neologism that is not of a slangy character is introduced. The first time *casualty ward* occurs (*SB* 242), it is in inverted commas, but not the second time (*PP* 32 438). This different treatment may well be accidental, however, since there is no consistency in Dickens's use of inverted commas; compare his vacillating practice with indirect speech (IV.6). Inverted commas further have the function of enabling the writer to comment, whether ironically or not, on the usage of his characters:

The waiters withdrew to 'clear away', or in other words, to appropriate to their own private use and emolument whatever remnants of the eatables and drinkables they could contrive to lay their hands on.(*PP* 7 93).

the poor soul ... sat down in a corner, and had what she termed 'a real good cry'. (*NN* 11 129).

There are many other references to the idiosyncrasies of Dickens's characters; here we have him on Miss Miggs, Mrs. Pipchin, and Miss Pross:

Miss Miggs, having undone her mistress, as she phrased it (which means, assisted to undress her), ... withdrew to her own apartment ... (*BR* 9 69).

'Mrs. Pipchin,' said Mr. Dombey, 'how do you do? '
'Thank you, sir,' said Mrs. Pipchin, 'I am pretty well, considering.'
  Mrs. Pipchin always used that form of words. It meant, considering her virtues, sacrifices, and so forth. (*DS* 11 138).

'Do dozens come for that purpose? '
'Hundreds,' said Miss Pross. — It was characteristic of this lady (as of some other people before her time and since) that whenever her original proposition was questioned, she exaggerated it. (*TC* II 6 89).

A favourite butt of Dickens's satire is linguistic pretentiousness. In *Pickwick Papers* we are introduced to grand Captain Boldwig, whose house is 'a villa' and whose land is 'grounds' (19 257). In *The Old Curiosity Shop* Mr. Swiveller invariably speaks of his single room as 'his rooms, his lodgings, or his chambers: conveying to his hearers a notion of indefinite space, and leaving their imaginations to wander through long suites of lofty halls' (7 53). In *Sketches by Boz* there occurs a reference to divided usage: 'The Miss Crumptons, or to quote the authority on the garden-gate of Minerva House, Hammersmith, "The Misses Crumpton"' (323). This is a discreet dig at gentility, which becomes more explicit in one of Dickens's letters: 'Pray convey my best regards ... to ... the Miss Powers — I can't say "the Misses Power", for it looks so like the blue board at the Gate of a Ladies' Seminary' (*Pilgr.* 3 402, 1842). The *OED* observes that the form *the Misses Smith* is regarded as 'grammatically the more proper' (*Miss* sb.[2], 2.); but it is obvious that Dickens found this form stilted.[14]

Dickens's playfulness comes out in a passage that describes Fanny Dorrit's wedding preparations:

The preparation consisted in the despatch of her maid to Paris ... for the purchase of that outfit for a bride on which it would be extremely low, in the present narrative, to bestow an English name, but to which (on a vulgar principle it observes of adhering to the language in which it professes to be written) it declines to give a French one. (*LD* II 15 608).

Here he is pretending to be in a cleft stick: on the one hand, if his description is to be stylistically appropriate to such a fashionable event, he cannot use a low English expression (like *kit*?); on the other hand, adopting a mock purist attitude, he will have no truck with the French loan-word *trousseau*. The word *wardrobe* is employed in the immediate sequel, so that Dickens's formulation is no more than an ironical comment on Fanny's wish to play a social role that is not natural to her.

Some Dickensian characters react against what they consider low or colloquial language. When Fanny Dorrit says that her uncle has 'tumbled over the subject', Mrs. General suggests that 'inadvertently lighted upon, or accidentally referred to' would be preferable expressions (*LD* II 5 482). In *Our Mutual Friend* young George Sampson is unfortunate enough to use the expression *go it!* to Lavinia, which makes her mother exclaim: 'What you may mean ... by your omnibus-driving expressions, I cannot pretend to imagine' (IV 16 805). Mrs. Wilfer is sniffy; on the other hand Kate Nickleby is over-modest and afraid of appearing to be proud, which is why she corrects herself: 'Reduced — I should say poor people' (*NN* 18 218); for the word *reduced* might carry a connotation of former grandeur that would perhaps not be acceptable to Kate's interlocutor Miss Knag.

Some of the perverted uses to which language is put by preachers and politicians are also satirized. Take the Rev. Mr. Chadband in *Bleak House*. Although he only appears a few times in the novel, his kind of oratory is unforgettable. In the first place he makes excessive use of repetition and variation. Addressing the crossing-sweeper Jo he says: 'My young friend, you are to us a pearl, you are to us a diamond, you are to us a gem, you are to us a jewel.' (19 269) And being well grounded in stock rhetorical devices, he goes on to inform Jo in the alliterative mode that he is not 'a stick, or a staff, or a stock, or a stone, or a post, or a pillar' (*ibid.*). Another prominent characteristic of his longwinded style is his peculiar technique of asking fatuous questions and answering them himself, one answer automatically leading to the next question:

My friends ..., what is this which we now behold as being spread before us? Refreshment. Do we need refreshment then, my friends? We do. And why do we need refreshment, my friends? Because we are but mortal, because we are but sinful, because we are but of the earth, because we are not of the air. (19 263).

Another of Dickens's pet aversions is political jargon. In *Sketches by Boz* he refers to 'the celebrated negative style adopted by great speakers', exemplifying it in his account of the election for beadle:

The captain replied in a similar parliamentary style. He would not say, he was astonished at the speech they had just heard; he would not say, he was disgusted (cheers). He would not retort the epithets which had been hurled against him (renewed cheering); he would not allude to men once in office, but now happily out of it, who had mismanaged the workhouse, ground the paupers, diluted the beer... (22).

The technical term for this is *occupatio*, a way of eating one's cake and having it too. In its lack of logic it is related to the wholly nonsensical use of language, as when a speaker eats his words by asserting that he has used a term 'in its Pickwickian sense' (*PP* 1 5, where *Pickwickian* has its modern parallel in the adjective *inoperative* that acquired notoriety during the Watergate scandal[15]). There is after all less camouflage about one of Mrs. Wilfer's formulations:

'I was about to say,' pursued Mrs. Wilfer, who clearly had not had the faintest idea of saying anything more: 'that when I use the term attractions, I do so with the qualification that I do not mean it in any way whatever.' (*OMF* I 16 207).

8. Sustained linguistic comment. Most of the examples we have considered above contain brief and indirect metalinguistic comment. But occasionally Dickens launches into regular little disquisitions which reveal him as an acute observer of linguistic matters. In *Little Dorrit* he makes what we would today call psycholinguistic comments on the layman's view of language teaching and learning, giving an amusing description of the behaviour of the inhabitants of Bleeding Heart Yard towards an Italian who only has a smattering of English, but who is struggling to learn it:

They spoke to him in very loud voices as if he were stone deaf. They constructed sentences, by way of teaching him the language in its purity, such as were addressed by the savages to Captain Cook, or by Friday to Robinson Crusoe. Mrs. Plornish was particularly ingenious in this art; and attained so much celebrity for saying 'Me ope you leg well soon', that it was considered in the Yard, but a very short remove indeed from speaking Italian. (I 25 303).

In *Nicholas Nickleby* the linguistic behaviour of the voluble Miss Knag gives rise to the following authorial aside:

Here Miss Knag paused to take breath, and while she pauses it may be observed —

not that she was marvellously loquacious and marvellously deferential to Madame Mantilini, since these are facts which require no comment; but that every now and then, she was accustomed, in the torrent of her discourse, to introduce a loud, shrill, clear, 'hem!' the import and meaning of which, was variously interpreted by her acquaintance; some holding that Miss Knag dealt in exaggeration, and introduced that monosyllable, when any fresh invention was in course of coinage in her brain; others, that when she wanted a word, she threw it in to gain time, and prevent anybody else from striking into the conversation. (17 210).

In sociolinguistic terminology Miss Knag is a faulty interactant who does not accept the rule of 'turn-taking' in conversation.

One of the most fascinating of the many idiolects that Dickens created is that used by Mr. Micawber, and it is the latter's 'formal piling up of words' that inspires Dickens to make the following remarks about grandiloquence and its psychological function:

In the taking of legal oaths ... deponents seem to enjoy themselves mightily when they come to several good words in succession, for the expression of one idea; as, that they utterly detest, abominate, and abjure, or so forth; and the old anathemas were made relishing on the same principle. We talk about the tyranny of words, but we like to tyrannise over them too; we are fond of having a large superfluous establishment of words to wait upon us on great occasions; we think it looks important, and sounds well ... (*DC* 52 754).

It is ironical that although Dickens heeds his own warning most of the time, he himself reveals a tendency to use several good words in succession for the expression of one idea (cf. III.20ff.), and he also has a penchant for Latinate vocabulary (cf. II.32).

Finally we may look at a very instructive passage in *Pickwick Papers* that provides us with valuable information about a special use of the phrase *never mind* at least in nineteenth-century English:

'Never mind, sir,' replied Mr. Magnus, striding up and down the room. 'Never mind.'
There must be something very comprehensive in this phrase of 'Never mind', for we do not recollect to have ever witnessed a quarrel in the street, at a theatre, public room, or elsewhere, in which it has not been the standard reply to all belligerent inquiries. 'Do you call yourself a gentleman, sir?' — 'Never mind, sir.' 'Did I offer to say anything to the young woman, sir?' — 'Never mind, sir.' 'Do you want your head knocked up against that wall, sir?' — 'Never mind, sir.' It is observable, too, that there would appear to be some hidden taunt in this universal 'Never mind', which rouses more indignation in the bosom of the individual addressed, than the most lavish abuse could possibly awaken. (*PP* 24 326).

9. Grammar and dictionary. Some of Dickens's statements about language may have been inspired by grammar and dictionary, and in a few cases it is possible to trace his probable sources. In *Dombey and Son* there occurs the following passage:

'... I'll introduce the party.'
 Running down-stairs ... Miss Tox got the party out of the hackney-coach, and soon returned with it under convoy.
 It then appeared that she had used the word, not in its legal or business acceptation, when it merely expresses an individual, but as a noun of multitude, or signifying many... (2 13).

This sounds like a grammatical definition, and in fact there is exactly the same formulation to be found on p. 94 of Lindley Murray's *English Grammar* (first published 1795, but there were several later editions): 'a noun of multitude, or signifying many'. Similarly, in *Sketches by Boz* a small boy who is being catechized about verbs regurgitates Murray's definition: 'A verb is a word which signifies to be, to do, or to suffer; as, I am — I rule — I am ruled...' (*SB* 319; this formulation is taken from Murray, p. 37). Elsewhere a vulgar speaker is said to express herself 'with a supreme contempt for the memory of Lindley Murray' (*SB* 299); there are other references to this grammarian, and it may be assumed that Dickens learnt his own grammar from an edition of Murray.
 Another passage from *Dombey and Son* suggests Dickens's indebtedness to a dictionary:

the smallest boy but one ... immediately began swarming upstairs after her — if that word of doubtful etymology be admissible — on his arms and legs ... (2 20).

The information about *swarm* is correct: the verb is of unknown origin. Neither Johnson's dictionary nor that of Charles Richardson, *A New Dictionary of the English Language* (1836-1837), contains any relevant information; but if we turn to John Walker's *Pronouncing Dictionary*, edited in 1836 by B.H. Smart, we may be on the right track. I have seen the fifth edition of 1857, which has the following comment on the word: 'for the sense of to climb a tree by embracing it with the arms and legs, there seems to be little authority'. Walker's dictionary was in Dickens's library at his death.[16]

 10. The textual problem. As mentioned, most of the quotations come from *The Oxford Illustrated Dickens.* This edition has been chosen because it is easily accessible, but it should be stressed that it is not fully reliable, being disfigured by misprints and corruptions. Some of these are easily recognizable as such: 'he bowed abstractly' (*PP* 31 429, for *abstractedly*); 'He felt silent' (*LD* II 5 480, for *fell*); 'the condition *in* which I had been *in*' (*GE* 54 412). Others are insidious. Thus there occurs the following passage in the Oxford edition of *The Old Curiosity Shop*:

Perhaps not one of the imprisoned souls had been able quite to separate itself in living thought from its old companion. (52 389).

Here *imprisoned* is a corruption of *unprisoned* 'released from prison', which according to the *OED* is a Dickensian neologism; in this case I have rejected the reading of the Oxford edition. A scholarly edition of the novels is in course of publication: the Clarendon Dickens (1967-), which establishes a critical text free from corruptions. Up till now five novels have been published: *Oliver Twist, Edwin Drood, Dombey and Son, Little Dorrit,* and *David Copperfield.*

We are in a better position as far as the letters are concerned: they are being published in the scholarly Pilgrim edition; so far five volumes have appeared, the last one covering the period 1847-1849. It will be a long time, however, before the entire Dickensian corpus becomes available in reliable editions. Meanwhile I can only hope that textual corruption has not affected the results of the present study.

CHAPTER II: VOCABULARY

1. Most neologisms unspectacular. At the outset it should be pointed out that when the expression 'Dickensian neologism' is employed, it is understood in a wide sense, comprising any kind of formal, semantic, or constructional innovation. Some of the innovations — but probably the minority — call attention to themselves even today: words and expressions like *to flummox, jog-trotty, a doormat* 'a despised passive person', and *to corkscrew one's way* come to mind. But most of the neologisms seem quite ordinary and unspectacular to the contemporary reader, though they appear for the first time in Dickens's writings; this is true of items like *abolitionist* in its general sense, of *matter-of-course* employed attributively, of compounds like *allotment garden* and *casualty ward*, of idioms like *an acquired taste* and *on the cards*, and of many others. These are all current today; but if it turns out that they were first used by Dickens, one can hardly escape the conclusion that cumulatively they must have produced an impression of freshness and novelty on nineteenth-century readers — a novelty that appears to have offended some of them.

2. The OED. The present analysis of Dickens's vocabulary could not have been undertaken without the *OED* and its Supplement. I have followed the classifications and the orthographic forms used by the *OED*. This means, for instance, that the form *kye-bosk* used by Dickens is listed under *kibosh* , and that the form *nev(v)y*, employed to suggest a substandard pronunciation of *nephew*, is given a separate entry.

The *OED* is an invaluable aid; and yet it must be recognized that it has its shortcomings and imperfections. The following remarks are made in no carping spirit, but in grateful acknowledgement of the wealth of information that can be culled from the pages of the Dictionary; at the same time it is necessary to realize its limitations if we are to assess properly the results that may be obtained by using it.

It is obvious that the editor, James Murray, held strong views on the criteria for admitting or omitting words. He fully agreed with the founders of the Philological Society's Dictionary in their statement (*c* 1860) that 'the literary merit or demerit of any particular writer, like the comparative elegance or inelegance of any given word, is a subject upon which the Lexicographer is bound to be almost indifferent'.[1] But criteria and axioms are one thing; another thing is how they worked out where many people had to co-operate. It also appears from the Murray bio-graphy that his associates did not always agree with him. Thus the sub-editor Henry Huck Gibbs, we are told, took a more rigid line about the admission of words, 'because his personal judgement was influenced by his literary prejudices'. [2] This sort of disagreement was bound to lead to some measure of inconsistency (cf. section 5).

3. Chronology. If one wishes to ascertain the extent to which Dickens is a lexical innovator, one naturally turns to the chronological infor-mation provided by the *OED*. Before long, however, one will find that in a great many cases the first appearances indicated by the *OED* can be antedated.

Though it is obvious that Dickens is a frequently quoted author, it has sometimes been overlooked that the first appearance of a word or phrase is in a Dickensian work; thus the idiom *rolled into one* is said by the *OED* to appear for the first time in 1862 in a book by Mrs Riddel (*roll* v.[1] , 8. *fig.*); it is used, however, in *The Old Curiosity Shop*: 'But, not fifty single gentlemen rolled into one could have helped poor Kit...' (60 452). At other times a word that is said to occur first in one Dickensian work actually makes its appearance in an earlier work of his; thus the first use of *mahogany* in the sense of 'a table, esp. a dining-table' (*OED* 3. *colloq.*) is stated to be in *The Old Curiosity Shop* (66 500), while it can be found as early as *Pickwick Papers*: 'the only other man visible above the mahogany' (49 683). The word *follower*, employed to refer to 'a man who courts a maidservant; esp. one who calls at the house to see her' (2.d. *colloq.*) is said to appear first in *Nicholas Nickleby*; I had found an earlier example in *Sketches by Boz* (112), when I came across the following observation: 'The *Gentleman's Magazine* (lix (1789), iv.) for 1789 exemplifies the word *Follower* in the sense of 'lover' about fifty years before the quotation from Dickens which O.E.D. gives as its first illustration...'[3] Very occasionally one may note another type of chronological oversight, as when the first quotation given to illustrate *angularly* (3. Of personal appearance) is from Poe 1846, the second from *Barnaby Rudge* 1849 (mistakenly for 184*1*).

4. The Supplement. So far I have been discussing the main body of the Dictionary, but we also have to consider briefly its supplementary volumes: *Supplement and Bibliography*, 1933; *Volume I, A—G*, 1972; *Volume II, H—N*, 1976; and *Volume III, O—Scz*, 1982. I have formed a rough idea of the extent of the revisions contained in the Supplement from the circumstance that when the third volume came out, I had to scrap about ten per cent of my candidates for first appearance in Dickens, but on the other hand I also spotted fresh examples of Dickensian neologisms documented in this volume. There are some oversights even in the supplementary volumes, and the last volume is not yet available. The lesson to be drawn from all this is that we should not entertain blind faith in the chronological information provided by the *OED*. But when this has been said, it seems reasonable to subscribe to the observation made by John Algeo: 'it is likely in most cases that the earliest date given by the OED is close to the initial appearance of the word in English'.[4]

5. Admission and omission. A regular user of the *OED* is bound to come up against another major problem, viz. the fact that not all words are admitted. In most cases this fact relates to the status of words. The bulk of lexical items are implicitly considered 'normal' and are accordingly included in the *OED* without comment. Then there are the minority categories, either *rare* words or *nonce-words* ('Words apparently employed only *for the nonce*', vol. I, p. xxx). But what about words that are not included in the Dictionary? It would be unrealistic to expect the lexicographer to be fully consistent, and no doubt some words have been left out through an oversight. In *Bleak House* there is a reference to a lady 'being *unproducible*' (25 356). This adjective is not in the *OED*, but if we look up the rare adjective *improducible,* we note that it is partly defined by *unproducible.* Although there is an observation in the *OED* about the impossibility of listing all forms (*un-*, prefix[1], 6.), it would perhaps have been reasonable to expect the Dictionary to list a form that is used elsewhere for definition. It is also a bit strange to find the form *ization* included ('He had no favourite ization that he knew of', *OMF* I 11 140), but not the form *ation* ('the whole of my right side has been benumbed, going on with your master about combustion, and calcination, and calorification, and I may say every kind of ation that could drive a poor invalid distracted',*HT* I 8 54). Similarly, the Dickensian coinage *cellarous*, used to describe the smell of a cellar (*LD* I 20 236), is included, but not the synonymous adjective *cellary* (*OMF* I 7 78). But after all, these are perhaps not very striking instances of inconsistency, nor is it particularly surprising to note that a special Dickensian use of the noun *accident* is left unrecorded. In *Pickwick Papers* a flippant young medical student remarks: 'Rather a good accident brought into the casualty ward.' (32 438), and in *Little Dorrit* an educated speaker asks: 'An accident going to the Hospital?' (I 13 162; this semantic extension corresponds to the one observable in other neologisms like *arrival* and *fraud* (section 40)). It is clear that in both cases the word denotes 'the victim of an accident'. If this use of the word is unattested in the *OED* (and in any other dictionary that I know of), it is perhaps because it was considered too private for inclusion.[5] There are numerous other instances of special Dickensian usage that have also been disregarded, probably for the same reason; see Appendix A.

   6. *Striking omissions.* There *are*, however, a number of omissions that appear striking, probably because they represent usage that is fully current today. It is very surprising that neither the *OED* nor the Supplement should record the use of *at least* for self-correction, = 'or rather'. This is common in Dickens, for instance: "'it's the dirty work I think sir — at least I don't know what it is, sir, but it's not my fault.'" (*NN* 8 93).[6] Other similar omissions are: *impossibly* 'to a preposterous degree': 'that slowest of all impossibly slow hackney Coaches' (*Pilgr.* 3 299, 1843); 'a shining white beaver bonnet, impossibly suggestive of a little feminine postboy' (*UT* 200); *to come up* 'to win (in a lottery)': 'I buy three numbers. If one of them come up, I win a small prize.' (*PI* 424)[7]; *depreciation* 'writing off': 'depreciation of plant in use (*UT* 256); *to disembarrass oneself of*: 'the triumphant manner in which he had disembarrassed himself of their company' (*DS* 42 588); *the price of* 'money enough to pay for': 'the man ... gave him the price of a supper and a night's lodging.' (*BH* 11 149); *a creature of habit*: 'If we were not such creatures of habit as we are, we shouldn't have reason to be astonished half so often.' (*DS* 53 745); *'He will never see sixty-five again'* (*BH* 2 10)[8].
   All the above examples have a modern ring, and they may well be Dickensian neologisms, as may the many more or less private words that are also unrecorded in the *OED* (see section 46); I have, however, no proof that this is so. Only extensive reading of Dickens's contemporaries and predecessors could give us proof positive.

   7. *Dickensian archaisms.* An analysis of Dickens's language reveals a large number of neologisms; but he is not just a neologist. It is striking — and indicative of his extensive linguistic repertoire — that he should also include in his vocabulary a number of lexical items that according to the *OED* are obsolete or archaic. Before embarking on a discussion of his neologisms we shall briefly illustrate Dickens's use of words that were obsolete in his day.
   In *Barnaby Rudge* there occurs the following passage:

It was not unusual for these running gentry, who carried it with a very high hand, to quarrel in the servants' hall...(16 123).

According to the *OED* (*carry* 22.b.) this sense of the verb: 'conduct matters, behave, act', is obsolete, the last example being from 1742. Compare further:

the lynx-eyed Ralph had already seen him in company with his unknown correspondent...(*NN* 51 677).

It is obvious from the context that *correspondent* here means 'a person who holds (secret) communication with another'; the last *OED* example of this sense dates from 1771. In *Our Mutual Friend* Silas Wegg refers to his wooden leg as 'that timber fiction' (II 7 303); the last *OED* illustration of *fiction* used to refer to 'that which is fashioned or framed' is from 1784. When Dickens writes in *David Copperfield*: 'I had not made much impression on the breakfast, for the black things destroyed my appetite' (9 126), the meaning is clear enough, and he may be harking back to the older use of *impression* for 'attack', employing it figuratively; there is a similar example in *Our Mutual Friend* (III 8 503).

Among other instances of obsolete terms that were revived by Dickens there is the verb *to bend*, which was employed in the sixteenth century in the sense of 'using for crooked purposes, perverting' *(OED* 15), a sense that fell into disuse. The first *OED* example of the revived use of the verb is from 1864, but this is anticipated by Dickens:

It has been claimed for our honourable friend, with much appearance of reason, that he was the first to bend sacred matters to electioneering tactics. (*UT* 565, 1852).

Similarly, the adjective *godfatherly* 'befitting a godfather' according to the *OED* was used once in the sixteenth century and was only revived in 1928; but Dickens uses it in one of his speeches:

I cannot disguise from you that I feel a kind of radiant godfatherly satisfaction in proposing the toast, for I can never forget that I had the honour of presiding over the first of its great meetings. (Fielding, p. 150, 1852).

In one passage it is obviously by accident, as it were, that a word introduced by Dickens as an analogical form characteristic of children's language comes to coincide with an obsolete verb:

'how would you support us? ' — The pirate-colonel replied in a courageous voice, 'By rapine! ' But his bride retorted, 'Suppose the grown-up people wouldn't be rapined? ' (*UT* 696, 1868).

The last *OED* example of the verb *to rapine* is from 1660.

8. Words used last by Dickens. All the examples given in section 7 are of words that were obsolete in Dickens's day. It may be added that in a number of cases he is the last to employ words in senses that have grown obsolete since the nineteenth century. We may consider the noun *mark* in the following quotation:

the French class becomes so demoralized that the Mark goes round as briskly as the bottle at a convivial party in the last century.(*ED* 3 21).

As used here, the word denotes a badge worn by the pupil who had last committed some particular fault. According to the *OED*, this sense of the word was shortlived, the first example being from 1832, the last from *c* 1855. Further, *to admire* is used in the sense of ''to wonder': 'Mrs. Chick admires that Edith should be, by nature, such a perfect Dombey.' (*DS* 31 446). And Dickens is the last to employ *middle-aged* as a synonym of 'mediaeval': 'the first chapter of a Middle-Aged novel' (*PI* 262).

Other obsolete or archaic words are listed in Appendix B.

9. Contemporary writers' neologisms. Before we proceed to a discussion of Dickens's own neologisms, it is worth noting that he was also very much alive to the neologisms introduced by other writers. It would be possible to draw up long lists of words and expressions employed by Dickens a very short time after they were first used by other writers, but let me give just a few examples from *Pickwick Papers*. Here he uses the colloquialism *on spec* (34 485), first recorded in 1832; further, the idiom *a drug in the market* (35 490), first recorded in 1833; and *to dissipate* (37 518) in its intransitive sense of 'engaging in dissolute pleasures', the first *OED* example of this sense being from 1836; besides several other recent neologisms.

10. Dated and current words. Some of Dickens's neologisms denote phenomena or processes that are not current or well known in twentieth-century civilization, and in that sense they have dated. Thus it is hardly customary any longer to *revive* one's faded clothes by applying the preparation termed a *reviver*. The occupation of *copying clerk* in the Dickensian sense (*SB* 120) hardly exists any more, nor does the *skeleton suit*: 'one of those straight blue cloth cases in which small boys used to be confined' (*SB* 75). Contrary to what modern readers might imagine, a *beer-chiller* (*SB* 239) was used, not to cool beer, but to take the chill out of it.

But most of the words or senses of words that Dickens introduced have full currency today; one might mention almost at random compound words like *casualty ward* (*SB* 242), *counter-accusation* (*DC* 32 469), and *season-ticket* (*SB* 102). The new senses that Dickens gave to words like *balloon* and *drag* have also come to stay; a *drag* is 'a heavy obstruction to progress' (*CB* 218), and the new sense of *balloon*: 'the outline enclosing words spoken or thought by a figure especially in a cartoon' is seen in this quotation:

Diabolical sentiments ... were represented as issuing from his mouth in fat balloons. (*MC* 31 501).

11. Arrangement of the material. The rest of this chapter will discuss important types of Dickensian neologisms: regular coinages, the use of existing words in novel senses or constructions, and new combinations of words; idioms will also be included in the discussion. For the sake of readability only select examples of each type will be given, and at the end of some sections there will be lists of additional examples that are illustrated in Appendix A. Four types are so numerous that it has been deemed most practical to identify them by means of superscripts in Appendix A: [1] stands for 'colloquialism, slang, humour', [2] for 'conversion', [3] for 'phrasal verb', and [4] for 'idiom'.

It has proved difficult to classify the neologisms in a satisfactory manner. I have employed formal, semantic, and stylistic criteria and combinations of these, but not all the categories form watertight compartments; for instance there are many phrasal verbs that are at the same time colloquialisms. But classification, though it may occasionally be felt as a Procrustean bed, nevertheless seems preferable to mere enumeration.

12. Idioms. Most of the idioms that are first recorded in Dickens have a colloquial ring. There are a number of catch-phrases like:

'Were you not a little surprised?' — 'I b'lieve you!' (*SB* 288, an expression of emphatic agreement, = 'certainly').

'What's the row, Sam?' (*PP* 2 8, = 'what's the matter?').

'You're a amiably-disposed young man, sir, *I don't think,*' resumed Mr. Weller, in a tone of moral reproof... (*PP* 38 541; used after an ironical statement to indicate that the reverse is intended).

'catch him who can; look on, keep your eyes open, and *niver say die!*' (*SB* 112; the first *OED* example is *a* 1865).

'is it brandy, rum, usquebaugh? ... Give it a name' (*BR* 8 62, = 'what would you like to drink?' In *GE* the formula is 'Put a name to it' (10 70)).

There are some of the idioms that are proverbial in character:

Ned would fetch up with a wet sail in good time, and carry all before him. (*DS* 17 228; cf. *OED wet*, adj., 6.d.: 'to make swift progress to victory, like a ship with sails wetted in order to keep close to the wind').

'You are in the same boat' (*BR* 45 347).

'We'll show 'em another pair of shoes than that, Pip; won't us? ' (*GE* 40 313).

Proverbial sayings often contain an implicit element of comparison. A related phenomenon is what Otto Jespersen terms 'veiled language'[9], i.e. a formulation that makes oblique reference to a state of things, etc., avoiding plain words. Dickensian examples are:

'Why,' said Mr. Roker, 'it's as plain as Salisbury! ' (*PP* 42 588 — a rather poor pun on *Salisbury Plain*).

'A new pal,' replied Jack Dawkins, pulling Oliver forward. — 'Where did he come from? ' — 'Greenland' (*OT* 8 56, i.e. 'the country of greenhorns').

Among idiomatic expressions that convey explicit comparison we find

Out flies the fare like bricks (*SB* 144).

'The wind,' cried Parkes. 'It's howling like a Christian...' (*BR* 33 250, = 'like a (decent) human being').

Some idioms are regularly associated with individual characters as their signature tunes. There is the familiar Wellerism, defined as 'an expression of comparison comprising a usually well-known quotation followed by a facetious sequel' (*Webster's Third New International Dictionary*): 'There's nothin' so refreshin' as sleep, sir, as the servant-girl said afore she drank the egg-cupful o' laudanum' (*PP* 16 211). A Wellerism is normally recognizable from the phrase 'as NN said when —'. It is more difficult to reduce Susan Nipper's rhetorical flourishes to a formula, but many Nipperisms are covered by the paraphrase 'though I possess or lack a certain quality, don't you draw any unwarranted conclusions from that fact':

'don't speak to me Miss Floy, for though I'm pretty firm I'm not a marble door-post' (*DS* 44 619).

'for though I may not gather moss I'm not a rolling stone' (*DS* 56 780).

Roger Riderhood in *Our Mutual Friend* identifies himself as 'a honest man as gets my living by the sweat of my brow', and Mr. Snagsby in *Bleak House* has a mannerism that he uses to excess:

'he ... was — not to put too fine a point upon it —', a favourite apology for plain-speaking with Mr. Snagsby, which he always offers with a sort of argumentative frankness, 'hard up! ' (*BH* 11 141f.).

A number of the idioms that appear first in Dickens have a quite modern ring; this is true of *an acquired taste* (*BR* 75 575) and of the phrase *going on for* that is synonymous with 'nearly': 'Noggs has lived in this house, now going on for five years' (*NN* 15 180). Other idioms appear in Dickens in a form that differs slightly from the one that is current today:

'... the other kind and gen'rous people o' the same purfession, as sets people by the ears, *free gratis for nothin'*...' (*PP* 26 362; now: '... and for nothing').

'Hooroar,' ejaculates a pot-boy in parenthesis, 'put the kye-bosk on her, Mary! ' (*SB* 70; the form *kibosh* is the current one today).

'It's a reg'lar holiday to them — all porter and skittles.' (*PP* 41 576; now: 'all beer and skittles', and usually in negative contexts).

The first *OED* example of (*one*) *in a million,* used to refer to an exceptional person, dates from 1900. There is a hyperbolical forerunner of this idiom in *Our Mutual Friend*: 'O Mrs. Higden, Mrs. Higden, you was a woman and a mother and a mangler in a million million!' (III 9 516).

For other idioms see the entries marked [4] in Appendix A.

13. Colloquialisms, slang, and humorous terms. Here, first, are a few colloquial neologisms:

At every bad attempt to catch, and every failure to stop the ball, he launched his personal displeasure at the head of the devoted individual in such denunciations as ... now, *butter-fingers, muff,* humbug, and so forth.(*PP* 7 91).

According to the *OED*, both the italicized words occur first here; but in fact there is an earlier Dickensian example of *muff* in *Sketches by Boz*: 'Blowed if hever I see sich a set of muffs!' (99). Another example is *oner* 'a unique person': 'Miss Sally's such a one-er for that' (*OCS* 58 430).

Among slang terms may be mentioned *governor* as a form of address: 'That is the intention, governor' (*OCS* 16 124), antedating the *OED* (which records the first example as being from *MC* 23 378); *magpie* 'a halfpenny' (*OT* 8 53); and *to flummox* (*PP* 33 455).

Humorous terms may be exemplified by *frog-eater* 'Frenchman' (*UT* 590), *gossamer* '(silk) hat of light material': 'Every hole lets in some air ... — wentilation gossamer I calls it.' (*PP* 12 154), and *slangular*:

Being asked what he thinks of the proceedings, characterizes them (his strength lying in a slangular direction) as 'a rummy start'. (*BH* 11 149).

For the numerous other members of this category see the entries marked [1] in Appendix A.

14. Conversion. This is the process whereby a word that belongs to one word-class is made to do duty in another word-class. There are numerous examples of nouns being turned into verbs, for instance:

'I have made up my mind ... to allowance him, ... to put him on a fixed allowance.' (*NN* 34 429).

When his guests had been washed, mended, brushed, and brandied... (*PP* 5 66; the *OED* has an example with *to brandy it a* 1819).

It is obvious that in the last quotation it is the context that has contributed to bringing about the process, a string of conventional past participles prompting the inclusion of the converted form. Binomial combinations, too, may become verbs: 'Five children milk-and-watering in the parlour' (*SB* 342), and the title of the work that Silas Wegg reads aloud to Mr. Boffin, *Decline and Fall of the Roman Empire,* is made into a weak verb [10] in

'Is it for him that I have declined and falled, night after night? ' (*OMF* III 14 582).

In *to yaw-yaw* we have an example of a supposed characteristic of affected pronunciation becoming a verb:

They liked fine gentlemen ... They became exhausted in imitation of them; and they yaw-yawed in their speech like them. (*HT* II 2 124).

Verbs may be converted into nouns:

Miss Squeers ... was ... taken with one or two *chokes* and catchings of breath... (*NN* 12 139)

'I may as well have a *rinse*,' replied Mr. Weller (*PP* 25 349).

Compare also the nominalizations exemplified in section 16.

A number of adjectives are used as nouns, for instance *professional* (*DS* 1 5), *temporary* (*DS* 3 31), *intended,* and *unchangeable*:

'What is the reason that men fall in love with me, whether I like it or not, and desert their chosen *intendeds* for my sake?' (*NN* 12 136).

... the three *unchangeables* who have been dancing the same dance under different imposing titles... (*SB* 671).

Compare also 'that man is *an unfathomable*' (*OCS* 56 416) and 'But, the lesser grindstone stood alone there in the calm morning air, with *a red* upon it that the sun had never given...' (*TC* III 2 250).

Several of the adjectives that are converted into nouns have an unmistakable colloquial ring. This is true of *germans* for 'German sausages' (*OMF* II 8 315), *green* for 'green man' (*SB* 172), *over-proof* for 'over-proof spirit' (*BR* 54 413), and *solitary* for 'solitary confinement' (*HT* I 5 24). Compare also *command* (performance) (*Pilgr.* 1 497, 1839) and *cottage* (piano) (Letter, 1850). Cf. the elliptical forms given at the end of section 38.

A special type of conversion is the one in which a premodifying name (which of course has an adjectival function) is made into a noun that denotes the content of premodifier + noun: 'a fragrant odour of full-flavoured Cubas' (*PP* 30 407, 'Cuba cigars'). In one of his letters Dickens substitutes *Sundays* for *Sunday papers*, which must have been highly unusual in the nineteenth century: '... the papers in which it [*sc.* an advertisement] must be inserted, which, indeed, are all the morning and evening ones. The Sundays we may leave alone.' (*Pilgr.* 2 225, 1841).

In *Our Mutual Friend* Bella Wilfer's sister Lavinia is referred to as 'the irrepressible Lavinia' at the beginning of the book (e.g. I 9 110); but towards the end this becomes 'the Irrepressible' (e.g. III 16 612). There is a similar change from 'the eminently practical father' to 'the eminently practical' in *Hard Times* (I 4 18). *The picturesque* is found from the mid-eighteenth century in an absolute function, but always with the definite article; Dickens, however, uses it with the indefinite article: 'let us ... try to associate *a new picturesque* with some faint recognition of man's destiny and capabilities' (*PI* 413).

In a couple of instances nouns are made into attributive adjectives: 'the *companion* passage of last year' (*AN* 1 4); 'The *regulation* cap to which the Miss Willises invariably restricted the ... tastes of female servants' (*SB* 15).

Pronouns are also made to extend their normal functions. Thus we find *something* employed as a regular noun, with a numeral and in the plural: 'one light carriage...; one something on wheels like an amateur carrier's cart' (*AN* 13 177); 'six somethings that he hadn't learnt yet, with three unknown something elses over' (*DS* 14 184). *Anything* has to do duty as a noun in 'a new dwarf or giant, a new chapel, a new anything' (*BH* 2 12) and as an adjective in 'I am not so clever, or so reasoning, or so eloquent, or so anything, as you are' (*DS* 5 46). A humorous use of *everything* in the plural is seen in 'But to be sure there were rum everythings' (*OMF* I 3 27).

For additional instances of conversion see the entries marked [2] in Appendix A.

15. Phrasal verbs. A phrasal verb is a combination of verb + preposition or of verb + adverb, the two elements forming a semantic whole. There is also a variant consisting of verb + adverb + preposition: *to come in for.* There occur many such new combinations in Dickens, for instance the graphic *to walk into*: 'I wish you could have seen the shepherd walkin' into the ham and muffins' (*PP* 22 298, 'devour greedily') and *to chime with*: 'if your inclinations chime with your sense of duty...' (*OT* 35 261). Examples in which the second element is an adverb are: 'Mr. Trabb, taking down a roll of cloth, and tiding it out in a flowing manner over the counter...' (*GE* 19 143, 'cause to flow as a tide or stream'); 'But [Mr. Snagsby] is immediately frowned down by Mrs. Snagsby.' (*BH* 19 263); and 'the Major wore [his hat] with a rakish air on one side of his head, by way of toning down his remarkable visage.'(*DS* 20 276). With *to come* as the verbal element we may note no fewer than five Dickensian neologisms recorded in the *OED*:

'Ha, ha! Join us. You shall come in cheap.' (*MC* 27 444; = 'to enter as a partner').

'You'll come in for it presently, I know you will!' (*BR* 1 7; = 'incur punishment').

'Oh, what a happiness it is when man and wife come round again! ' (*BR* 19 148; = 'become reconciled').

He had bought a half-ticket for the twenty-five thousand prize, and it had come up. (*CS* 215; = 'win').

'Then, come up,' said the carrier to the lazy horse; who came up accordingly. (*DC* 5 63; = 'move! ').

It may be added that *come out* = 'come out of curl' is not recorded by the *OED*: '... her luxuriant crop of hair arranged in curls so tight that it was impossible they could come out by any accident' (*NN* 39 503).

For additional examples of phrasal verbs see the entries marked [3] in Appendix A.

16. Nominalizations. Some phrasal verbs are nominalized: *to come back* produces *a come-back*. There are a few examples of this type in Dickens:

'... so produce the sustainance [sic] , and let's have a quiet fill-out for the first time these three days!' (*OT* 25 182, a colloquialism for 'a meal'; not in the *OED*).

... with a kick-up of his hindlegs... (*GE* 3 14).

'Suppose I was to give you a look in, say at half-arter ten to-morrow morning' (*BH* 49 676; antedates the *OED*).

'If he took it into his head that I was coming here for such or such a purpose, why, that's his look-out.' (*MC* 27 441).

'That's rayther a sudden pull-up, ain't it, Sammy?' inquired Mr. Weller. (*PP* 33 454).

'She must just hate and detest the whole set-out of us...' (*HT* I 8 50; = 'company, party').

17. Nouns in -er. There is no better illustration of Dickens's talent for exploiting the potential of English than his use of suffixes for creating new words, mainly nouns and adjectives. Such words can be formed freely as occasion demands; they are part of an open-ended system.

Let us begin by considering nouns in *-er*. Most of them are agent nouns with a colloquial ring:

'It's Destiny, and mine's a crusher!' (*OCS* 50 374).

'Like you, you fool!' said she to Joe, 'giving holidays to great idle hulkers like that...' (*GE* 15 106).

'He's what you may call a rasper, is Nickleby.' (*NN* 57 748).

Mr. Swiveller replied that he had very recently been assuaging the pangs of thirst, but that he was still open to 'a modest quencher' (*OCS* 35 266).

That Dickens is an innovator in his use of *-er* nouns appears from the fact that some of them antedate the *OED*, and others are not even listed in the Dictionary. Sometimes they are nominalizations born of the context, as in the railroad between Leghorn and Pisa, which is a good one, and has already begun to astonish Italy with a precedent of punctuality, order, plain dealing, and improvement — the most dangerous and heretical astonisher of all. (*PI* 359).

There are some of these *-er* neologisms that are not agent nouns. This is true of *searcher* in

Waterloo [a toll-taker] received us with cordiality, and observed of the night that it was 'a Searcher'. (*UT* 529).

which presumably means that it was so dark a night that it called for searching. Similarly, *a six-footer* (*BH* 33 467) is a colloquial designation of a coffin, and *a minder* (*OMF* I 16 199) means 'a child who is minded or taken care of at a minding school'.[11]

For further examples see *beamer, bender, codger, fast-goer, freshener, giver up, knifer, merry-go-rounder, putter in, refresher, refreshmenter, right-hander, shark-header, short-timer, six-roomer, squeaker, taker out, tickler,* and *town-mader* in Appendix A.

18. Nouns in -ment. There occur one or two rather odd-looking Dickensian neologisms that are formed with the suffix *-ment*; we hear of the *embowerment* of Mrs. Pipchin (*DS* 8 99) and of the *bewigment* of the Canterbury amateurs (*Pilgr.* 5 138, 1847). In *Household Words* there is a reference to 'the cabs, in every degree of *ramshacklement*' (*HW* I 244, 1851). This form does not appear to have taken root, but other writers must have felt in need of a noun corresponding to the adjective *ramshackle*: we now have the forms *ramshackleness* (1922) and *ramshackledom* (1962). Compare also *jostlement* and *reconsignment* in Appendix A.

19. Nouns in -ness. Dickens's use of the *-ness* suffix is also unconventional. In principle almost any word can be turned into an abstract noun by the addition of *-ness,* but most readers will probably be rather surprised when they come across the word *kitchen-pokerness*:

He ... had a clean-cravatish formality of manner, and kitchen-pokerness of carriage, which Sir Charles Grandison himself might have envied. (*SB* 431).

Sometimes the suffix is resorted to in a passage where it seems as if Dickens has contrived to create a need for such a noun. Here, first, is an example from *Pickwick Papers*:

'All fun, ain't it?' — 'Prime!' said the young gentleman... The young gentleman, notwithstanding his primeness and his spirit, ... reclined his head upon the table, and howled dismally. (40 565).

This may be compared with the *bandiness* that is asserted to characterize Miss Sally Brass:

The law had been her nurse. And as bandy-legs or such physical deformities in children are held to be the consequence of bad nursing, so, if in a mind so beautiful any moral twist or bandiness could be found, Miss Sally Brass's nurse was alone to blame. (*OCS* 36 270).

Compare further *cheesiness, coachfulness, coachlessness, dovetailedness, excitableness, gashliness, mirthfulness, rumness,* and *touch-me-not-ishness* in Appendix A.

20. Adjectives in -ed: type 'thief-dreaded'. Dickens employs a number of compound adjectives that are not new as types, but he tends to use them in unconventional fashion. We may begin by considering the type consisting of noun + past participle: 'his thief-dreaded watch' (*GE* 36 276), in which the noun is equivalent to the agent in an abbreviated postmodified construction: 'his watch (which was) dreaded by thieves'. Further examples are: 'the amateur-painted ... scenery' (*SB* 423), 'one of the chateau's four extinguisher-topped towers' (*TC* II 9 113), 'his weather-ploughed-up nose' (*AN* 16 227), 'the sun-and-shadow-chequered colonnade' (*BH* 12 153). Such premodified constructions are more striking than the corresponding postmodified constructions would be — for two reasons. In the first place a construction with qualifiers preceding the head noun is often felt to be heavy, and in the second place premodification tends to imply the idea of a permanent state of things.[12] Thus a locality may be characterized as being 'God-forsaken', while in 'he felt forsaken by God' we have a free syntactic postmodification that is typically used to refer to an individual situation. It is therefore less striking to read of 'the many house-encompassed churches' (*OMF* II 15 393) than of 'monsieur the marquis, flambeau preceded' (*TC* II 9 112); in the latter case, the formulation that would normally be preferred to describe an individual situation is 'the marquis, preceded by flambeaux'.

21. Adjectives in -ed: type 'sedentary-pursuited'. Another type that has a superficial resemblance to the one just dealt with is seen in 'a sedentary-pursuited Waiter' (*CS* 321) and 'a copper-saucepaned laboratory' (*LD* II 15 610) where the adjectival *-ed* suffix is, however, added to either a compound noun or to a set phrase consisting of adjective +

noun. Again, the type as such is not Dickens's contribution, but he exploits it freely to form striking adjectives. Compare further examples like 'circular-visaged males' (*PP* 5 65), 'proud-stomached teachers' (*NN* 13 149), 'a small, green-baized, brass-headed-nailed door' (*SB* 86), and 'a low-crowned, flower-pot-saucer-shaped hat' (*SB* 267). In *Pictures from Italy* there is a reference to 'Queer old towns, draw-bridged and walled' (264). Cf. *bulbous-shoed* in Appendix A.

22. Adjectives in -ing: type 'promise-breaking'. Attributive compounds consisting of a noun + a transitive present participle that takes the noun as its object are Dickensian favourites. Some of them appear never to have taken root: 'town-surprising theatrical announcements' (*SB* 121), 'any ... duty-doing man' (*GE* 14 101), 'a ghost-seeing effect' (*GE* 27 209). But in a number of instances, listed by the *OED* as first occurrences, such forms have acquired currency: 'a company-keeping, love-making, pleasant sort of manner' (*NN* 12 138), 'a ... promise-breaking ... person (*Pilgr.* 3 146, 1842), 'the misery-making money' (*OMF* II 14 379). — In a few cases Dickens uses condensed premodified constructions as in 'circulating-library-subscribing daughters' (*SB* 92) and 'a ... hackney-coach-jostling ... world' (*DC* 19 286), where the corresponding postmodified constructions would be explicit as far as the prepositions are concerned ('jostling *with* each other *for* hackney-coaches').

23. Adjectives in -ish. There occur a few adjectives formed with the suffix *-ish*, for instance *raspish* 'irritating, irritable' (*HT* II 5 152) corresponding to *rasper* (section 17), and *vixenish* 'characteristic of a vixen': 'a short, thin, squeezed-up woman, with a vixenish countenance' (*OT* 4 27). See *cheekish* and *spoffish* in Appendix A, and compare the noun *touch-me-not-ishness.*

24. Adjectives in -less. Adjectives formed with this suffix are normally employed to refer to institutionalized concepts, or in other words, an adjective in *-less* typically describes a well-known situation as do, for instance, *careless* and *penniless.* Some Dickensian adjectives of this type are, however, ad hoc coinages, which is why they seem odd. Not many people possess ravens; Dickens did, and when his raven died, he referred to himself as *ravenless* (*BR*, preface). A similar example is:

she was already reflecting how she would flourish these very same Boffins and the state they kept, over the heads of her *Boffinless* friends. (*OMF* I 9 113).

where the oddnes of the formulation is caused by too high a degree of specificity in the element   preceding -less: one can be *friendless,* but hardly, say, **Joanless.*[13]

Further examples, listed in Appendix A, are *bibless, conversationless, dollarless, fireworkless, mugless, nephewless, pastureless, pupil-less, spongeless,* and *theatreless.*

25. Adjectives in -ous. Examples of Dickensian neologisms of this type are:

Mr. Lammle takes his gingerous whiskers in his left hand. (*OMF* I 10 123).

his philanthropy was of that gunpowderous sort that the difference between it and animosity was hard to determine. (*ED* 6 57).

Further examples, listed in Appendix A, are *blisterous, cellarous, dollarous, prisonous, spumous, tinderous,* and *veinous.*

26. Adjectives in -y. These are particular favourites of Dickens's, perhaps because they are easily formed colloquialisms that are often of a humorous character. Many nouns can be given an adjectival function if they are employed attributively, but not if they are used predicatively, and in the latter case an adjective in *-y* comes in handy: '... his amiable old walnut shell countenance very *walnut-shelly* indeed as he smiles...' (*CS* 330). Other examples are:

'Legs shaky — head queer — round and round — *earthquaky* sort of feeling — very.' (*PP* 45 639).

'It's rather *jog-trotty* and humdrum.' (*BH* 17 230).

I suppose myself to be better acquainted than any living authority, with the *ridgy* effect of a wedding-ring, passing unsympathetically over the human countenance. (*GE* 7 48).

In a couple of passages it is clear that a new form in *-y* owes its creation to rhyming adjectives in the context:

'For that [*sc.* smell] ... is musty, leathery, feathery, *cellary,* gluey, gummy...' (*OMF* I 7 78).

'You're as moody and *broody* a lad as never I set eyes on yet.' (*UT* 737).

Further examples, listed in Appendix A, are *beamy, dolly, fluey, fluffy, fruity, ginger-beery, gold-dusty, hearth-broomy, hunchy, mil-*

dewy, mortary, mumbly, oystery, pepper-corny, sawdusty, seedy, sneezy, soupy, staggery, streety, touchwoody, trembly, turfy, velveteeny, vinegary, waxy, and *windmilly.*

27. The prefix un-. Dickens coins several adjectives beginning with the negative prefix *un-* , for instance: 'She said it finally and in ... an *undiscussible* way' (*GE* 8 51); *'undistinctive* Death' (*UT* 526); 'an ungrateful and *unpensioning* country' (*BH* 40 565); for *unproducible* see section 5. What attracted him about such forms may have been the fact that they are succinct and economical, packing into one word ideas that would otherwise have to be conveyed through several words. There are also a few neologisms in which the prefix combines with a verb in the sense of undoing the action described, for instance:

Madame Bouclet now traced the line with her forefinger, as it were to confirm and settle herself in her parting snap at Monsieur Mutuel, and so placing her right hand on her hip with a defiant air, as if nothing should ever tempt her to *unsnap* that snap... (*CS* 331).

Other examples, listed in Appendix A, are *unapproachable, unbear, unboy, unchangeable, uncommercial, unholy, unpost, unprisoned, unravenlike, unruffable, unruffianly, unscratchable, unshiplike,* and *unweighable.*

28. Verbs in new constructions. In addition to what was said about verbs in sections 14 and 15, it may be noted here that another source of neologisms is Dickens's use of verbs in new constructions. If the syntactic function of a word is altered, this normally entails some semantic change.

In a number of cases transitive verbs are pressed into service as intransitive verbs, a function they did not have before Dickens:

'Do you suppose there has been much violence ... among these cases?' — 'I don't suppose at all about it ... I ain't one of the supposing sort' (*OMF* I 3 23; cf. *OED suppose* 8.g.).

'You rayther want somebody to look arter you, sir, wen your judgment goes out a wisitin'.' (*PP* 22 312; cf. *OED visit* 8.e.).

The absolute use of the verbs in the passages quoted below is not recorded in the *OED*:

'[My brother] Was pitchforked into the Navy, but has not circumnavigated...' (*OMF* I 12 146f.).

vapours issue forth that blind and suffocate... (*AN* 6 90).

in its soft and gentle influence, [the rising of the moon] seems to comfort while it saddens. (*AN* 16 226).

Conversely, intransitive verbs may be employed as transitive verbs:

[a description of Epsom] ... until at last we are drawn, and rounded, and backed, and sidled, and cursed, and complimented, and *vociferated* into a station on the hill... (*HW* I 306, 1851; antedates the *OED*).

There occur two transitive uses, both neologisms, of the predominantly intransitive verb *to stand*: (1) 'to pay for', (2) 'to cause to stand':

Mr. Augustus Cooper ... 'stood' considerable quantities of spirits-and-water. (*SB* 260).

The pretty housemaid had stood the candle on the floor... (*PP* 25 356).

Occasionally a verb is employed in a new reflexive function: 'a concerted plot ... having for its object the inducing Mr. Swiveller to *declare himself* in time' (*OCS* 8 65). This, according to the *OED*, is the first occurrence of the construction when it means 'propose marriage'. The following two are unrecorded:

the back compartment of the vehicle ... had an ... alarming tendency ... to hiccup itself away from the front compartment. (*OMF* I 9 102).

Tippins the divine has dined herself into such a condition by this time that... (*OMF* III 17 624).

According to the *OED*, the first example of *to confide* + object + *to* (= 'to entrust (an object of care, a task, etc.) *to* a person...') is from 1861; but Dickens has the construction as early as 1838:

Nicholas stooped over her, for a few seconds, and placing her gently in a chair, confided her to their honest friend. (*NN* 20 254; also *BH* 14 192).

29. Adverbs. The first point that may be noted is Dickens's innovations within colloquial adverbial usage; thus *again* is used 'in request for a repetition of what has previously been said': '"You know Mr. Skimpole?" said I. "What do you call him again?" returned Mr. Bucket.' (*BH* 57 774; cf. *NN* 21 263f.). Dickens is also the first writer to employ *never* in emphatic denial: 'could such things be tolerated in a Christian land? Never!' (*SB* 35), and he uses *any day* in the sense of 'without doubt':

'Why, *you* are a good deal better-looking than her, Barbara.' – 'Oh, Christopher! ' said Barbara... – 'You are, any day,' said Kit. (*OCS* 39 294).

The first *OED* example of *ever so* as an intensifier, = 'vastly', 'immensely', is from 1858, but we find this use as early as *Pickwick Papers*:

'There was something behind the door, sir, which perwented our getting it open, for ever so long, sir,' replied Sam. (25 356).

Most of Dickens's adverbial neologisms are, however, forms in -*ly*; there are more than thirty of them, and it must be said that he tends to put them to rather strained use. Here are some examples:

For some little time the Jurymen hang about the Sol's Arms colloquially. (*BH* 11 149, i.e. 'in colloquy', a sense not recorded by the *OED*).

the upholsterer's foreman skirmishingly measuring expensive objects... (*DS* 35 497).

In Dickens's account of the Paris morgue there occurs the following passage:

Indeed, those two [bodies] of the back row were so furtive of appearance, and so (in their puffed way) assassinatingly knowing as to the one of the front, that it was hard to think the three had never come together in their lives... (*UT* 191).

Another coinage is the adverb *cherubically*, and where it occurs, it is put to a rather peculiar use, conveying agency rather than manner: 'the family retired; she [*sc.* Mrs. Wilfer] cherubically escorted...' (*OMF* I 4 42, i.e. she was escorted *by* her husband, nicknamed the cherub). In *Bleak House* the adverb *nomadically* is employed figuratively to describe the gait of a drunken person: 'a man so very nomadically drunk as to stray into the frigid zone' (58 796).

30. Prepositions. There are not many neologisms among prepositions. It is interesting to note, however, that in the same novel Dickens employs the preposition *pending* first in its traditional function, = 'during', and next in the sense of 'until', which is the first example of this recorded by the *OED*:

Pending the utterance of these frantic cries... (*NN* 15 181).

pending his return, Kate and her mother were shown into a dining-room... (*NN* 21 265).

In one or two other instances we find the semantic range of a preposition extended. With reference to a pub, etc., *by* is used synonymously with 'kept by (as licensee)': 'This is the Valiant Soldier, by James Groves' (*OCS* 29 219). The first *OED* example of *for* 'in preparation for or anticipation of (the stated time of a dinner, etc.)' is from 1900, but this use of the preposition is frequent in Dickens's letters, for instance: 'dine ... at 5 o'Clock for half past exactly' (*Pilgr.* 1 329, 1837).

The first Supplement example of the combination *at about* with indications of time is from 1843, but Dickens used it one year earlier: 'at about half-past six that evening' (*AN* 8 115). For the elliptical use of *with* and *without* see Appendix A.

31. Interjections. Mention has already been made (I.8) of the phrase *never mind* which Dickens is the first to use in its offensive sense 'it is none of your business'. There are one or two other neologisms: *bother!* is employed as a mild imprecation: 'To this amorous address Miss Brass briefly responded "Bother!"' (*OCS* 33 248), and another phrase voicing dissatisfaction is *drop it!* 'have done!': 'Drop it, I say!... Drop it — now and for ever.' (*MC* 20 331). For *charmed!* see Appendix A.

32. Latinisms. Much of the preceding discussion has been concerned with the native resources of English; but Dickens commands the entire gamut of the language, and he has a penchant for exploiting the Latinate element (and a few Greek words) for humorous purposes. In the early nineteenth century it was believed by penny-a-liners and some of their readers that the use of stock Latin phrases made for a vivid and humorous style, and it should not be forgotten that such phrases also added to the length of a description, thus increasing the authors' earnings.[14] In *Pickwick Papers* we find examples like 'He ... was under the painful necessity of admitting the veracity of his optics' (2 21) and 'a grin which agitated his countenance from one auricular organ to the other' (5 64). It may further be noted that in some passages a phenomenon is referred to in plain English at first mention, while at second mention a Latin term is substituted:

Grandfather Smallweed immediately throws the cushion at her...
    The effect of this act of jaculation is twofold. (*BH* 21 289).

some unmannerly drinking-house ... opens its mouth at intervals and spits out a man too drunk to be retained ... [one page later] Unmannerly drinking-house expectorates as before. (*CS* 745f.).

There occurs another variant that exploits the contrast between plain and Latinate terms; it may be exemplified in Mr. Micawber, who typically moves from a resounding formulation to its bathetic counterpart: 'It is not an avocation of a remunerative description – in other words, it does *not* pay.' (*DC* 27 409).

Dickens also creates his own Latinisms, which he launches with mock pomposity in formulations like 'aquatic recreations' (*SB* 97), 'vocular exclamations' (*OT* 7 45), and 'ventriloquial chirping' (*SB* 255). These examples are from his early works; but he never lost interest in this element of lexis, as may be seen from his last novel:

'I am as well,' said Mrs. Billickin, becoming aspirational with excess of faintness, 'as I hever ham.' (*ED* 22 249).

This unconventional and jocular use of the adjective ('pronouncing an *h* where none is warranted'; not in the *OED* in this sense) may be paralleled by the use of adverbs in passages like the following:

the regular water-drinkers ... took their quarter of a pint, and walked constitutionally. (*PP* 36 506, i.e. 'by way of a constitutional').

The two brutal casts [of hanged criminals]... seemed to be congestively considering whether they didn't smell fire at the present moment. (*GE* 51 388; this should be compared with the first description of the casts: 'two dreadful casts ... of faces peculiarly swollen, and twitchy about the nose' (20 154)).

sneaking Calais, prone behind its bar, invites emetically to despair. (*UT* 179).

Occasionally Dickens had second thoughts about his use of facetious Latinisms. Thus the *OED* (s.v. *mangle, sb.*[3], 1.a.) gives a quotation from *Sketches by Boz* that runs as follows: 'The only answer we obtained was a playful inquiry whether our *maternal parent* had disposed of her mangle.' (As the *OED* informs us, 'The question "Has your mother sold her mangle?" ... was at one time the commonest piece of 'chaff' used by London street-boys'). This is the original formulation. In the Preface to *Sketches by Boz* as published in book form Dickens tells us that he has left the text unchanged, apart from 'a few words and phrases here and there'; among the changes he introduced was *mother* for *maternal parent* (*SB* 175). – Compare III.12 (elegant variation).

Other neologisms, listed in Appendix A, are *acidulation, admonitorial, aquatically, auriferously, bacchanalially, condonatory, conductorial, constabular, corporational, dilapidative, dissective, excursional, pastorial, perspirational, polygamically, proctorial, sassagerial,* and *uvularly.*

33. Gallicisms. Considering his interest in France and his knowledge of French, it is perhaps a bit surprising that there should be few French-inspired expressions in Dickens's language. In one passage he comments on his own usage: 'I ... assisted — in the French sense — at the performance of two waltzes' (*CS* 92); *to assist* 'to be present as a spectator' is a French idiom which he uses elsewhere without comment (*OMF* I 3 19). Besides, we may note the following French-inspired neologisms:

the triumphant manner in which he had disembarrassed himself of their company... (*DS* 42 588; French *se débarrasser de*).

The British Consul hadn't had such a marriage in the whole of his Consularity. (*LD* II 15 609; probably inspired by *consularité*).

... the gloomy staircase on which the grating gave. (*LD* I 1 2; cf. French *donner sur*; this antedates the *OED* example from *UT*, 1860).

There is one other area where French influence makes itself felt, albeit not in an artistically very convincing manner. This is in the speech of some characters of French extraction which is stamped by what may be termed covert Gallicisms: Dickens provides unidiomatic translations of some of the words and expressions used by these characters. Thus the French maid in *Bleak House* says: 'I know that I should *win* less, as to wages here.' (23 319; French *gagner*). Monsieur Blandois in *Little Dorrit* uses the term of address *my Cabbage* (I 30 362; French *mon chou*), and one of his oaths is *holy blue* (I 30 360; French *sacrebleu*).

34. Americanisms. During his visit to America in 1842 Dickens wrote to Forster: '... but that for an odd phrase now and then — such as *Snap of cold weather*; *a tongue-y man* for a talkative fellow; *Possible?* as a solitary interrogation; and *Yes?* for indeed — I should have marked, so far, no difference whatever between the parties here and those I have left behind.'[15] In a later letter to Forster Dickens is much more critical of American English: 'I need not tell you that out of Boston and New York a nasal drawl is universal, but I may as well hint that the prevailing grammar is also more than doubtful; that the oddest vulgarisms are received idioms...; and that the most fashionable and aristocratic (these are two words in great use), instead of asking you in what place you were born, inquire where you "hail from"!!'[16]
There is a sprinkling of Americanisms in Dickens's writings, mainly in *American Notes* and *Martin Chuzzlewit,* some of them neologisms:

'A dance? It shall be done directly, sir: "a regular breakdown."' (*AN* 6, 91, 'a riotous dance'; antedates the *OED* quotation *a* 1864).

'Here's full particulars of the patriotic loco-foco movement yesterday, in which the whigs was so *chawed up*' (*MC* 16 255, = 'demolish, do for, smash'; this is the first *OED* example).

'They rile up, sometimes; but in general we have a hold upon our citizens...' (*MC* 16 263, = 'get angry'; first *OED* example).

... the mysteries of Gin-Sling, Cocktail, Sangaree, Mint Julep, Sherry-Cobbler, *Timber Doodle*, and other rare drinks. (*AN* 3 60; another neologism).

When Dickens introduces Americanisms, it is often for the sake of ridiculing or poking gentle fun at them. It is clear that he disapproves of the expression *hail from* quoted above, and there is no mistaking his attitude towards it when he uses it in *Martin Chuzzlewit*:

'Pray, sir! ' said Mrs. Hominy, 'where do you hail from? ' — 'I am afraid I am dull of comprehension,' answered Martin... — '... where was you rose? ' (22 369).

where significantly it is equated with a piece of bad grammar. Sometimes he supplies a translation of American English expressions: 'pants are fixed to order; or in other words, pantaloons are made to measure.' (*AN* 8 116).

In *American Notes*, at the beginning of chapter 10, Dickens notes with obvious amusement the many uses to which the verb *to fix* is put in American English: *fixing oneself* = 'dressing'; *fixing the tables* = 'laying the cloth'; *fix the luggage* = 'fetch it'; the doctor will *fix you* = 'cure you'; etc. There is also the noun *fixing,* used to refer to a dish of food. It occurs here and in chapter 13 in the following passage:

He had ordered 'wheat-bread and chicken fixings', in preference to 'corn-bread and common doings'. The latter kind of refection includes only pork and bacon. The former comprehends broiled ham, sausages, veal cutlets, steaks, and such other viands of that nature as may be supposed, by a tolerably wide poetical construction, 'to fix' a chicken comfortably in the digestive organs of any lady or gentleman. (180).

The words in inverted commas appear in almost identical form in Edmund Flagg's *The Far West* (New York 1838):

the first inquiry made of the guest by the village landlord is the following: 'well, stran-ger, what'll ye take: wheat-bread and *chicken fixens,* or corn-bread and *common doins*? ' by the latter expressive and elegant soubriquet being signified bacon. (Quoted from a 1906 reprint (Cleveland, Ohio), p. 324).

Unless there is a common source of the two passages, it looks as if

Dickens had a look at Flagg's book: the culinary terms are the same, though Dickens embroiders a bit on their interpretation. *The Far West* is not, however, listed in the inventory of contents of 1 Devonshire Terrace (*Pilgr.* 4 704ff.) or in the Gadshill *Catalogue of the Library of Charles Dickens,* but according to the former inventory there were several groups of unspecified books.

There is another interesting point about the Flagg passage: the spelling of the word *stran-ger*. This use of the hyphen is presumably meant to convey level stress,[17] and Dickens repeatedly employs the device in *Martin Chuzzlewit: a-dopted, do-minion, po-ssession,* etc. Could he have been inspired by Flagg to adopt this practice? — In other respects there do not appear to be linguistic points of resemblance between Flagg and Dickens.

35. Theatre and circus terms. Dickens's vivid interest in the stage manifests itself in a number of technical terms, all neologisms. In the quotation that follows:

he put his head out of the practicable door in the front grooves O.P. (*NN* 22 281).

practicable is applied to a door that can actually be used in the play, and the *grooves* are slides in which the scenery may be pushed back. In

Little Swills, in what are professionally known as 'patter' allusions to the subject, is received with loud applause... (*BH* 39 558).

the technical term means 'rapid speech introduced into a song'. An actor who is good at memorizing his lines is said to be 'a quick study' (*NN* 23 292); but the stage is also peopled by 'wretched supernumeraries, or sixth-rate actors' (*SB* 179f.). When Vincent Crummles tells Nicholas about the prospect of an addition to his family:

'I thought such a child as the Phenomenon must have been a closer; but it seems we are to have another.' (*NN* 48 628).

he is making figurative use of the term *a closer*: 'a number or play that brings a programme to a close'. — Among circus terms we may note *to miss one's tip* 'to fail in one's aim' (*HT* I 6 31; also used in a speech made by Dickens in 1855 (Fielding p. 184)), and *garters* 'tapes held up for a circus performer to leap over' (*HT* I 6 31).

Other examples, listed in Appendix A, are *circuit, gag, half-price, a hurry, incidental music, a Jeff, to make up, to mug, ponging, to produce, reception, to ring up,* and *a wait.*

36. Dickensian institutions. Among his contributions to the English language we should not forget the names of Dickens's own characters; many of these names have become institutions, epitomizing typical behaviour or typical qualities, and some of them have given rise to derivations introduced by later writers.

The phrase *in a Pickwickian sense* is well known, and in recent years the medical profession has begun to operate with the concept of a *Pickwickian syndrome,* which occurs in obese adults (an allusion to the fat boy in *Pickwick Papers*; see the *OED* Supplement). Sam Weller's characteristic manner of introducing graphic examples has produced the term *Wellerism* (see section 12), and there are two adjectives available to characterize this procedure: *Welleresque* and *Wellerian.* Mr. Bumble in *Oliver Twist* is responsible for *Bumbledom,* which means 'fussy official pomposity and stupidity' (*OED*), and for *bumble* = 'beadle', though Jespersen rightly points out that 'the common name *bumble* was already in existence' when Dickens wrote *Oliver Twist* 'and was a very expressive word (cf. *jumble, grumble, bungle,* etc.)'.[18] While we are on the subject of officialdom it is natural also to mention the *Circumlocution Office* described in *Little Dorrit.* This novel further contains the famous advice on elocution given by Mrs. General:

'Papa is a preferable mode of address,' observed Mrs. General. 'Father is rather vulgar, my dear. The word Papa, besides, gives a pretty form to the lips. Papa, potatoes, poultry, prunes, and prism, are all very good words for the lips: especially prunes and prism.' (II 5 476).

The phrase *prunes and prism(s)* has come to stand for affected and priggish speech or behaviour, and it has produced the adjectival phrases *prunes and prismy* and *pruny and prismy.*

In *David Copperfield* we are introduced to Mr. Dick, who is unable to finish his memorial because he cannot keep *King Charles's head* out of his thoughts; this phrase has come to be applied to an obsession (ch. 14). The gaily dressed *Dolly Varden*'s apparel (in *Barnaby Rudge*) has caused her name to be associated with a print dress or a large hat (besides being used to refer to a Californian species of trout or char). The name of Sarah *Gamp* (in *Martin Chuzzlewit*) has also undergone commonization, so that *gamp* is synonymous with either a disreputable nurse or an umbrella. The name of the arch-hypocrite *Pecksniff* in the same novel has spawned at least the following forms: *Pecksniffery, Pecksniffian, Pecksniffism, Pecksniffianly,* and *Pecksniffingly. Dombey* appears to have produced only one derivation: *Dombeyism,* while several other characters' names have been more prolific: *Micawberish(ly), Micawberism, Micawberite (David Copperfield); Gradgrinding,*

Gradgrindism (Hard Times); Podsnappery, Podsnap(p)ian, Podsnapism (Our Mutual Friend).

Sometimes Dickens's use of sayings and phrases that existed long before his time has resulted in their acquiring added currency and popularity. Thus, in *Dombey and Son* he makes use of the name of a children's game, *Tom Tiddler's ground,* in describing Mr. Dombey's dining-room, which 'might have been taken for a grown-up exposition of Tom Tiddler's ground, where children pick up gold and silver.' (36 512). According to the *Oxford Dictionary of English Proverbs* the name has acquired proverbial status. The same is true of the saying *the Law is an ass,* which was first used by Chapman *c.* 1634, but which has become immortalized in Mr. Bumble's version:

'If the law supposes that,' said Mr. Bumble ... 'the law is a ass – a idiot.' (*OT* 51 399).

Yet other household words might be added to the list; but such examples suffice to show that Dickens's creation of these names and characters has enriched the English language both directly and indirectly.

37. Changed collocational range. Words may undergo greater or lesser degrees of semantic change when their collocational ranges are extended. A careful reading of the context will usually suggest the new use of a word. Let us consider some examples.

Until 1848 the adjective *rough* meant 'unrefined' without any admixture of redeeming qualities; but in *Dombey and Son* the word is placed in a context that warrants the definition 'unrefined (but kindly or friendly)' (*OED* 14.c.): '... the generous ... youth, whom he had loved, according to his rough manner' (32 455). Until 1839 the noun *belligerent* according to the *OED* denoted 'a nation, party, or person waging regular war (recognized by the law of nations)'; but in *Nicholas Nickleby* the noun is extended to refer to policemen: 'a loud shout attracted the attention even of the belligerents' (2 13). Before the publication of *Bleak House* the figurative meaning of *cheek* was 'insolent speech', but in that novel the word is used in the sense of 'impudent behaviour': 'they killed him... on account of his having so much cheek' (54 730). A word that is used to describe a person may come to be humorously applied to non-persons; this is true of the adjective *brazen-faced*, which appears in *Bleak House* in the following passage: 'Law and Equity, those teak-built, copperbottomed, iron-fastened, brazen-faced ... Clippers' (19 258; the first *OED* illustration of this use is from 1864). Conversely, a word that was not originally employed to describe personal appearance may have its collocational range extended to include this, as in a passage from *Barnaby Rudge*: 'his limbs all *angular* and rigid' (37 280; the first *OED* example of the word in this sense is from 1850).

In the following sections we shall look at various types of semantic change, illustrating them with examples that are all neologisms.

38. Pregnant senses. Given a suitable context, a word that is basically neutral may take on a pregnant sense. Thus *language* comes to mean 'bad language' in

What was more conclusive was, Mr. Victualler's assurance that he 'never allowed any language, and never suffered any disturbance.' (*UT* 45; the first *OED* example dates from 1886).

and *on terms* is equivalent to 'on friendly terms' in

'the time is come ... when the lion should lie down with the lamb, and my family be on terms with Mr. Micawber.' (*DC* 54 772; the first *OED* example is from 1864).

Dickens is the first to employ the adjective *common* in the sense of 'vulgar' (of persons):

'And I told you, Mrs. Merdle,' said Fanny, 'that we might be unfortunate, but were not common.' (*LD* I 20 241; first *OED* example 1866).

In 1842 he had been criticized for using *mutual friend* instead of *common friend* in *American Notes*;[19] but he may well then have been alive to the new sense of *common,* which might create ambiguities, and it was presumably the same consideration that made him decide on *Our Mutual Friend* in 1864.

In this connexion it may be mentioned that Dickens makes use of a handful of elliptical forms, the correct interpretation of which depends on the context: *breach* 'breach of promise' (*OCS* 8 61); *call* 'call to the bar' (*SB* 357); *flint* 'skinflint' (*NN* 41 539); *House* 'workhouse' (*SB* 2); *lock* 'lock-keeper' (*OMF* III 8 508); and *mill* 'treadmill' (*SB* 273).

39. Euphemism. A special case of the use of neutral terms in pregnant senses is euphemism. The examples given below are characteristic of spoken language:

'We knew pretty well that we were *helping ourselves,* before we met here, I believe. It's no sin' (*CB* 62, = 'steal'; first *OED* example 1868).

'It'll be a deuced unpleasant thing if she takes it into her head to *let out*, when those fellows are here, won't it? ' (*PP* 32 434, = 'use strong language'; first *OED* example 1840).

Victorian conventions of linguistic propriety are behind vapid periphrases like 'more farewells, more something else's' (i.e. kisses; *MC* 53 675), and particularly behind Dickens's way of suggesting oaths and imprecations; he employs a number of variants:

Bark's parts of speech are of an awful sort — principally adjectives. I won't, says Bark, have no adjective police and adjective strangers in my adjective premises! (*UT* 524).

'Capital D her! ' burst out Caroline. (*CS* 375).

He flung out in his violent way, and said, with a D, 'Then do as you like.' (*GE* 11 76).

he says ... that he'll be de'ed if he doesn't think he looks younger than he did ten yers ago. (*SB* 600).

'Gorm the t'other one...' (*DC* 21 312; a vulgar substitute for '(God) damn').

'He's a' — National Participled — 'fool! ' said the Englishman... So he had National Participled the unconscious Corporal... (*CS* 337f.).

he wished he might be something or othered if he didn't make an Autumnal excursion to this place... (*Pilgr.* 4 578, 1846).

'Is it blessed? ' — '... Blest? I should think it was t'othered myself...' (*BH* 16 225).

40. Beyond conventional semantics. In Chapter III we shall examine how Dickens's unconventional view of the world is reflected stylistically over extended narrative passages. In the present chapter it may be fitting to call attention to some semantic peculiarities that may perhaps also be seen as reflections of Dickens's world view.

In our conventional world there are human beings — men and women — , animals, and 'things'; it may, however, be noted that some of Dickens's semantic innovations entail a reclassification of these categories.

In section 5, mention was made of the extended use of *accident*: 'the victim of an accident'. There are a number of parallel cases in which an abstract noun comes to denote a person, namely the words *arrival, fraud, half-price, prose, tease,* and *title*:

The popular Mr. Hilton was the next arrival... (*SB* 329; the first *OED* example is from 1847).

He is one of the most shameless frauds and impositions of this time.(*UT* 379).

... the curtain drawn up for the convenience of the half-price on their ejectment from the ring... (*SB* 107).

'I verily believe you have said that fifty thousand times, in my hearing. What a Prose you are! ' (*MC* 37 586).

'what a teaze you are' (*BH* 30 416).

Miss Teresa went to bed, considering whether, in the event of her marrying a title, she could conscientiously encourage the visits of her present associates... (*SB* 361; first *OED* example 1900).

In other cases an abstract noun is used to refer to a group of people. According to the *OED*, Dickens is the first to make 'quasi-personified' use of *gentility*:

Here were poor streets where faded gentility essayed with scanty space and ship-wrecked means to make its last feeble stand... (*OCS* 15 115).

while the corresponding use of the following abstracts goes unrecorded in the *OED*:

shabby magnificence flaunted its threadbare liveries and tarnished cocked hats... · (*PI* 405).

Mendicity on commission stooped in their high shoulders, shambled in their unsteady legs... (*LD* I 9 91).

... her determination ... to bring actions for trespass against the whole donkey proprietorship of Dover (*DC* 13 198).

In the last examples we note the rather striking numerical vacillation which manifests itself in the nouns and pronouns that refer back to the personified abstracts (cf. III.8).
In one or two cases the transfer of a sex-bound word to the other sex gives rise to neologisms:

he would sometimes reward her [Miss Sally Brass] with a hearty slap on the back, and protest that she was a devilish good fellow... (*OCS* 36 271).

'She contended that any reference to a flannel petticoat was improper ... I pleaded my coverture; being a married man.' (*SB* 435; *coverture* means 'the condition or position of a woman during her married life').

41. Animals, things, and people. There is nothing particularly striking about the application to people of the names of animals, for this is a time-honoured tradition. Still it may be noted that Dickens introduces some neologisms. In *Sketches by Boz* a stupid person is termed *a donkey* (286); in *Pickwick Papers* a boy who is given to puffing and blowing is called *a young grampus* (25 350); and in one of his letters Dickens describes 'a human Prawn' (*Pilgr.* 4 253, 1845). He is also the originator of the use of *animal* to refer to a person:

Misty ideas of being a young man at my own disposal, of the importance attaching to a young man at his own disposal, of the wonderful things to be seen and done by that magnificent animal ... lured me away. (*DC* 19 273).

More striking are the passages in which a 'thing' word is applied to a human being, for instance:

So he stopped the unstamped advertisement — an animated sandwich, composed of a boy between two boards (*SB* 257).

'Here you are, sir,' shouted a strange specimen of the human race. (*PP* 2 6).

'What does this allusion to the slow coach mean? ...It may be a reference to Pickwick himself, who has ... been a criminally slow coach during the whole of this transaction.' (*PP* 34 474; this and an 1837 quotation from Marryat are the first two *OED* examples of figurative use).

'She'll learn to like me better, when I'm not a drag upon her' (*CB* 218, 1845, 'a heavy obstruction to progress'; first *OED* example 1857).

Worth quoting here is also the graphic use of *doormat* in 'She asked me and Joe whether we supposed she was door-mats under our feet, and how we dared to use her so.' (*GE* 12 91).

42. Animation. All the instances of metaphorical usage given so far have involved the depersonalization of human beings. Conversely, we sometimes find Dickens's mind moving in the opposite direction, when he endows inanimate objects with human qualities. Thus there occurs in *Dombey and Son* a description of 'dining-tables, *gymnastic* with their legs upward on the tops of other dining-tables' (9 114); in *Bleak House* there is a reference to 'a lame invalid of a sofa' (4 37); and on two occasions Dickens employs the verb *to languish* — which normally has a person as its subject — in a peculiar manner:

The robbery at the Bank had not languished before, and did not cease to occupy a front place in the attention of the principal of that establishment now. (*HT* III 4 246).

Lightwood retained no other affairs in his hands than such as still lingered and languished about the undiscovered criminal (*OMF* I 16 194).

Again, in two passages we find the anatomical adjective *knock-kneed* cropping up outside its normal sphere of application: in 'knock-knee'd sugar-tongs' (*DS* 9 119), and — rather more strikingly — in a description of George Sampson's mind which, we learn, 'was constitutionally a knock-knee'd mind, and never very strong upon its legs' (*OMF* III 4 457; this, according to the *OED*, is the first figurative use of the adjective in the sense of 'halting; feeble').

43. From physical to non-physical. There are still other instances of metaphorical usage; they do not always lend themselves easily to classification, but perhaps we may recognize one type of metaphor in which terms that basically denote some kind of physical action or characteristic come to be employed in various non-physical senses. This applies to verbal expressions like *cork down, touch,* and *be on the move,* which are all put to new uses by Dickens:

'That chap ... though he has all his faculties about him..., bottled up and corked down, has no more imagination than Barnaby has' (*BR* 11 86).

'Is there one of you that could touch him or come near him on any scent!Eh?' (*OT* 43 330; 'attain equality with').

'Dombey,' said the Major, 'your wife's mother is on the move, sir.' (*DS* 40 572; = 'dying').

Similarly, *a whitewasher* is used of a person who tries to conceal another's faults (*LD* I 11 127); and among adjectives we may mention *dim* 'somewhat stupid' (*DS* 31 439), *foggy* 'not clear to one's mind' (*PP* 55 772), and *vinegary* 'morose' (*DS* 31 436).

No matter what their interpretation is, the examples of unconventional semantics listed here and in the preceding sections must have struck nineteenth-century readers as zestful and original — or alternatively as artificial and strained — for they were new then. It may be difficult for a modern reader to grasp this fully since he is familiar with the figurative uses of the words. Most of them are in the *OED*, which suggests that they were not considered unduly private. However, an overall characterization of Dickens's vocabulary will have to consider less well-known strata as well: rare words, nonce-words, decided oddities, and words that must be said to be private and occasional, having arisen in special contexts.

44. Rare words and nonce-words. Dickens is the creator of a sprinkling of words that are labelled 'rare' by the *OED*, for instance:

The 'prentices no longer carried clubs wherewith to mace the citizens. (*BR* 4 34; 'to strike (as) with a mace').

... tear-blotted copy-books, canings, rulerings... (*DC* 7 106; 'beatings with a ruler').

'He ain't ill. He's only a little swipey, you know.' (*MC* 28 456; 'tipsy').

There are, further, a number of nonce-words, labelled as such by the *OED*. We note converted forms like *to butler* (*LD* II 13 613; probably by now ousted by the back-formation *to buttle*), *to message* (*BR* 24 186), *to mother-in-law* (*LD* II 14 590), and *to wrong* as in 'the ship rights. Before one can say 'Thank Heaven!' she wrongs again.' (*AN* 2 12). There is the adjective *draggle-haired* 'with hair hanging wet and untidy' (*OMF* III 10 544), formed on the analogy of *draggle-tailed.* Further, there are fanciful words like the adjective *sofane* 'relating to a sofa' (*UT* 56) and the noun *touch-me-not-ishness* (*PP* 8 96).

Additional examples, listed in Appendix A, are *admonitorial, coachfulness, coachlessness, conductorial, to counterpray, distributionist, jog-trotty, kitchen-pokerness, to look out, meltability, to opium-smoke, to poor, somethingean, stage-stricken, stand-up* (adj.), *velveteeny, vocular, waiterhood,* and *wide-awake.*

45. Fanciful words. It is a somewhat arbitrary matter to label words on the fringe of the language. Thus, though they seem to be on a par, the *OED* describes the two words *coachfulness* and *coachlessness* as 'nonce-word' and 'rare', respectively, and some of Dickens's coinages have apparently been considered so fanciful as not to deserve admission to the *OED*:

'I only hope she's not a *Pagodian* dissenter.' (*LD* I 13 152).

... a thing that ... might obtain some promotion for the Major — which he well deserves and would be none the worse for ... *L.S.D.-ically. (CS* 390).

... wickedly, falsely, traitorously, and otherwise *evil-adverbiously*... (*TC* II 2 59).

'But a architectural lodging!' That seemed to trouble the waiter's head, and he shook it. — 'Anything *Cathedraly,* now,' Mr. Datchery suggested. (*ED* 18 207).

But when Dickens coins an unusual word, he generally contrives to make it, if not acceptable, at least intelligible to the reader by placing it in helpful surroundings. In most cases a semantically related conventional term precedes the neologism:

The egotistical couple may be young, old, middle-aged, well to do or *ill to do*... (*SB* 588).

... that class which is so aptly and expressively designated as 'shabby-genteel' ... this compound of the two — this *shabby-gentility* — is as purely local as the statue at Charing Cross (*SB* 262).

... a flushed page ... who seemed to have in part outgrown and in part *out-pushed* his strength... (*DS* 21 287).

her eyes would play the Devil with the youngsters before long — 'and the *oldsters* too, sir, if you come to that,' added the Major (*DS* 10 127).

There is a moral sinuosity about her — a kind of *corkscrewism*... (*Pilgr.* 5 375, 1848).

'We'll break it to you gently, dearest Pa,' said Bella. — 'My dear,' returned the cherub,'you broke so much in the first — Gush, if I may so express myself — that I think I am equal to a good large *breakage* now.' (*OMF* III 16 607).

Compare *beamy, pooh-pooher, raspish, round-elbowed,* and *tickler* in Appendix A.

In introducing the blend *wiglomeration* Dickens makes it sum up all the forbidding aspects of a Chancery lawsuit:

'The whole thing will be vastly ceremonious, wordy, unsatisfactory, and expensive, and I call it, in general, Wiglomeration...' (*BH* 8 98).

This is a telescoping of the words *wig* and *conglomeration,* suggesting 'ceremonious fuss in legal proceedings'. There are few blends before the Victorian Age,[20] and I have only found one other word in Dickens that may belong to the same type, the word *prejoction* (for which see Appendix A).

Sometimes there is, however, no supporting word in the context, so that the reader has to interpret an expression on the basis of his knowledge of parallel expressions. This is true of the following passage:

Her systematic manner of flying at her and pouncing on her ... is wonderful; evincing an accomplishment in the art of *girl-driving,* seldom reached by the oldest practitioners. (*BH* 21 293f.).

which presupposes a knowledge of the word *slave-driving*.

On related phenomena illustrating the stylistic cohesion that is so characteristic of Dickens see III.24.

46. Private and occasional. The language of Dickens's letters throws an interesting sidelight on the language he uses in his fiction. In his fictional prose he had to consider the general reader, and he normally toned down his natural linguistic exuberance; but he obviously felt that in his private correspondence he need not discipline himself to the same extent. Here we find extravagant language that would not have been suitable in the novels, and there is room for private allusions and jokes. Let me exemplify.

In 1839 an actor friend was playing Trinculo, and Dickens wrote to him: '... if you will come in when you have done Trinculizing...' (*Pilgr.* I 506). In a letter from 1841 he refers to the death of little Nell as 'that Nellicide' (*Pilgr.* 2 228). A favourite word of Dickens's youth is *flare,* which he employs both as a noun and as a verb: 'an unpremeditated flare at the English Opera House last night with the ladies' (*Pilgr.* 1 40, 1834; here the word seems to mean 'convivial activities'); 'I am most happy to hear my Godson ... is flaring up so rig'lar' (*Pilgr.* 1 39, 1834; the verb probably means 'flourish'). He even forms an irregular past of the verb, on the analogy of *bear/bore*: 'On the preceding day I was at Northampton, and 'flore' slightly' (*Pilgr.* 1 110, 1835; an editorial comment informs us that 'the allusion here is probably to some convivial party') He creates the verb *to ball* 'to give a ball in honour of': '... how I have been dined, and balled (there were 3000 people at the ball) and feted in all directions' (*Pilgr.* 3 115, 1842), and we note his predilection for adjectives in *-y* in forms like *sea-sicky* (of lakes; *Pilgr.* 3 182, 1842), *Adam-and-Evey* (of a dedication; *Pilgr.* 3 297, 1842), and *public-housey*: 'I call him so, [*sc.* Skittles] from something skittle-playing and public-housey in his countenance' (*Pilgr.* 4 659, 1846). The suffix *-y* competes with *-ish*: elsewhere Dickens suggests that a friend and he might be *public house-ish* (*Pilgr.* 2 60, 1840).

Such more or less fanciful words are scattered all over his letters. To a friend with a black eye he puts the question: 'Did you take it naturally or bacchanalially?' (*Pilgr.* 1 618, 1839), and his advice to another friend goes: 'You must regard his invitation (Manchesterially speaking) as a great compliment.' (*Pilgr.* 4 404, 1845). On the basis of *prompter* he coins the adjective *prompterian* (*Pilgr.* 5 354, 1848), and about Lord Lansdowne he makes the following observation: 'There has been a kind of grim imbecility and gouty Chesterfieldianity about Ld. Lansdowne this year' (*Pilgr.* 5 580, 1849). In his letters Dickens writes without restraint.

47. Dickens's contribution assessed. I have found a total of 1,059 neologisms in Dickens's fiction, periodical essays, and letters, most of them in the novels. No doubt I have overlooked a few, or perhaps more than a few; but even that figure suggests a very high degree of creativity and originality. The majority of these neologisms — 732 — have been established as such on the authority of the *OED*. To this figure should be added 176 words and phrases which have been overlooked by the *OED* as Dickensian neologisms. There is an additional batch of 151 words and phrases that are unrecorded in the *OED*, but which may have been coined or introduced by Dickens.

If we consider these lexical innovations from the point of view of word-class representation, we find the following distribution:

Nouns	449
Adjectives	241
Verbs	206
Adverbs	52
Prepositions	6
Interjections	4

To these figures should be added 101 idioms first used by Dickens. It will be seen that nouns heavily outnumber the other classes, but that adjectives and verbs also loom large.

If the question is asked whether Dickens is equally creative throughout his career, it may be answered by a look at the number of neologisms found in the individual works. Below I shall give my figures for *Sketches by Boz* and the novels, leaving out of account the letters and periodical articles, which would not present a very clear picture since they span a long period. Besides, if we want to assess Dickens's contribution to English, it is natural to focus on the novels, which were read in his day, while his letters only began to be studied after his death.

	neologisms
Sketches by Boz	120
Pickwick Papers	106
Oliver Twist	34
Nicholas Nickleby	73
The Old Curiosity Shop	33
Barnaby Rudge	31
Martin Chuzzlewit	26
Dombey and Son	66
David Copperfield	28
Bleak House	86

	neologisms
Hard Times	32
Little Dorrit	39
A Tale of Two Cities	17
Great Expectations	35
Our Mutual Friend	56
The Mystery of Edwin Drood	10

It will be seen that the beginning of Dickens's career marks his largest contribution to the vocabulary. Each of his first two published works contains more than a hundred neologisms; apparently there is a heavy decline in *Oliver Twist* as compared with *Nicholas Nickleby,* but that is probably accounted for by the fact that the latter novel is approximately twice the length of *Oliver.* From *The Old Curiosity Shop* onwards Dickens's lexical innovation is on a more modest scale, though certain figures stand out: those for *Dombey and Son, Bleak House,* and *Our Mutual Friend.* It is probably impossible to draw any specific conclusions from this statistical material; why, for instance, should the figures for *Martin Chuzzlewit* and *David Copperfield* be so comparatively low? But at least the figures show that Dickens begins his career with a burst of creativity, and that even in as late a work as *Our Mutual Friend* his linguistic fertility is very far from having left him.

Otto Jespersen states that 'poets and novelists are responsible for extremely few word-coinages: what they have done is chiefly to give literary currency to words that were already used in everyday speech.'[21]. Giving literary currency to already existing words was no doubt part of Dickens's endeavour; it may be relevant to quote here what Hans Aarsleff says about innovators in intellectual history and the history of science: 'the innovative ideas of individuals play an important role, but they occur in particular contexts.'[22] It is, however, hard to agree with Jespersen's generalization, for it seems preposterous for anybody to assert that the majority of the numerous neologisms that Dickens has to his credit simply testify to his undoubtedly fine ear for contemporary speech. It should appear from this chapter how Dickens exploits — and in some cases perhaps over-exploits — the possibilities of English. He is a large-scale contributor to the vocabulary of English.

CHAPTER III: SYNTAX AND STYLE

1. Existing patterns exploited. In this chapter we shall consider how much foundation there is for the nineteenth-century criticism of Dickens's 'fine, manly disregard of syntax' (I.4). In the first sections we shall examine some striking aspects of his syntax; but it should be stated at once that he is not a syntactic innovator in the sense that he introduces a lot of new constructions. What he does in a number of cases is to exploit — and occasionally to over-exploit — the syntactic potential of English. Thus his syntactic behaviour may be said to form a parallel to some of his procedures as a lexical neologist: we may, for instance, compare his very free use of conversion (II.14) with the liberties he takes with premodified constructions and with collective nouns. There is no doubt that in some respects he tends to go beyond the limits of normal grammar.

2. Archaisms. Before we proceed to a discussion of Dickens's syntactic peculiarities, it may be fitting to consider briefly the question of archaisms. As in the case of the vocabulary, we have to distinguish between features that were archaic in Dickens's day and features that have become archaic since then. Some examples of the latter category were given above (I.3). If we look for instances of features that were archaic in the nineteenth century, we shall find that they are few and far between. There is the striking use of *the which* as a relative:

... two young ladies ... wearing miraculously small shoes, and the thinnest possible silk stockings: the which their rocking-chairs developed [i.e. displayed] to a distracting extent. (*MC* 17 285).

According to Jespersen[1] *the which* practically died out in the first half of the eighteenth century.

It is also a bit surprising to find Fascination Fledgeby — who is a speaker of Standard English — making use of the typical eighteenth-century combination *you was* (*OMF* II 5 271); of course Dickens's substandard speakers make frequent use of it. A further point worth listing here is a type of interrogative clause that was common in Old and Middle English, but which died out before 1600; this type is a simple direct question introduced by the particle *whether,* 'as if depending on a principal clause understood' (*OED, whether,* 2):

Whether myrmidons of Justice ... would be lying in ambush behind the gate? (*GE* 12 87).

Occasionally Dickens uses the old subjunctive construction for exhortation: '*Turn we* our eyes upon two homes...' (*DS* 33 471). If it is added that he sometimes employs the *-th* ending instead of the *-s* ending in the third person singular in order to convey a note of (mock) solemnity: 'what is called the world — a conventional phrase which, being interpreted, often signifieth all the rascals in it' (*NN* 3 28), this practically exhausts the number of syntactic archaisms to be found.

3. Premodification. One area in which Dickens's unconventionality is particularly prominent is in his handling of premodified constructions. We have already commented on some of the striking adjectival types (II. 20-22) which make for semantic density. Add to this that the sheer length of some of these constructions is remarkable. We may consider the strings of parallel attributive adjectives that are so frequently met with in Dickens to be a combined outcome of his exuberance and of his wish to convey a lot of information in brief compass: 'stagnant, slimy, rotten, filthy water' (*AN* 13 178); 'a silly, old, meek-faced, garlic-eating, immeasurably polite Chevalier' (*PI* 272); 'a bawling, splashing, link-lighted, umbrella-struggling, hackney-coach-jostling, patten-clinking, muddy, miserable world' (*DC* 19 286). These are attempts to overcome the linearity of language by packing a lot of information into one construction.

Some of the excessively long premodified constructions strike a humorous note owing to their very length; this is true of the bogus company styled 'the United Metropolitan Improved Hot Muffin and Crumpet Baking and Punctual Delivery Company' (*NN* 2 10) as well as of the reply made by the voluble Sam Weller when he is asked if he has no eyes:

'Yes, I have a pair of eyes ... and that's just it. If they wos a pair of patent double million magnifyin' gas microscopes of hextra power, p'raps I might be able to see through a flight of stairs! ' (*PP* 34 484).

In such examples it is mainly the length of the construction that is striking; in other cases it is the peculiar semantic relationship between premodifier and noun that calls attention to itself, as when we read of Mr. Squeers that he not infrequently purchased the bodies of horned cattle which had died a natural death 'for boy consumption' (*NN* 7 81), a sequence that at least in principle is ambiguous between a subjective and an objective interpretation. In *Dombey and Son* there is a description of

a musty little back room usually devoted to the consumption of soups, and pervaded by *an oxtail atmosphere.* (38 532).

In a couple of passages Dickens makes highly idiosyncratic use of the indefinite pronoun *no* preceded by a possessive:

It may have arisen ... out of a woman's quick association of ideas, or out of a woman's no association of ideas... (*LD* II 27 732).

The French gentleman, though he had no eyes, ... appeared ... to open and shut his no eyes (*OMF* III 14 576).

Such formulations involve a paradoxical manipulation of phenomena that are assumed or asserted to be non-existent.

4. *String-compounds.* If an entire sentence or phrase is given attributive function, we speak of string-compounds;[2] examples are:

a little man with a puffy Say-nothing-to-me,-or-I'll-contradict-you sort of countenance (*PP* 7 93).

I am not up to the wanting-employment-in-an-office move (*CS* 358),

These are nonce-formations, and the same is true of examples like 'a show-fight little island' (*CS* 332) and 'a curious up-all-night air' (*LD* I 20 233); on the other hand the Dickensian coinages seen in 'the cool matter-of-course manner of this reply' (*BR* 404) and 'an odd-job-man' (*TC* II 1 51) have become current.

String-compounds can be freely formed, and Dickens appears to have been one of the first to make extensive use of them. Perhaps the culminating instance of the type occurs in one of his letters, where he felt no need to restrain himself: 'that long-deferred-but-never-sufficiently-to-be-considered-and-never-to-be-approached-though-not-yet-planned-or-named Periodical' (*Pilgr.* 5 582, 1849), with a string of no less than twenty premodifiers.

5. *Second mention condensed.* One sort of collocational oddity that is sometimes met with in the nominal group is accounted for by a look at Dickens's stylistic habit of condensing a phrase the second time it appears. If we consider in isolation a sequence like *the mashed potatoes messenger* (*LD* I 10 113), it seems peculiar (and is perhaps open to more

than one interpretation); however, the reader is supposed to remember that one page earlier he was introduced to 'a messenger who ... was eating mashed potatoes and gravy'. Similar examples are: 'a young fellow in mulberry-coloured livery − − The mulberry man' (*PP* 16 212f.), 'every gentleman seems to have pen and ink in his pocket − − One of the pen and ink gentlemen' (*DS* 59 830ff.), and the following passage from *Our Mutual Friend*:

'I always was a pepperer. You Bob Gliddery there, put the chain upon the door and get ye down to your supper.' − With an alacrity that seemed no less referable to the pepperer fact than the supper fact, Bob obeyed... (I 6 67).

The principle of condensation at second mention is a recognized stylistic device, but Dickens tends to go rather far in using it, and he resorts to other striking devices when he is in need of back-reference to nouns. One of them is the use of initials, as in *Our Mutual Friend*, where a 'gruff and glum old pensioner' becomes first 'Gruff and Glum', next 'G. and G.' (IV 4 664f.); similarly, it is 'Toddles and Poddles' at first mention, 'T. and P.' at second mention (*ibid.*, I 16 203). − Compare the discussion of non-pronominalization in section 12.

6. Articles and determiners. In Standard English there are certain rules governing the use of articles and determiners with nouns. This is an area in which Dickens's language is often unconventional. Sometimes he deviates from normal usage in order to conform to a special type of story-telling that resembles telegraphese and tends to become breathless, as it were, as the narrator gets into his stride:

'... He must have been a boy of spirit and resource ... he burst in on his father, and pleaded his sister's cause. Venerable parent promptly resorts to anathematisation, and turns him out. Shocked and terrified boy takes flight... (*OMF* I 2 15).

We note that the absence of determiners goes hand in hand with a switch into the dramatic present. But the device is also Dickens's own. It occurs, for instance, in *Bleak House*, where we are first introduced to *the beadle* and *the policeman,* after which the account continues: 'Beadle goes into various shops and parlours ... Policeman seen to smile...' (11 144); here another characteristic of telegraphese is the omission of a finite verb. In *Pictures from Italy* Dickens tells us of a little old, swarthy woman, who is first referred to as *this She-Goblin,* subsequently becoming plain *Goblin* (275); that is, the word is treated as a kind of proper name. The articles may also be dispensed with for the purpose of suggesting the rapid succession of events:

Sound of advancing voices, sound of advancing steps. Shuffle and talk without. Momentary pause. Two peculiarly blunt knocks or pokes at the door... (*OMF* III 2 442).

At the dinner party given by the Merdles (*LD* I 21 248f.) we learn that a lot of magnates are present, among them *Bishop magnates* and *magnates from the bar*; they are introduced to the reader in these terms, but subsequently the guests are simply referred to as *Bishop* and *Bar:* 'Bishop said he was glad to think...'; 'Bar, with his little insinuating Jury droop...' Here again, we have a highly unconventional transition from common names to proper names, and the fact that only one from each group of magnates is heard to speak suggests that he is meant to be the typical representative of his group.

7. Countable and uncountable nouns. Many nouns are either countable or uncountable, depending on the context in which they occur; compare 'Indian *teas*' with 'He likes *tea*'. Some nouns, however, are only (or practically only) countable (for instance, *a loaf*), others only (or practically only) uncountable (for instance, *money*). Now it is characteristic of Dickens that he tends to reclassify nouns that are normally countable, as uncountable, often for humorous purposes. In *Our Mutual Friend* we read how Georgiana 'preceded six feet one of discontented footman (an amount of the article that always came for her when she walked home)' (II 4 260); in *Pickwick Papers* there appear two poor relations, 'all smiles and shirt collar' (57 798); and in *Little Dorrit* we are given this account of a wedding: 'It was the peculiarity of the nuptials that they were all Bride. Nobody noticed the Bridegroom.' (II 15 609). Of Inspector Bucket in *Bleak House* we learn that 'through the placid stream of his life, there glides an undercurrent of forefinger' (63 712); there are a number of previous references to the Inspector's forefinger — large, fat, and active — which immediately before this passage is raised to the status of a familiar demon that is consulted by its owner. This change of grammatical status causes the word involved to be viewed as an amorphous and more or less abstract concept; compare the following example from *Great Expectations*: 'from head to foot there was Convict in the very grain of the man' (40 319).

Sometimes this unconventional treatment of nouns that are typical countables is brought about by their being made to appear in construction with a noun that normally combines with abstract uncountables: we talk, for instance, of 'a long stage of inactivity'; but Dickens flouts this convention:

I thought the windows ... were in every stage of dilapidated blind and curtain, crippled flower-pot, cracked glass, dusty decay, and miserable makeshift... (*GE* 21 162)

where only the last two nouns are in normal collocation with *stage*.

While such examples are very numerous, there are occasional instances of reclassification working in the opposite direction, from uncountable to countable. Thus, in *Sketches by Boz* we find *two breads* used for 'two portions of bread' as well as *a cheese* for 'a portion (or piece) of cheese' (216). Mention may also be made of an unconventional use of abstracts in the plural; the *OED* has no examples of the plural of the following words:

His manner of coming and going between the two places, is one of his *impenetrabilities.* (*BH* 42 583; = 'instances of inscrutable behaviour').

their ... *amiabilities* (*NN* 48 635).

William Buffy carries one of these *smartnesses* from the place where he dines, down to the House (*BH* 58 787; = 'specimens of smart town talk').

According to the *OED*, Dickens is the first to convert *frivolity* into a countable noun: 'Mr. Nickleby glanced at these frivolities with great contempt' (*NN* 3 20), but this example can be antedated by a passage from *Oliver Twist*: 'your mother, wholly given up to continental frivolities' (49 375). In a passage from *Martin Chuzzlewit*: 'self; with its long train of suspicions, *lusts,* deceits, and all their growing consequences' (52 796) the italicized form is understandable, occurring as it does in a context of plurality; in normal usage, however, *lust* is treated as a countable only if it is qualified in some way (*fleshly lusts, the lusts of the flesh*).

8. Collective nouns. There is another number-related phenomenon that calls for comment, viz. Dickens's treatment of collective nouns. In principle, collectives — or nouns of multitude, to use Lindley Murray's term[3] — can combine with either singular or plural verbs and pronouns (in British English), depending on whether the emphasis is on a unitary or a plural concept; compare contemporary examples like 'His family is an old one' and 'His family are early risers'. But Dickens produces a striking effect when he combines the unitary concept with plurality in the same construction:

The whole court, adult as well as boy, is sleepless for that night, and can do nothing but wrap up its many heads. (*BH* 33 458).

We note that *court* is treated as a grammatical singular, and that this creates a slightly humorous clash with *its many heads,* although it may have been the author's prime concern to suggest that all the inhabitants of the court react in the same way. I append a few similar examples, which in some cases involve a clash not only as far as number is concerned, but also a clash between the pronoun *it* and a verb that normally has a human agent as its subject:

... a full account of what the government had said in a whisper the last time they dined with it, and how the government had been observed to wink when it said so... (*NN* 2 12).

The public, represented by a boy with a comforter, and a shabby-genteel man secretly eating crumbs out of his coat pockets, was warming itself at a stove in the centre of the court. (*DC* 23 352).

Yet now, the inconstant public turned its back upon them, and even leaned its elbows carelessly against the bar ... and shook off the mud from its shoes, and also lent and borrowed fire for pipes. (*UT* 191).

The village itself was so steeped in autumnal foliage ... that one might have fancied it was out a bird's-nesting, and was (as indeed it was) a wonderful climber. (*CS* 256).

In the last quotation *village* is used ambiguously: at the beginning of the passage it means 'collection of houses', at the end 'villagers', and this ambivalence is what creates the oddity. Similar examples are the following:

'the omnibus,' as Miss La Creevy protested, 'swore so dreadfully, that it was quite awful to hear it.' (*NN* 38 488; the driver or the passengers collectively?)

If your business necessitated your seeing 'the House', you were put into a species of condemned hold ..., where you meditated on a misspent life, until the house came with its hands in its pockets (*TC* II 1 49f.).

The house here means 'the manager of the bank' (a sense not attested by the *OED*). In the following passage Dickens also plays a trick on the reader, in order to give vent to his humorous bent:

The day-scholars ... had hooted the beadle, and pelted the constabulary — an elderly gentleman in top-boots (*PP* 24 328).

Constabulary means 'an organized body of constables', but the context forces it into the unconventional sense of 'a constable'. A similar procedure is followed with the word *bodyguard*: 'attached to Mrs. Pott's person was a bodyguard of one, a young lady' (*PP* 18 239). This, however, turns out to be an innovation that was destined to take root. Until the publication of *Pickwick Papers* the word was only used of a group of persons, so that this is presumably the first — and at the time of its appearance mildly humorous — example of a neologism that nobody smiles at today. The case is interesting; it shows that what began as a mild joke came to be established usage: 'a person whose duty it is to guard an important person'. In his next novel Dickens makes unreserved use of *bodyguard* in its new sense: 'Oliver ... had been walking in the streets, with Mr. Giles for a bodyguard' (*OT* 41 309).

9. 'Person' and related matters. As we have just seen, an expression that is grammatically singular may imply a plurality, and this is why we find a plural possessive referring back to *every person* in 'every person should have their rights' (*BH* 22 309). Compare further

The person, whoever it was, had come in suddenly and with so little noise, that Mr. Pickwick had had no time to call out, or oppose *their* entrance. (*PP* 22 308).

where, although it is obvious that only one person is involved, the unknown sex of that person may have prompted the avoidance of *he*; it is in fact a lady who enters. If Lindley Murray had dealt with such examples, he would no doubt have condemned them, since he proscribes the use of plural pronouns to refer back to indefinite pronouns;[4] this is usage that is often found in Dickens, for instance: 'Let us give everybody their due' (*NN* 41 532); 'Nobody cares about me now, and it's very nat'ral they shouldn't (*PP* 28 382). But sometimes he follows the rule of prescriptive grammar: 'Everybody should know his own business' (*GE* 51 388).

If an expression that is grammatically singular may imply a plurality and is treated accordingly, it is not surprising that we should also find grammatical plurals with a singular demonstrative pronoun: 'in the course of that three minutes' (*NN* 33 425); 'that ten thousand pounds' (*NN* 56 739). There are also occasional constructions in which a binomial subject has a singular verb, probably owing to the influence of a singular predicative: 'old Arthur Gride and matrimony is a most anomalous conjunction of words' (*NN* 47 614).

10. 'Every gum'. There is a final point concerning number that should be mentioned. It is part and parcel of the English grammatical system to distinguish between 'two' and 'more than two'; this is reflected, for instance, in the distinction between *both* and *all, neither*[5] (of them) and *none* (of them). When we read of Mr. Carker:

As Mr. Dombey raised his eyes, it [*sc.* the face of Mr. Carker] changed back ... to its old expression, and showed him every gum of which it stood possessed. (*DS* 26 365, a variant of *every tooth* (26 363); there is a similar formulation at 27 391).

the use of *every* goes against normal usage, suggesting more than two as it does; it is clear that the narrator has chosen this hyperbolic expression in order to place extra emphasis on Mr. Carker's dominant physical characteristic.

11. 'We' and 'our'. In some respects Dickens's use of the personal pronouns is striking. According to Poutsma it was Walter Scott who was the first writer to employ the so-called 'paternal *we*'[6], used jocularly for example by a doctor to his patient. Examples of this occur in Dickens; in fact the first *OED* instance of *our* in paternal use comes from *Little Dorrit*: 'Now, let's see whether there's anything else the matter, and how our ribs are? ' (I 13 164). Somewhat different is the use of *we* and *our* in Mr. Murdstone's ominous speech to his refractory stepson: 'We shall soon improve our youthful humours' (*DC* 4 46). And an element of irony or sarcasm seems to be present in Pip's use of *we* when the deafness of the Aged causes a hitch in the wedding ceremony where Pip acts as best man: 'I had doubts for the moment whether we should get completely married that day.' (*GE* 55 431). — For Dickens's peculiar treatment of *we* and *our* in reported speech see IV.5, 8.

12. Non-pronominalization. The normal procedure when a noun or a name has been introduced is to employ a pronoun for back-reference. Dickens has, however, a very strong tendency to avoid using pronouns for this purpose. He contrives to avoid pronominalization in two ways: either by repeating the nominal or by introducing a variant, and both procedures involve a greater or lesser degree of deviation from normal style. Let us consider repetition first. Sometimes the repetition of a noun merely serves to underline the thoroughness of a process, as in

Bella soaped his face and rubbed his face, and soaped his hands and rubbed his hands... (*OMF* IV 5 684f.).

Or what is conveyed is a feeling of frustration in somebody who is unsuccessful in his attempt:

Fledgeby knocked and rang, and Fledgeby rang and knocked, but no one came. Fledgeby crossed the narrow street and looked up at the house-windows, but nobody looked down at Fledgeby. (*OMF* II 5 275).

But more often non-pronominalization is a vehicle for irony or humour; in the first quotation given below, repetition seems very apt for suggesting pompous Mr. Bumble's irritation:

'The Clerkinwell Sessions have brought it upon themselves, ma'am,' replied Mr. Bumble; 'and if the Clerkinwell Sessions find that they come off rather worse than they expected, the Clerkinwell Sessions have only themselves to thank.' (*OT* 17 120).

Or what is conveyed is the narrator's ironical attitude towards self-important characters:

Thomas Gradgrind now presented Thomas Gradgrind to the little pitchers before him (*HT* I 2 3).

Mr. Podsnap was well to do, and stood very high in Mr. Podsnap's opinion. (*OMF* I 11 128).

In numerous cases there is a semantic variant at second mention: 'elegant variation'. This is one of Dickens's mannerisms, no doubt intended to be humorous, but often somewhat contrived, and it is probably the overdose that produces this effect. Here are a handful of examples:

a shirt collar − − that appendage (*PP* 30 407).

the Annual Register − − that ingenious compilation (*OMF* III 5 467).

A carriage was hired from the Town Arms, ... and a chariot was ordered from the same repository (*PP* 15 198).

one of the pockets of his square blue coat − − that repository (*DS* 9 119).

gentlemen students, who bought live donkeys, and made experiments on those quadrupeds (*DC* 27 400).

a meal of chaff − − that equine provision (*LD* II 9 537).

I took the opportunity of being alone in the courtyard, to look at my coarse hands and my common boots. My opinion of those accessories was not favourable. (*GE* 8 57).

As will be noted, this mannerism may create stylistic tension between a plain English word at first mention and a Latinate term at second mention; compare II.32 and IV.4.

13. Adjectives reclassified. As was noted in section 7, Dickens has a tendency to reclassify nouns. A similar tendency manifests itself in his handling of some adjectives. This word-class may be divided into two groups: descriptive (or gradable) adjectives, which may take modifiers like *very,* and classifying (or non-gradable) adjectives, which do not normally take modifiers: either somebody is, or is not, say, *English*; however, it is possible to say 'he is very English', and as this example suggests, non-gradable adjectives can be reclassified. This is sometimes done by Dickens for humorous purposes:

He said, however, that the delight was mutual, and Lord Frederick added that it was mutual, whereupon Messrs. Pyke and Pluck were heard to murmur from the distance that it was very mutual indeed. (*NN* 27 352).

The Doctor ... had ... a chin so very double that it was a wonder how he ever managed to shave into the creases. (*DS* 11 142).

I found ... my easy chair imitating my aunt's much easier chair in its position at the open window. (*DC* 35 515).

He had doubts whether references to any individual capital, or fortune, might not seem a wretchedly retail affair to so wholesale a dealer. (*LD* II 16 616).

Similarly, the *light porter* (a porter whose task is (was) to carry light luggage only) referred to in *Hard Times* (II 1 113) is later described as being 'a very light porter indeed', and in one of his speeches Dickens employs the expression 'a very home-made fishing-rod' (Fielding, p. 271). In 'the small gentleman ... got very tenor indeed, in the excitement of his feelings' (*SB* 128) a noun that is often used as a non-gradable attributive adjective is given predicative function *and* a modifier. Occasionally an adverb is given the same treatment: 'the Printers ... maimed my last communication, most surgically' (*Pilgr.* 3 352, 1842).

There occurs one further deviation from normal adjectival usage. When one has to state the length or breadth of something, it is customary to use positive (or unmarked) adjectives like *long* and *wide* ('how long is it? ') or the corresponding nouns. But this rule is broken in *American Notes* with the implication that an abnormal state of things requires abnormal usage:

I am afraid to tell how many feet short this vessel was, or how many feet narrow; to apply the words length and width to such measurement would be a contradiction in terms. (5 73).

14. The use of the present tense. The so-called historic or dramatic present is a traditional device that an author may resort to in order to lend a particular degree of vividness to his story. Dickens makes occasional use of it in its traditional form. In *Pickwick Papers* the first paragraph of chapter 28 continues the narrative in the preterit, which had been used up till then — the normal tense; after this there follow a couple of paragraphs containing a panegyric on Christmas, and here the present is employed, which is natural enough, since what is said about Christmas is in the nature of an eternal truth. But the use of the present tense is continued when the narrative is resumed after the digression, and it is only three or four pages later that we return to the normal narrative tense: 'Such was the progress of Mr. Pickwick and his friends...' (28 378). The account of their progress is highlighted through the use of the present tense.

This example is not particularly striking, but it should be noted that in some of his later works Dickens exploits the contrast between the tenses with great artistry. If the preterit is the normal (unmarked) narrative tense, this means that the passages in which the present is used are somehow foregrounded. Most of *Dombey and Son* is told in the preterit, but on a few occasions the narrator switches into the present, which is employed, for instance, to bring home to the reader the muted atmosphere reigning after young Paul has died (chapter 18); when the narrator returns to the preterit, we feel that we have now returned to comparatively normal conditions. Later in the novel the present is again made use of, this time to describe the special atmosphere surrounding Mr. Dombey's second wedding — not a happy event either (chapter 31). Most of *David Copperfield* is in the preterit; however, in the first pages of chapter 2 the narrator switches into the present when trying to conjure up his early childhood memories, and in the four retrospective chapters he once more resorts to the present for the purpose of focussing sharply on four stages of his life.

Bleak House represents Dickens's most sustained attempt at exploiting this tense contrast stylistically. In roughly one half of the book we find an almost consistent use of the present tense; this is the half that is stagemanaged by the more or less omniscient narrator, and it contrasts with the preterit used in the other half, where the spokesperson is Esther Summerson. This is probably a deliberate attempt at conveying (comparatively) normal points of view through the normal tense, the preterit, while the present tense is employed to foreground the key theme of the law's delay — one manifestation of a corrupt society. Perhaps the present tense is also meant to symbolize the interminable dragging of the lawsuit, but its main function is to conjure up the peculiar and sinister atmosphere.

There can be no doubt that Dickens's use of the present in *Bleak*

House is highly unconventional. We have proof of this in the fact that the compositors were occasionally disconcerted by it, with the result that 'half a dozen preterites were substituted for presents here and there'[7].

15. Finite verbs dispensed with. Another remarkable feature of Dickens's verbal syntax is that he sometimes chooses to do completely without finite verbs. The best-known example is probably the opening of *Bleak House*: 'London. Michaelmas term lately over, and the Lord Chancellor sitting in Lincoln's Inn Hall. Implacable November weather...'[8] There are other similar instances of nominal style, thus one from *Dombey and Son*: 'The time, an hour short of midnight; the place, a French apartment, comprising some half-dozens rooms...' (54 755), where the device is clearly intended as a kind of stage-direction. Elsewhere in *Dombey and Son* there is the famous description of the rapidly moving train. It is an iconic[9] description that goes on for a page and a half. In the first paragraph, quoted below, there are no finite verbs, but Dickens manages to conjure up a fascinating illusion of the speed and noise of the train; he does this by making use of devices like repetition, alliteration, sound symbolism, parallel present participles, and not least an emphatic string of prepositional phrases, all with *through*:

Away, with a shriek, and a roar, and a rattle, from the town, burrowing among the dwellings of men and making the streets hum, flashing out into the meadows for a moment, mining in through the damp earth, booming on in darkness and heavy air, bursting out again into the sunny day so bright and wide; away, with a shriek, and a roar, and a rattle, through the fields, through the woods, through the corn, through the hay, through the chalk, through the mould, through the clay, through the rock, among objects close at hand and almost in the grasp, ever flying from the traveller, and a deceitful distance ever moving slowly within him; like as in the track of the remorseless monster, Death! (20 280f.).

Such deviations from normal syntax should of course be looked at in context. The specimens that have been given here (compare also the second passage from *Our Mutual Friend* quoted in section 6) are parts of grim or uncanny situations which they intensify. They are thus entirely different in tone from the type of disjointed syntax favoured by Mr. Alfred Jingle, which in one of its manifestations does largely without verbs and articles:

'Ah! fine place,' said the stranger, 'glorious pile — frowning walls — tottering arches — dark nooks — crumbling staircases — old cathedral too — earthy smell...' (*PP* 2 13).

But here Dickens is trying to give us an impression of an extremely whimsical idiolect.

There is another situation in which finite verbs are often dispensed with, namely where there is traditionally a reporting clause (like *he said*) to identify a speaker and a speech. The context may be clear enough without such a clause, which can be rather cumbrous, and instead of it other information may be provided:

'Hallo! what's that!' looking at Oliver, and retreating a pace or two. (*OT* 14 98).

'And I may take it for granted, no doubt,' with a little faltering, 'that you would be quite as contented yourself, John...' (*OMF* IV 5 688).

Dickens is not, however, the first writer to do without an *inquit*; there are similar examples in Jane Austen.[10]

16. The passive of phrasal verbs. Phrasal verbs in the passive are very numerous in Dickens. This construction is much older than the nineteenth century[11], but he has a tendency to go beyond its normal limits. A combination of verb + preposition may have the same function as a transitive verb (*look at — consider*), and in that case the complement of the preposition is 'affected' in the same way that the object of a transitive verb is.[12] In the passive it is the subject that is affected, as in 'Sometimes he will be appealed to by a poor relation' (*SB* 218), which is a normal example of the construction. But consider the following instances:

every inch of the carpet was walked over with similar perseverance; the windows were looked out of, often enough to justify the imposition of an additional duty upon them. (*PP* 51 713).

They [*sc.* cows] are presided over, and slept with, by an old man (*PI* 286).

... as if the wildness of a momentary terror, or distraction, had been struggled with and overcome... (*PI* 395).

'my daughter has been turned away from, and cast out' (*DS* 58 824).

'... it might be skilfully led up to.' (*OMF* III 12 560).

Mr. Sapsea 'dresses at' the Dean; has been bowed to for the Dean, in mistake... (*ED* 4 31).

One has to strain one's imagination to see how the subjects can be affected here. The choice of the passive in such examples is bound up with the narrator's wish to emphasize a particular element in the context: it is the subject of the construction that is foregrounded, and this suggests a somewhat odd interpretation of the situation. As is often the case, Dickens really lets himself go in a letter: '... an unfortunate young orphan who after being canvassed for, subscribed for, polled for, written for, quarreled [sic] for, fought for, called for, and done all kinds of things for..., was floored at the last election' (*Pilgr.* 5 532f., 1849).

17. Inversion. If the verb *to say* forms part of a sentence-opener, we can find instances of inversion — verb before subject — much earlier than Dickens; the *OED* has an example from 1700. In Dickens there are sentence-openers like 'Says Twemlow...' (*OMF* II 3 245) and 'Said Mr. Podsnap to Mrs. Podsnap' (*OMF* I 11 130) which serve to inject an extra degree of vividness into the narrative; but he also uses inversion with other verbs than *to say*: 'Whispered Wegg to Venus...' (*OMF* IV 3 652); 'Answered Gruff and Glum...' (*OMF* IV 4 667). A poetical use of inversion is seen in 'Howls the shrill wind round Chesney Wold' (*BH* 29 401), and we have a parody of this function in 'Howls the sublime, and softly sleeps the calm Ideal, in the whispering chambers of Imagination' (*MC* 34 542). In the quotation that follows there are first three examples of straight word-order, next two cases of inversion:

To-morrow comes, the savoury preparations for the Oil Trade come, the evening comes. Comes, Mr. Snagsby in his black coat; come, the Chadbands... (*BH* 25 356).

where the change of word-order and sentence-rhythm serves to increase attention. The last two verbs are in the nature of stage-directions (*enter Hamlet*), and the commas after them have the function of colons.

A special type of inversion is the one that offended a nineteenth-century critic (and possibly also the shade of Lindley Murray),[13] the tag statement seen in 'He had a very broad chest had Miss Snevellicci's papa' (*NN* 30 389). The *OED* has a single example before Dickens (from 1828, s.v. *be*, 9.d. in the Supplement), but Dickens is the first writer to make extensive use of it, and he introduces a negative variant: 'He isn't altogether bowled out, yet, Sir, isn't Bagstock.' (*DS* 10 128). Jespersen says about it that it is employed 'to make it clear who or what is meant by a pronoun used loosely in the first sentence',[14] but that is hardly correct. What can be said about it is that in most cases at least it conveys an emotional note, whether one of sentimentality or one of irony:

'He suffered heavily, did my unfortunate boy...' (*OMF* IV 9 732).

They were in a charming state of mind, were Mr. and Mrs. Lammle... (*OMF* IV 2 641).

18. Emphasis. The preceding sections have mainly dealt with phenomena that traditionally fall under the domain of syntax, although some of them also belong to style. In the rest of this chapter we shall be concerned with features that are central to style, and here again we shall see that Dickens is sometimes on the periphery of the norm, or even that he goes beyond it. If we generalize about his style, we may say that it is above all an emphatic style: he likes to 'pitch it strong', and he often does so by resorting to textures of concord, i.e. cohesive devices whose elements support each other. But emphasis may also be achieved through the use of textures of discord, i.e. stylistic devices that produce a shock effect because they somehow thwart the reader's expectations. Another point that has already been touched on above (I.6 and II.40ff.) is that Dickens's language is coloured by his idiosyncratic world view; this will be given further consideration in sections 33ff.

19. Superlatives. In *Sketches by Boz* Dickens pokes gentle fun at the poetical young gentleman whose adjectives 'are all superlatives. Everything is of the grandest, greatest, noblest, mightiest, loftiest' (537). But Dickens himself has the same tendency to heighten the effect, not infrequently through the use of superlatives: 'the bedstead, and such few other articles of necessary furniture ... were of the commonest description, in a most crazy state, and of a most uninviting appearance' (*NN* 57 747); 'every house is the whitest of the white; every Venetian blind the greenest of the green; every fine day's sky the bluest of the blue.' (*AN* 5 71). But this tendency takes several other shapes.

20. Keywords, variation, and tautology. When Dickens introduces a keyword, he often does so with a vengeance. In *Little Dorrit* we are told that it was Mrs. General's aim in life to *varnish,* i.e. gloss over, shocking things:

The little that was left in the world, when all these deductions were made, it was Mrs. General's province to varnish. In that formation process of hers, she dipped the smallest of brushes into the largest of pots, and varnished the surface of every object that came under consideration. The more cracked it was, the more Mrs. General varnished it.
    There was varnish in Mrs. General's voice, varnish in Mrs. General's touch, an atmosphere of varnish round Mrs. General's figure... (II 2 450f.).

In other passages the same action is referred to in a succession of synonymous expressions:

The bill paid, and the waiter remembered, and the ostler not forgotten, and the chambermaid taken into consideration — in a word, the whole house bribed into a state of contempt and animosity, and Estella's purse much lightened — we got into our post-coach... (*GE* 33 254).

Yet another device that serves to drive home a point is the conjoining of words that have the same semantic range: tautology or semantic concord. We note agreement between adjectives and nouns in 'the munificent liberality of these noble brothers' (*NN* 61 793), in 'Mrs. Nickleby's prophetic anticipations' (*NN* 65 829), and in 'modern innovations' (*PP* 10 118). There is agreement between verb and adverb in 'he stalked majestically after his friend' (*PP* 3 43) and in 'the misdemeanour she had so flagrantly committed' (*NN* 63 818).

21. Syntactic support. Semantic repetition often goes hand in hand with the repetition of syntactic patterns, and this kind of double parallelism is particularly emphatic:

the impotence of his will, the instability of his hopes, the feebleness of wealth, had been so direfully impressed upon him. (*DS* 20 272).

Mr. Pancks wouldn't hear of excuses, wouldn't hear of complaints, wouldn't hear of repairs, wouldn't hear of anything but unconditional money down. (*LD* I 23 279).

An even greater degree of foregrounding is achieved when a syntactic minority construction is employed; in the example that follows we find predicatives as sentence-openers:

Bright the carriage looked, sleek the horses looked, gleaming the harness looked, luscious and lasting the liveries looked. (*LD* II 16 614).

22. Doublets and triplets. Striking examples of textures of concord are the numerous doublets whose chief function appears to be to intensify the description: 'symptoms ... caused and occasioned by violent love' (*NN* 27 351); 'various other acts and deeds' (*PP* 30 408); 'this parlour ... was cut off and detached from all the world' (*BR* 4 31); 'Miss Sally Brass had been the prop and pillar of his business' (*OCS* 36 270); 'Foul and filthy as the room is...' (*BH* 10 137).; etc.

A special type of doublet is the one in which a preposition is repeated for the sake of emphasis; this is a favourite of Dickens's:

the figure ... stood at the speaker's elbow, motioning across and across its windpipe (*CS* 464).

we started away again round and round the room. (*GE* 11 79).

I walked through and through the town all the rest of the day... (*PI* 339).

Less frequently it is synonymous prepositions that are coordinated:

a little quiet conversation about and concerning all their particular friends and acquaintance... (*PP* 26 359).

Tom ... twined himself yawning round and about the rails of his chair... (*HT* I 8 52).

An occasional vehicle for emphasis is the repetition of a verb or noun: 'And so busy had he been..., piling and piling weights upon weights of earth above John Harmon's grave...' (*OMF* II 13 378).

There are also a fair number of triplets, for instance: 'people of all sorts, kinds, and descriptions' (*SB* 163); 'he unbent, relaxed, stepped down from his pedestal' (*PP* 18 236); 'here was good cause, reason, and foundation for pretending to be angry' (*OCS* 8 63); 'the Freedom ... to be savage, merciless, and cruel' (*AN* 17 228), where we find near-synonyms combined. There is another type of triplet in which a verb is repeated for the purpose of calling attention to a protracted process, the third time with *-ing* added:

I used to sit, think, think, thinking (*SB* 27).

All night the faithful Cricket had been Chirp, Chirp, Chirping on the Hearth. (*CB* 214).

I went on prose, prose, prosing (*BH* 23 334).

where the items repeated have a symbolic or iconic function.

In normal prose the last two items of an enumeration are linked by *and*: 'all sorts, kinds, and descriptions'; but deviations from this practice occur with special stylistic implications. We sometimes see Dickens resorting to polysyndeton, i.e. the insertion of a conjunction between any two members of a long enumeration:

Colonel Bulder ... galloping first to one place, and then to another, and backing his horse among the people, and prancing, and curvetting, and shouting..., and making himself very hoarse in the voice, and very red in the face... (*PP* 4 46).

This conveys an overwhelming impression of one action rapidly succeeding another. Paradoxically enough, we also find deviation in the opposite direction, in the form of an asyndetic construction that entirely dispenses with conjunctions:

'It ... is not likely to enrich me in reputation, station, fortune, anything.' (*GE* 44 340).

... steam ferry-boats laden with people, coaches, horses, waggons, baskets, boxes ... (*AN* 5 79).

where the absence of a conjunction between the last two members of an enumeration suggests that the list of items could be indefinitely extended; both polysyndeton and asyndeton, being deviations from the norm, have the function of foregrounding the passages in which they appear.

23. Sound effects. The triplets discussed above conveniently lead on to a discussion of the use of some phonetic devices: rhyme, assonance, and alliteration. They were probably more effective in Dickens's day, when his works were read aloud, than today; but even a contemporary reader cannot help being struck by their frequency.

Here, first, are some examples of rhyme:

Away we go, by muddy roads, and through the most shattered and tattered of villages (*PI* 428).

'Sit down, you dancing, prancing, shambling, scrambling poll-parrot!' (*BH* 33 465).

... a politico-diplomatic hocus pocus piece of machinery, for the assistance of the nobs in keeping off the snobs (*LD* I 10 116).

Wemmick was at his desk, lunching — and crunching — on a dry hard biscuit (*GE* 24 188).

One of the uses to which rhyme can be put is what may be termed Dickens's name game, which he introduced quite early in his career. The first example I have noted occurs in *Pickwick Papers*:

'Call Elizabeth Cluppins,' said Serjeant Buzfuz ...
    The nearest usher called for Elizabeth Tuppins; another one ... demanded Elizabeth Jupkins; and a third rushed in a breathless state into King Street, and screamed for Elizabeth Muffins ... (34 475).

The slight distortion of the name as it is shouted from person to person is convincing enough. Where it occurs in *Bleak House*, the name game is, however, given a symbolic function. Here we are presented with long lists of politicians' names which differ only in their initial sounds:

He [Lord Boodle] perceives ... that the limited choice of the Crown in the formation of a new Ministry, would lie between Lord Coodle and Sir Thomas Doodle — supposing it to be impossible for the Duke of Foodle to act with Goodle, which may be assumed to be the case in consequence of the breach arising out of that affair with Hoodle. Then, giving the Home Department and the Leadership of the House of Commons to Joodle, the Exchequer to Koodle, the Colonies to Loodle, and the Foreign Office to Moodle, what are you to do with Noodle? (12 160).

Just after this there follows a similar list including names like *Juffy, Kuffy,* and *Luffy,* and the device is obviously employed here to voice Dickens's disgust with politicians; there is not much to choose between them.[15] The name game is resumed once again in *Our Mutual Friend,* as a mere joke without any symbolic significance, when an office boy runs through the supposed names of the day's appointments: 'Mr. Aggs, Mr. Baggs, Mr. Caggs, Mr. Daggs, Mr. Faggs, Mr. Gaggs, Mr. Boffin' (I 8 86).

There are occasional instances of assonance: two words may be sufficiently similar phonetically to be associated with each other, the association being reinforced by their semantic similarity:

placards ... which were plentifully pasted on the walls, and posted in the windows of the principal shops. (*SB* 20).

'their child ... is petted and patted' (*DS* 5 51).

'Neither of the three served, or saved me.' (*BH* 3 33).

That Dickens realized the effectiveness of alliteration would appear from an example like the following:

'I lost money by that man, and by his guzzlings and his muzzlings' — Mrs. Mac Stinger used the last word for the joint sake of alliteration and aggravation, rather than for the expression of any idea... (*DS* 39 555).

although he mistakes rhyme for alliteration here. He appears himself sometimes to succumb to the temptation of making pairs of words begin with the same sound 'for the joint sake of alliteration and aggravation', witness the following quotation:

But, at all the dismal dinners, leaden lunches, basilisk balls, and other melancholy pageants, her mere appearance is a relief. (*BH* 40 565).

82

For what exactly is meant by 'a basilisk ball'? — a ball that kills? Generally, however, we find the device of alliteration competently handled; compare examples like 'an ambitious and aspiring soul' (*BR* 4 34), 'the torture and torment of His Majesty's liege subjects' (*PP* 31 418), and 'an old house, dismal, dark and dusty' (*NN* 51 667).

24. Imagery. Dickens's descriptions of people and things abound in detailed observations, among them comparisons of various types: 'So she sat, corpse-like, as we played at cards' (*GE* 8 55); 'Mr. Pecksniff continued to keep his mouth and his eyes very wide open, and to drop his lower jaw, somewhat after the manner of a toy nut-cracker' (*MC* 2 11); 'Sometimes a face would appear behind the dingy glass of a window, and would fade away into the gloom as if it had seen enough of life and had vanished out of it.' (*LD* I 3 30). An explicit comparison between two phenomena is set up by the use of *as if, as, like,* and similar words, and it is characteristic of the way Dickens's imagination works that many of his similes become metaphors, explicit comparisons developing into implicit ones:

As the sombre wheels of the six carts go round, they seem to plough up a long furrow among the populace in the streets. Ridges of faces are thrown to this side and to that, and the ploughs go steadily onward. (*TC* III 15 353).

Mr. Bounderby, with his hat in his hand, gave a beat upon the crown at every little division of his sentences, as if it were a tambourine ... Having come to the climax, Mr. Bounderby, like an oriental dancer, put his tambourine on his head. (*HT* II 8 184f).

In such examples we find the metaphor just a couple of lines after the simile. But sometimes the reader must be prepared to recognize a metaphorical expression that crops up many pages after the introduction of the corresponding explicit comparison:

He [Mr. Kenge] said this at the stair-head, gently moving his right hand as if it were a silver trowel, with which to spread the cement of his words on the structure of the system, and consolidate it for a thousand ages ... (*BH* 62 844); 'you are to reflect, Mr. Woodcourt,' observed Mr. Kenge, using his silver trowel, persuasively and smoothingly, 'that this has been a great cause' (*ibid.,* 65 866).

This is a good illustration of the cohesiveness of Dickens's style, a cohesiveness that makes great demands on the reader's attention. A reader who considers the following passage from *Great Expectations* in isolation

When I did at last turn my eyes in Wemmick's direction, I found that he had unposted his pen, and was intent on the table before him. (51 390).

would hardly be able to make sense of the sequence *unposted his pen*; this verb is not in the *OED*. A careful reader will not, however, have forgotten that when Wemmick is first introduced, his mouth is described as being 'such a post-office of a mouth' (21 162) and that this image recurs on several occasions. With such examples we may compare the account given in *Bleak House* of an election campaign, in the course of which 'Doodle has found that he must throw himself upon the country - chiefly in the form of sovereigns and beer' (i.e., bribery and treating; 40 562); this connects with a passage three pages later referring to 'all those particular parts of the country on which Doodle is at present throwing himself in an auriferous and malty shower' (40 565).

Metaphorical sequences like *the cement of his words* and *a post-office of a mouth* may be paraphrased 'his words were cement' and 'his mouth was (like) a post-office'. This is a formula that is a favourite with Dickens; compare 'For six entire weeks after the bankruptcy this miserable foreigner [the Native] lived in a rainy season of boot-jacks and brushes' (*DS* 58 815).

25. Extended metaphor. Sometimes, as has just been noted, a metaphor is briefly introduced and may then lie dormant for several pages before it is resumed. In other passages we see that once his imagination has hit on an image, Dickens may grow so fond of it as to extend it over a prolonged passage, being unable to resist the introduction of further parallels. This leads to some odd collocations of adjectives and nouns in his comparison of Dr. Blimber's school with a hothouse:

In fact, Doctor Blimber's establishment was a great hot-house, in which there was a forcing apparatus incessantly at work. All the boys blew before their time. Mental green-peas were produced at Christmas, and intellectual asparagus all the year round. Mathematical gooseberries (very sour ones too) were common at untimely seasons, and from mere sprouts of bushes, under Doctor Blimber's cultivation. Every description of Greek and Latin vegetable was got off the driest twigs of boys, under the frostiest circumstances. (*DS* 11 141).

A less strained example is the one in which Mrs. Boffin's social gaucherie is compared with ice skating:

when she made a slip on the social ice on which all the children of Podsnappery ... are required to skate in circles, or to slide in long rows, she inevitably tripped Miss Bella up...and caused her to experience great confusion under the glances of the more skilful performers engaged in those ice-exercises. (*OMF* II 8 307).

26. *Contextual pressure.* Dickens's imagination undoubtedly has a tendency to run away with him. Once he has decided on an epithet or an image, he feels bound to keep it up, so that sometimes it becomes a kind of straitjacket. The result may be that owing to pressure from the context a word is forced into strange collocations. In such cases it may be said that it is no longer the author who is in charge; his medium has taken over, at least for a time. This tendency is illustrated in the quotations given below, where the adjective *prosperous* and the verb *to tick* are put to rather strained uses:

He was a prosperous old bachelor, and his open window looked into a prosperous little garden and orchard, and there was a prosperous iron safe let into the wall (*GE* 19 142).

There was a grave clock, ticking somewhere up the staircase; and there was a songless bird in the same direction, pecking at his cage, as if he was ticking too. The parlour-fire ticked in the grate. There was only one person on the parlour-hearth, and the loud watch in his pocket ticked audibly. — The servant-maid had ticked the two words 'Mr. Clennam' so softly that she had not been heard (*LD* I 13 145).

Sometimes the mention of a physical act gives rise to a metaphorical variant of the act; in the quotation that follows the reference to the use of a gimlet leads to the creation of a corresponding verb that is figuratively employed:

the purple-faced vintner, who, gimlet in hand, had projected an attack upon at least a score of dusty casks, and who stood transfixed, or morally gimleted as it were, to his own wall... (*BR* 13 102).

In another passage we are given a description of the wind, which is said to saw rather than to blow; this leads to streets being equated with sawpits and pedestrians ('passengers') being dubbed *under-sawyers* ('subordinate or inferior people'):

The grating wind sawed rather than blew; and as it sawed, the sawdust whirled about the sawpit. Every street was a sawpit, and there were no topsawyers; every passenger was an undersawyer, with the sawdust blinding him and choking him. (*OMF* I 12 144).

Compare II.45.

27. *Idioms varied.* In the preceding section the term 'straitjacket' was employed to suggest the kind of consistency that Dickens feels impelled to stick to once he has hit on an image. Idioms are another kind of

linguistic straitjacket; for they are normally invariable. But since people who know English are familiar with English idioms, it is possible to introduce variants that play on the conventional forms. Thus the expression *Ordeal by General* (*LD* II 7 503), containing a reference to Mrs. General, is modelled on the idiom *ordeal by fire*. In *Pickwick Papers* there occur two variants of the idiom *to look daggers*: 'If he played a wrong card, Miss Bolo looked a small armoury of daggers' (35 503) and 'the old lady ... drew herself up, and looked carving-knives at the hard-headed delinquent' (6 69). The reference in *Nicholas Nickleby* to Kate's patroness, who was sometimes 'taken literary' (28 359), is a variant of the idiom *to be taken ill* (cf. *OED take* v., 7.d.) and is clearly ironical, and so is the 'creature discomforts' that we come across elsewhere (*OMF* II 12 352), being modelled on *creature comforts*. Sometimes two idioms are conflated: in 'How the Circumlocution Office ... tossed the business in a wet blanket' (*LD* I 10 120) we have a combination of *to toss somebody in a blanket* (as a punishment) and *a wet blanket* (something that acts as a damper to activity) — thus a very strong negative expression. Dickens also employs the procedure of taking a set phrase and contrasting it with a non-existent antonym:

'*On* the whole then; observe me,' urges Twemlow with great nicety, as if, in the case of its having been off the whole, he would have done it directly — '*on* the whole, I must beg you to excuse me from addressing any communication to Lord Snigsworth.' (*OMF* II 3 245).

28. Punning. The last quotation is in the nature of a pun. Punning is a foible of Dickens's; he does not always resist the temptation of introducing rather feeble word-play for no very obvious reason. In fact one sometimes has the impression that the moment a given word has slipped into his text, it is the language that runs away with him, and he almost automatically creates ambiguities:

the mail ... just then passes by ... Mr. Todd's young man, who being fond of mails, but more of females, takes a short look at the mails, and a long look at the girls... (*SB* 49).

The literary gentleman was then about to be drunk [i.e. toasted], but it being discovered that he had been drunk for some time in another acceptation of the term ..., the intention was abandoned... (*NN* 48 635).

[a pig] goes grunting down the kennel, turning up the news and small-talk of the city in the shape of cabbage-stalks and offal, and bearing no tails but his own... (*AN* 6 86).

'Miss Ferdinand is at present weighed down by an incubus' — Miss Twinkleton might have said a pen-and-ink-ubus of writing out Monsieur La Fontaine ... (*ED* 9 92f.).

As will be noted, such examples occur both early and late in Dickens's career. But it would be unfair not to add that he sometimes does better than that. Thus he is the originator of quite respectable punning coinages like *everbrowns* and *irrelative*:

[a description of a desolate London garden] the scanty box, and stunted everbrowns, and broken flower-pots, that are scatterered mournfully about — a prey to 'blacks' and dirt. (*NN* 2 8).

'*Which,* was you pleased to observe, Miss Varden?' said Miggs, with a strong emphasis on the irrelative pronoun. (*BR* 71 546).

29. Textures of discord. The stylistic devices found in Dickens's prose may be arranged on a scale whose extremes are textures of concord and textures of discord. Typical examples of the former that have already been surveyed are, for instance, doublets and rhyme, in which the elements support each other. With punning we have arrived at the middle range of the scale: an ambiguous expression, it is true, serves to link two elements of description, but at the same time it conveys a note of discord. In the following sections we shall be concerned with textures of discord which in various ways run counter to the reader's stylistic expectations.

30. Common-sense expectations disappointed. A collocation is a habitual juxtaposition of a particular word with other particular words. Now, since language is linear, this means that the first member of a collocation prepares the reader for a compatible member to follow. Given the verb *to cross-examine* we feel sure that what follows as the object must be the designation of a person, most often a witness. And yet we find Mr. Jaggers described as cross-examining 'his very wine when he had nothing else in hand' (*GE* 29 229). Given the sequence *he died of...* we confidently expect to be informed of the name of some disease or other similar cause. And yet Mrs. Pipchin is referred to as the 'relict of a man who had died of the Peruvian mines' (*DS* 11 136). The words given as examples here of course point to known facts in our world (concerning the legal system and concerning medicine), and there are numerous other facts and causal relationships which we are familiar with and usually take for granted without a moment's reflection. When we are suddenly confronted with an unconventional collocation, we feel surprised (and perhaps amused) because our expectations have somehow been thwarted.

Two short passages from the beginning of *Oliver Twist* run counter to our notions of common sense:

The board ... took counsel together on the expediency of shipping off Oliver Twist, in some small trading vessel bound to a good unhealthy port. (4 22).

It was a nice sickly season just at this time. In commercial phrase, coffins were looking up... (6 39).

Positive and negative terms are unequal yokefellows; here they are combined to convey, in very patent fashion, the narrator's feelings towards the callous people who were responsible for Oliver's fate. When we read of Mr. Wopsle's great-aunt that she 'conquered a confirmed habit of living into which she had fallen' (*GE* 16 115), it is ironically suggested that being alive may be a bad habit, although we normally consider the instinct of self-preservation something positive. The word *infliction* is a negatively loaded term which collocates with something unpleasant (for instance, punishment). When it appears in an unusual collocation, as in

Even the calm and patient face of Doctor Strong expressed some little sense of pain ... under the infliction of these compliments. (*DC* 45 650).

we are not in doubt as to the narrator's attitude towards the inflictor of the compliments.

31. Some other unequal yokefellows. The clash between positive and negative terms is not the only kind of semantic incompatibility that we find in Dickens. Sometimes he flouts the normally accepted distinction between intentional and involuntary behaviour:

'Trouble?' echoed my sister, 'trouble?' And then entered on a fearful catalogue of all the illnesses I had been guilty of, and all the acts of sleeplessness I had committed... (*GE* 4 24).

and the one between halting and fluent speech:

When the time comes for Veneering to deliver a neat and appropriate stammer to the men of Pocket-Breaches... (*OMF* II 3 251).

Some verbs necessarily collocate with subjects that denote a number of people. This convention is given cavalier treatment in *Our Mutual Friend*, where we learn that 'Mrs. Sprodgkin was left still unadjourned in the hall' (IV 11 748), a formulation that appears unmotivated and merely whimsical. But in a suitable context other unequal yokefellows may be only seemingly discordant; with our knowledge of Mr. Micawber it makes sense to read of him that he was 'boastfully disparaging himself' (*DC* 36 532).

Some words combine with static nouns, others with dynamic ones. Thus the sequence *in a state of* is regularly followed by a specification of the condition referred to, while *a burst of* requires as its continuation a word that denotes violent activity; but Dickens creates highly unorthodox collocations:

Sitting opposite to them was a gentleman in a high state of tobacco, who wore quite a little beard, composed of the overflowings of that weed... (*MC* 34 536).

'Do not,' he would sometimes add, in a burst of Deportment, 'even allow my simple requirements to be considered' (*BH* 50 684).

The former example appears strained; as for the latter example, the word *Deportment* in collocation with *burst* is admittedly given a semantic value that is alien to it, but this nevertheless conveys an apt suggestion of Mr. Turveydrop's hypocritical behaviour.

Compare also the deviations analysed in sections 33ff.

32. Syllepsis. One of Dickens's mannerisms is his use of syllepsis, a figure of speech that consists in applying a word to two or more words in different senses. This entails an unexpected combination of disparate spheres of life:

she fell into a chair and a fainting fit, simultaneously. (*NN* 21 261).

Mr. Ben Allen and Mr. Bob Sawyer sat together in the little surgery behind the shop, discussing minced veal and future prospects ... (*PP* 48 668, with a pun on *discuss* (1) 'consume', (2) 'debate').

His looks were starched, but his white neckerchief was not ... (*PP* 27 365).

it *was* whispered that Miss Buffle would go either into a consumption or a convent ... (*CS* 412).

'But, excuse me,' says Podsnap, with his temper and his shirt-collar about equally rumpled ... (*OMF* IV 17 817).

In one passage the same preposition is made to govern a succession of nouns, not all of which are equally compatible with it:

Angelo Cyrus Bantam, Esq. ... emerged from his chariot ... in the same wig, the same teeth, the same eyeglass, the same watch and seals, the same rings, the same shirtpin, and the same cane (*PP* 35 499).

It is not all the occurrences of such more or less lopsided constructions that exactly fit the definition of syllepsis given above. But common
to all of them is the element of surprise, thus also in the following quotation, in which the third occurrence of *over* introduces the surprise element:

Twemlow, sitting over his newspaper, and over his dry toast, and weak tea, and over
the stable-yard in Duke Street ... (*OMF* I 10 115).

And in Augustus Moddle's letter to Miss Pecksniff the reader is led de-
lightfully astray by the first predicative, which clashes absurdly with the
second:

Ere this reaches you, the undersigned will be — if not a corpse — on the way to Van
Dieman's Land. (*MC* 54 835).

Sometimes we find an adjective transferred from the position that
would logically be required, to another position (hypallage). Typically,
an epithet that properly characterizes a person is moved to a position in
which it describes an action performed by that person: 'the little man
took an argumentative pinch of snuff' (*PP* 10 124). Compare also: 'I
sent a penitential codfish and barrel of oysters to Joe' (*GE* 30 233, i.e.
'by way of penance').

33. Animism and automatism. In I.6 Dickens's idiosyncratic view of
the world was briefly touched on, and in II.42f. examples were given of
the animation of non-persons and of the use of terms denoting physical
acts outside their proper spheres. Here we shall take a look at the way in
which Dickens's vision manifests itself linguistically in more extended
passages. There are two complementary angles from which the world is
viewed. On the one hand, the animistic angle endows dead things with
human attributes, while on the other hand the angle of automatism
transforms human beings into mere puppets or things.[16]
There is no better illustration of animism than Dickens's descriptions of houses, for instance:

the old house looked as if it were nodding in its sleep. Indeed, it needed no very great
stretch of fancy to detect in it other resemblances to humanity... (*BR* 1 2).

Impassive, as behoves its high breeding, the Dedlock town house stares at the other
houses in the street of dismal grandeur, and gives no outward sign of anything going
wrong within. (*BH* 56 760).

Objects used by human beings may, as it were, become upgraded and acquire near-human status when they appear in collocation with terms that normally take human collocates. Thus we *consort with* and *are grouped with* or *attended by* other people; but Dickens substitutes things:

I often paid him a visit in the dark back-room in which he consorted with an ink-jar, a hat-peg, a coal-box, a string-box, an almanack, a desk and stool, and a ruler ... (*GE* 34 260).

... Mr. Turveydrop; whom we found, grouped with his hat and gloves, as a model of Deportment, on the sofa in his private apartment (*BH* 23 326).

Young Barnacle appeared, attended by his eye-glass (*LD* I 17 207).

In these passages the narrator may be satirizing the inordinate importance that such characters attach to things: this is second nature with Mr. Turveydrop as a model of Deportment; and as for Young Barnacle, we have been told earlier (I 10 108) of the important role played by his 'superior eye-glass'. Other examples of this kind appear to be mere jokes without any ulterior significance: of a constable's staff of office we hear that it 'had been reclining indolently in the chimney-corner' (*OT* 30 221) and of a wheeled chair that it 'passed the night in a shed' (*DS* 21 292).

34. Articles of clothing. Articles of clothing are often made to stand for persons; this appears psychologically quite convincing in a child's view of adults:

The child glanced keenly at the blue coat and stiff white cravat, which, with a pair of creaking boots and a very loud ticking watch, embodied her ideas of a father... (*DS* 1 3).

Dickens repeatedly invites the reader to adopt the child's visual angle by looking impressionistically at his surroundings, and this has linguistic implications. At the beginning of the following two quotations we find articles of clothing collocating with verbs that normally require a human agent as their subject, but there is enough supplementary information for the reader to grasp the situation:

a hackney-coach drives into the square, on the box of which vehicle a very tall hat makes itself manifest to the public. ... the tall hat (surmounting Mr. Smallweed the younger) alights (*BH* 33 464).

Raising his eyes thus one day, he was surprised to see a bonnet labouring up the step-ladder. The unusual apparition was followed by another bonnet. He then perceived that the first bonnet was on the head of Mr. F's Aunt, and that the second bonnet was on the head of Flora. (*LD* I 23 267).

The breaches of collocation brought about by such descriptions have a humorous effect, but this is not just whimsicality: there appears to be a genuine artistic endeavour behind the wording of these passages, where we are invited to focus impressionistically on dominant phenomena. On the other hand we probably have just an example of Dickens's technique of abbreviation in a passage from *American Notes* where we are told that 'The straw hat then inquires of the brown hat, whether...' (14 191); here 'the straw hat' is short for 'a gentleman in a straw hat' (cf. section 5).

35. Parts of the body. It is not only articles of clothing that may be given an autonomous status; the same is true of parts of the body. An extreme example is seen in the following quotation, where there appears to be a complete split between a character's voice and the rest of the person:

the Commander [of the *Cautious Clara*], addressing himself to nobody, thus spake; or rather the voice within him said of its own accord, and quite independent of himself, as if he were possessed by a gruff spirit, — 'My name's Jack Bunsby!' ... When it had pursued its train of argument to this point, the voice stopped, and rested. ... The voice here went out of the back parlour and into the street, taking the Commander of the *Cautious Clara* with it ... (*DS* 23 338).

Another peculiar example is Dickens's description of Mr. Carker. When we are first introduced to him, we are informed that he has 'two un-broken rows of glistening teeth, whose regularity and whiteness were quite distressing' (*DS* 13 171). The teeth dominate the person to such an extent that they tend to take over:

Mr. Carker the Manager did a great deal of business in the course of the day, and be-stowed his teeth upon a great many people. In the office, in the court, in the street, and on 'Change, they glistened and bristled to a terrible extent. Five o'clock arriving, and with it Mr. Carker's bay horse, they got on horseback, and went gleaming up Cheapside. (22 308).

The last *they* here is perhaps ambiguous: it may mean either 'his teeth' or 'Mr. Carker and his teeth', but even under the latter interpretation the teeth and their owner are coordinate entities. The promotion to inde-pendence of teeth, legs, whiskers, etc. probably strikes most readers as farfetched, and it results in a number of extremely odd collocations. Further examples, more or less peculiar, are the following:

92

Miss Knag ... said with great solemnity, that it would be a warning to *her*, and so did the young ladies generally, with the exception of one or two who appeared to entertain doubts whether such whiskers [i.e. Mr. Mantalini's] could do wrong. (*NN* 44 578).

The wooden leg looked at him with a meditative eye. (*OMF* I 5 48).

a monotonous appearance of Dutch cheese at ten o'clock in the evening had been rather frequently commented on by the dimpled shoulders of Miss Bella (*OMF* I 4 40).

Mr. and Mrs. Boffin ... perceived three pairs of listening legs upon the stairs above, Mrs. Wilfer's legs, Miss Bella's legs, Mr. George Sampson's legs. (*OMF* I 9 106f.).

36. Oblique subject. If an article of clothing or a part of the body is made the subject of a sentence, this entails the dethronement of a character from the role it normally performs: that of being the actor, the one who initiates events. The types of deviant sentence organisation that have just been reviewed are paralleled in a striking manner by another Dickensian peculiarity: in numerous sentences a word that denotes a human being is ousted from its subject function by a psychological noun. This term covers words like *imbecility* and *sagacity; generosity* and *rapacity; delicacy* and *gallantry,* i.e. words that denote normally permanent characteristics of the personality, whether intellectual, moral, or emotional.
Let me exemplify the words given above:

Mrs. Gradgrind faintly looked at the tongs, as the most appropriate thing her imbecility could think of doing. (*HT* I 4 15).

The sagacity of the man of business perceived an advantage here, and determined to hold it. (*TC* II 18 187).

He reddened deeply, as if his natural generosity felt a pang of reproach (*BH* 37 525).

'you must prepare to disgorge all that your rapacity has become possessed of...' (*DC* 52 758f.).

To this proposal, however, Mr. Pickwick's delicacy would by no means allow him to accede ... (*MH* III 55).

Even Sir Leicester's gallantry has some trouble to keep pace with her. (*BH* 16 218).

It appears that what makes the syntactic and semantic promotion of these psychological nouns odd is the fact that they denote permanent traits; there is nothing striking about an example like 'our anxiety was not much relieved by him' (*BH* 24 336), for *anxiety* here points to a temporary frame of mind.

In order to account for this peculiarity it may be helpful to look briefly at modern case grammar.[17] In this type of grammar a case is a semantic function, and we need only consider the first of these, the so-called agentive (roughly equivalent to 'actor'), which is the case of the typically animate perceived instigator of the action identified by the verb. Now the rule is posited that if an agentive is present, it will become the subject of an unmarked sentence. Unmarked versions of the examples just given (where an agentive *is* present) would then be: 'In his sagacity, *the man of business* perceived ...'; 'disgorge all that *you* have become possessed of in your rapacity'; etc. Dickens's versions are all marked: they deviate from the preferred or normal kind of sentence organization by demoting a person and foregrounding a psychological element. It is interesting to note that Seymour Chatman discusses a similar phenomenon in Henry James, who also tends to submerge his characters grammatically. Under the heading of 'Obliquity' Chatman observes that 'by nominalizing verbs of mental action, James makes *them*, rather than the mere human to whom they attach, the topic of the discourse. Grammatically, this entails the partial or total elimination of the real actor, his removal to an oblique position or even complete disappearance'.[18]

37. The status of human beings reduced. The foregoing discussion has concentrated on the unconventional raising of non-persons to subject status. We may conclude the discussion by considering the other side of the coin: the reduced status of human beings. There are passages in which this status is explicitly indicated. In section 7 it was noted how a footman is made a grammatical uncountable and is referred to as 'an amount of the article that always came for her when she walked home'. Pancks in *Little Dorrit* is compared with a tug (e.g. I 13 151), and Twemlow is regarded by the Veneerings as 'an innocent piece of dinner-furniture' (*OMF* I 2 6). Of Mr. Toddle it is remarked that he was 'never out of children, but always kept a good supply on hand' (*DS* 38 534), and a similar view of children is expressed by a clergyman in *Our Mutual Friend*: " 'We have orphans, I know,' pursued Mr. Milvey, quite with the air as if he might have added, 'in stock' " (I 9 105).

In some passages it is interesting to note the words used by a character to refer to a part of his own body. The verb *to adjust* normally takes as its object an article of clothing, yet we read of Mr. Micawber 'genteelly adjusting his chin in his cravat' (*DC* 52 753). We are shown another instance of split personality in 'The Captain then stood himself up in a corner, against the wall.' (*DS* 25 353). This verb normally takes a thing as its object; the *OED* (s.v. *stand,* 65.b.) gives this as the first example of the rare reflexive construction.

It may be added that in several passages persons and things are lumped together, both being given the same characterization, so that either things are raised to the level of human beings or human beings reduced to the level of things:

an unusual quantity of carpet-bags and small portmanteaus, no less apoplectic in appearance than the Major himself (*DS* 20 276).

what was observable in the furniture, was observable in the Veneerings – the surface smelt a little too much of the work-shop and was a trifle sticky. (*OMF* I 2 6).

there was a faded look about her, and about the furniture, and about the house. (*NN* 21 265).

Mute, close, irresponsive to any glancing light, his dress is like himself. (*BH* 2 11).

his manner is a little sombre. His room is a little sombre, and may have had its influence in forming his manner. (*ED* 2 8).

In a final example it may be noted how the normal roles have been inverted: objects are endowed with human features, and a person becomes an article:

The travellers' room at the White Horse Cellar is of course uncomfortable; it would be no travellers' room if it were not. It is the right-hand parlour, into which an aspiring kitchen fire-place appears to have walked, accompanied by a rebellious poker, tongs, and shovel. It is divided into boxes, for the solitary confinement of travellers, and is furnished with a clock, a looking-glass, and a live waiter: which latter article is kept in a small kennel for washing glasses, in a corner of the apartment. (*PP* 35 490f.).

38. Summing up. After we have now surveyed a number of syntactic and semantic phenomena that deviate more or less from normal nineteenth-century prose, it is time for a few concluding remarks. Dickens does not create new patterns, though he is the first writer to make extensive use of a pattern that was very recent when he began to write (section 17). What makes his language striking in a number of respects is his penchant for pitching it strong: he introduces excessively long premodified constructions, he takes liberties with the conventional distinction between countable and uncountable nouns and treats collectives as it suits his humorous bent, he goes against the rules governing pronominalization, and he makes very free with phrasal verbs in the passive. His artistic exploitation of the contrast between the tenses is remarkable, and so is the occasional absence of finite verbs. His tendency to go the extreme animal is again noteworthy in his use of metaphor which sometimes verges on the artificial, and it is startling to observe the way in which he disregards the conventional dichotomy between human beings and things and the sentence organization that goes with it. If by 'syntax' we understand the normal, unspectacular arrangement of words in sentences, the nineteenth-century reference to Dickens's 'fine, manly disregard of syntax' is not unfounded.

CHAPTER IV: NARRATIVE AND SPEECH

1. Realism vs. conventions. The present chapter will be concerned with Dickens's rendering of speech and with the interplay of speech and the narrative voice. Dickens is generally acclaimed for the masterly realism of his speech-rendering. This is a verdict that I do not wish to quarrel with, although it must be qualified by the comment that fictional speech is never fully realistic. It must also be added that Dickens is not in all respects a realist. It has already been noted how he suggests oaths and imprecations euphemistically (II.39); the closest approach to an actual oath is its initial letter: 'The individual ... demanded in a surly tone what the — something beginning with a capital H — he wanted.' (*PP* 42 590). This is a stylistic strategy that was dictated by Victorian conventions of propriety.

Speakers of substandard English abound in the novels, and their speech is realistic enough in most respects, though they are not allowed to bring a blush into the cheek of the young person. Dickens stated in his preface to *Oliver Twist* that he saw no reason why the dregs of life should not serve the purpose of a moral 'so long as their speech did not offend the ear'. There are some Dickensian characters whose speech is hardly realistic; is it likely, for instance, that Oliver Twist, who comes from the workhouse and is forced to associate with low characters, should speak Standard English? The reason why he does so may be that he is meant to be an idealized and incorruptible young hero, and that Dickens believed it was difficult to reconcile substandard speech with dignity and moral worth.[1] If this is true, it must be said that here Dickens is adhering to a stylistic convention that is acceptable to few twentieth-century readers.

2. Narrative modes. In telling his story the novelist has at his disposal a number of traditional narrative modes: his own report or narrative, the direct speech of his characters, indirect speech, and free indirect speech. To this list must be added a fifth mode: free direct speech, which will be discussed below. There are certain stylistic conventions that regulate the use of these modes, and they are kept apart by traditional writers. Dickens also to some extent adheres to the conventions; but what is noteworthy about his literary artistry is that he frequently flouts conventions and combines the modes in striking ways. This he does with great virtuosity, particularly in his later works, where he has arrived at full stylistic maturity, a circumstance that has led some modern critics to hold that these writings are the forerunners of the twentieth-century experimental novel.[2] To start with, it may be useful to sketch the conventions.

3. The conventions. The author's own report of events is usually intended to give the illusion of being factual and comparatively unemotional. The tense that is normally used is the preterit, but it may alternate with the historic or dramatic present, which suggests greater immediacy, and this alternation between the tenses, as we have seen (III. 14), may be exploited stylistically. When faced with such a report, the reader feels that he is hearing the voice of the authorial persona.

In order to make his narrative more vivid and in order to strengthen the impression of authenticity the novelist frequently has his characters use direct speech. The guarantee of authenticity is assumed to be the use of inverted commas or quotation marks. The speaker is identified by a reporting clause like *John said,* which may precede or interrupt or follow the statement; in suitable circumstances it may be replaced by other information (III.15).

Indirect speech is heralded by a reporting clause: *John said (that)...* There are pronoun shifts, and tense shifts if the reporting clause is in the preterit: first and second person pronouns become third person pronouns, and the present tense of direct speech is shifted to the preterit. Compare a direct statement like *I like it* with its indirect equivalent *He said (that) he liked it.* Indirect speech generally conveys a more muted tone than direct speech: it lacks the immediacy of the present tense; it is not always possible to reconstruct the precise wording of the corresponding direct statement; and items like interjections and vocatives — which are common in direct speech — are not transferred into conventional indirect speech.

Free indirect speech is the mode of speech-rendering that is characterized by not being dependent on a reporting clause. From a formal point of view this mode may be identical with authorial report, but in most cases a given context will enable the reader to distinguish between the two. Seen in isolation a sequence like *Dolly hoped that he was not angry with her* could be either one or the other; but usually the context will help us to decide whether we are given the author's information about Dolly's state of mind, or the sequence means 'Dolly expressed the hope that...'

After this brief sketch of conventional usage we shall now proceed to a discussion of Dickens's unconventional handling of the narrative modes.

4. Report. We shall start with examples in which the basic mode is the author's report, and consider how this may incorporate elements from other modes. Here, to begin with, is a passage that describes Mrs. Nickleby:

Mrs. Nickleby went on to entertain her guests with a lament over her fallen fortunes, and a picturesque account of her old house in the country: comprising a full description of the different apartments, not forgetting the little storeroom, and a lively recollection of how many steps you went down to get into the garden, and which way you turned when you came out at the parlour-door, and what capital fixtures there were in the kitchen. This last reflection naturally conducted her into the wash-house, where she stumbled upon the brewing utensils, among which she might have wandered for an hour, if the mere mention of those implements had not ... instantly reminded Mr. Pyke that he was 'amazing thirsty'. (*NN* 27 347).

It is obvious that this bit of narrative is a report on Mrs. Nickleby's flow of words; this appears from the presence of the verb *entertain* and the nouns *lament, account, description, recollection, reflection,* and *mention.* It is, however, hardly possible to reconstruct Mrs. Nickleby's *ipsissima verba.* This type of report has been termed 'submerged speech'[3]: though it is about words being uttered, the formulation is dominated by the author as stage-manager. It may, for instance, be noted how the sequence 'This last reflection naturally conducted her into the wash-house' is completely divorced from its literal, physical meaning and is made to describe verbal behaviour. But even if we cannot reconstruct more than a few of the actual words used, we are nevertheless given an excellent illustration of how Mrs. Nickleby's mind works, and how she gives utterance to her ideas, moving by loose association from one boring detail to another. This kind of reporting confirms the impression of rambling and desultoriness that we have previously formed by 'listening to' Mrs. Nickleby's direct speech.

There is another type of report in which authorial manipulation is obvious; consider these examples:

Mr. Winkle ... was feebly invoking destruction upon the head of any member of the family who should suggest the propriety of his retiring for the night (*PP* 8 99).

The officiating undertakers made some protest against these changes in the ceremonies; but, the river being alarmingly near, and several voices remarking on the efficacy of cold immersion in bringing refractory members of the profession to reason, the protest was faint and brief. (*TC* II 14 149).

These are both reports of speech events, and they are couched in deliberately formal, not to say stilted, language which contrasts humorously with what was most probably actually said; we cannot reconstruct this with certainty, but in the first example it seems likely that the direct-speech equivalent of 'the propriety of his retiring for the night' was something like 'you had better go to bed'. Further light may be shed on how this kind of manipulation is effected if we look at the following passage:

> 'I say, old boy, where do you hang out?'
> Mr. Pickwick replied that he was at present suspended at the George and Vulture. (*PP* 30 416).

What Dickens is doing here is to translate a colloquialism from direct speech into its formal equivalent, which is not strictly speaking applicable here except as a joke, and Mr. Pickwick is not a punster: it is the author's joke (cf. II.32).

Sometimes the author's report is so worded as unmistakably to give us an idea of some of the actual words uttered by the characters involved. Thus we read in the account of a party given by the Veneerings: 'Mrs. Veneering welcomes her sweet Mr. Twemlow. Mr. Veneering welcomes his dear Twemlow.' (*OMF* I 2 7), where we are not in doubt as to the terms of welcome used by hostess and host. In the account of the inquest given in the same novel we are told:

> It was also made interesting by the testimony of Job Potterson ... that the deceased Mr. John Harmon did bring over, in a hand-valise with which he did disembark, the sum realized by the forced sale of his little landed property. (I 3 31).

Here the two occurrences of *did* carry a clear legal flavour (which is not the witness's). In such examples the author is again reporting on speech events: the verb *to welcome* and the noun *testimony* imply the use of words, a few of which can be reconstructed.

We come next to the type of report in which snippets of direct speech crop up as vivifying elements. In the quotation that follows the author dexterously incorporates a couple of colloquialisms from the idiolect of the two ladies involved, by putting them in inverted commas; these items clash stylistically with the formal authorial tone:

> Mrs. Perkins, who has not been for some weeks on speaking terms with Mrs. Piper, in consequence of an unpleasantness originating in young Perkins having 'fetched' young Piper 'a crack', renews her friendly intercourse on this auspicious occasion. (*BH* 143).

In another passage a vocative makes its appearance in the author's report as an illustration of one of the idiosyncrasies of the Major's speech:

The Major ... now sits over his pint of wine, driving a modest young man ... to the verge of madness, by anecdotes of Bagstock, Sir, at Dombey's wedding... (*DS* 31 451).

We also occasionally note an abrupt transition from report to direct speech as in the following passage from *Bleak House,* where Mr. Guppy has just said, 'What do *you* take, Chick?':

Chick, out of the profundity of his artfulness, preferring 'veal and ham and French beans — And don't you forget the stuffing, Polly' (20 275).

There are yet other ways in which report can combine with other modes. Let us consider two passages in which we find a mixture of report and free indirect speech:

Surely there never was such fragile china-ware as that of which the millers of Coketown were made. Handle them never so lightly, and they fell to pieces with such ease that you might suspect them of having been flawed before. *They were ruined,* when they were required to send labouring children to school; *they were ruined* when inspectors were appointed to look into their works... (*HT* II 1 110; my italics).

parties of diggers were formed to relieve one another in digging among the ruins. *There had been a hundred people in the house* at the time of its fall, *there had been fifty, there had been two.* Rumour finally settled the number at two; the foreigner and Mr. Flintwich. (*LD* II 31 794; my italics).

The italicized sequences are free indirect speech. In the first quotation it is the repetition that opens our eyes and ears to the millers' complaint (corresponding to 'we are/shall be ruined' in direct speech), and what makes the presence of free indirect speech obvious in the second quotation is the word *rumour* that points back to the competing assumptions. Owing to the formal identity between narrative and free indirect speech the reader is slightly surprised by the time he realizes that there has been a switch of modes; for more striking examples of this see sections 7 and 8.

5. Borrowing. In many passages we find Dickens manipulating his narrative in a characteristic way: he borrows a word or phrase from the speech of one of his characters and inserts it in his own report; for instance

she was much touched with this proof of his devotion, and protested, with great admiration, that he was indeed a dove.
The dove then turned up his coat-collar, and put on his cocked hat... (*OT* 27 200).

'Augustus, my sweet child, bring me a chair.'
The sweet child did as he was told (*MC* 46 703).

I term this device 'borrowing'; it is roughly equivalent to the term 'speech allusion' employed by Leech and Short,[4] but I find my own term preferable since it has a wider scope and also covers the peculiar use of first-person pronouns and of 'here-and-now' adverbs discussed below. The device conveys an ironical tone owing to the fact that the narrator pretends for a moment to accept a formulation used by one of his characters. Its use may entail deviation from grammatical convention, as in

'He thought to squeeze money out of us, and he has done for himself instead, Bella, my dear!'
Bella my dear made no response... (*OMF* III 15 595).

where a first-person pronoun appears in a third-person narrative. There are several instances showing a *we* where a *they* would be the expected form. Depending on the context, this use of *we* may suggest different things. In one passage it is only mildly surprising, suggesting perhaps that the narrator has for a moment entered into the situation of his characters:

'Can we get anything hot to drink?'
We could, and we did. In a public-house kitchen with a large fire. We got hot brandy and water, and it revived us wonderfully (*OMF* I 14 176).

Here the first-person pronoun appears in a third-person narrative, and the same is true of the following example:

'The road is clear, my dearest. So far, we are not pursued.'
Houses in twos and threes pass by us ... The hard, uneven pavement is under us, the soft, deep mud is on either side. Sometimes we strike into the skirting mud (*TC* III 13 339).

where the first-person pronouns are continued till the end of the chapter. This is highly unconventional, and possibly the device is resorted to here because the author is endeavouring to heighten the sense of danger by showing empathy with the fugitives. In *Dombey and Son* there occurs a passage in which the extremely affected Mrs. Skewton's statement is followed by an authorial one-line paragraph:

'... We are so dreadfully artificial.'
We were indeed. (*DS* 21 289).

102

This is the narrator's acid comment (compare the use of *we* discussed in III.11). Such cases, in which he comments on his characters, reveal the presence of the author's 'second self'.[5]

This sort of comment is very different in tone from those passages in which Dickens apostrophizes a character in melodramatic fashion:

Awake, unkind father! Awake now, sullen man! The time is flitting by; the hour is coming with an angry tread. Awake! (*DS* 43 609).

It is relevant to quote here a passage from *Edwin Drood* that illustrates a peculiar combination of direct speech and the report of it: there are tense-shifts, but the first-person pronouns have been retained, as have a vocative and an interjection:

Miss Twinkleton then said: Ladies, another year had brought us round to that festive period at which the first feelings of our nature bounded in our — Miss Twinkleton was annually going to add 'bosoms', but annually stopped on the brink of that expression, and substituted 'hearts'. Hearts; our hearts. Hem! (13 143).

And here is a final striking example of the way Dickens breaks down the barrier that is normally erected between two modes:

Dombey and Son was no more — his children no more. This must be thought of, well, to-morrow.
    He thought of it to morrow... (*DS* 59 842).

The word *to-morrow* is a 'here-and-now' adverb that is usually employed with reference to the moment of speaking (or thinking); in this passage it first occurs in free indirect thought and is then conveyed into the author's report, where it is stylistically extremely odd, involving as it does a breach of grammatical and semantic convention.

6. Direct speech and free direct speech. When a novelist makes his characters use direct speech, it is meant to lend a stronger air of vividness and authenticity to his narrative than is conveyed by indirect speech. It is normal nineteenth-century practice to indicate direct speech by means of quotation marks or inverted commas, and this is indeed what Dickens usually does; he is, however, not quite consistent in such typographical matters. Occasionally he employs inverted commas with indirect speech:

Mr. Chitling wound up his observations by stating that he had not touched a drop of anything for forty-two mortal long hardworking days; and that he 'wished he might be busted if he warn't as dry as a lime-basket.' (*OT* 18 133).

The presence of inverted commas here may be due to the elements of substandard language. In *Bleak House*, on the other hand, there occurs a passage whose opening is authorial report combined with comment (in the parenthesis), but whose latter half can only be interpreted as direct speech — or rather direct thought; there are, however, no quotation marks:

It must be very puzzling to see the good company going to the churches on Sundays, with their books in their hands, and to think (for perhaps Jo *does* think, at odd times) what does it all mean, and if it means anything to anybody, how comes it that it means nothing to me? (16 220).

Conventionally, the use of quotation marks is intended to guarantee the authenticity of a character's speech; but as has been interestingly shown by Mark Lambert, there are ways in which an author can manipulate his characters' speeches, one of them being the 'suspended quotation', i.e. a protracted interruption of a speech on the part of the narrator. The interruption may accommodate information about gestures, facial contortions, etc., thereby deflecting the reader's interest from the character to the author: 'the more one distorts a character's *ipsissima verba* the more one injures that character'.[6] Lambert has noted many more such suspensions in Dickens's early works than in his late works and advances the hypothesis that the young Dickens was jealous of his characters, but that after he had acquired fame he had less cause for jealousy. Whatever we may think of this, it is no doubt true that the authentic ring of direct speech may suffer from such suspensions:

'The best of her is,' said the dwarf, advancing with a sort of skip, which, what with the crookedness of his legs, the ugliness of his face, and the mockery of his manner, was perfectly goblin-like; — 'the best of her is that she's so meek...' (*OCS* 4 36).

If direct speech is identified as such through the use of inverted commas and is introduced by a reporting clause, what are we to think of passages like the following?

Sir Leicester receives the gout as a troublesome demon, but still a demon of the patrician order. All the Dedlocks, in the direct male line ..., have had the gout. It can be proved, sir. (*BH* 16 218).

Now. Is there any other witness? No other witness.
Very well, gentlemen! Here's a man unknown... (*BH* 11 148).

In the first quotation Sir Leicester appears to be suddenly addressing the reader directly. In the second, the Coroner is addressing the court and the jury; this is something we must deduce from the context, since the narrator has refrained from guiding us and from making it explicit in the normal way that this is direct speech. It is direct speech of a special kind. Leech and Short label it 'free direct speech' and define it as a form in which 'the characters apparently speak to us more immediately without the narrator as an intermediary'.[7] Compare the following example, where we have what may be termed 'free direct thought':

So! Anger, and fear, and shame. All three contending. What power this woman has to keep these raging passions down! Mr. Tulkinghorn's thoughts take such form as he looks at her... (*BH* 41 575).

7. Indirect speech. We may begin by considering a passage that might perhaps equally well have been dealt with under the heading of direct speech:

But Mr. Spenlow argued the matter with me. He said, Look at the world, there was good and evil in that; look at the ecclesiastical law, there was good and evil in *that*. It was all part of a system. Very good! There you were! (*DC* 33 479).

Judging from the introductory *He said,* followed by a comma, we are led to believe that what follows is direct speech. There are, however, no inverted commas, and present-tense verbs have been shifted into the preterit. On the other hand imperatives and exclamations have been retained, and on balance this specimen is perhaps closer to indirect than to direct speech.

Dickens often employs unconventional forms of indirect speech, incorporating in it items from direct speech like *sir* and *you know*, besides elements of substandard language:

He ... whispered in his ear, that she was a woman of extraordinary charms, sir... (*DS* 26 375).

he informed her and the Captain ... that now he was sure he had no hope, you know, he felt more comfortable (*DS* 56 794).

Mrs. Wickam often said she never see a dear so put upon. (*DS* 8 90).

The shifting of a first-person pronoun to the third person is also sometimes omitted, as in

Mr. Plornish ... said ... that people did tell him as Mr. Merdle was *the* one, mind you, to put us all to rights in respects of that which all on us looked to, and to bring us all safe home as much as we needed, mind you, fur toe be brought. (*LD* II 13 571).

where the unshifted pronouns clash oddly with the shifted tenses. Sometimes there is actual transition from indirect to direct speech in mid-sentence, indicated by inverted commas:

she ... only led the way up-stairs again; informing us ... that her landlord was 'a little — M —, you know!' (*BH* 5 54).

Another passage begins with indirect speech and inverted commas, after which there is an abrupt switch into direct speech:

Silas ... sulkily opines 'that it must be the fault of the other people. Or how do you mean to say it comes about?' he demands impatiently. (*OMF* I 7 80).

Finally let us consider a passage in which what begins as indirect speech is cut off by authorial intrusion:

She then remarked that she would not allude to the past, and would not mention that her daughter had for some time rejected the suit of Mr. Tackleton; and that she would not say a great many other things which she did say, at great length. (*CB* 199).

where the last twelve words are the narrator's.

8. Free indirect speech. Since Dickens mingles the narrative modes, we have already come across some instances of free indirect speech in the preceding sections. We may now consider free indirect speech in more detail.

This mode is characterized by not being dependent on a reporting clause and is therefore sometimes identical with narrative, so that some kind of contextual support is needed for its correct interpretation. In the first quotation to be given it is the word *revilings* that is the clue to the stylistic nature of the sequel:

the lady and daughter were both out of temper that day, and the poor girl came in for her share of their revilings. She was awkward — her hands were cold — dirty — coarse — she could do nothing right; they wondered how Madame Mantalini could have such people about her... (*NN* 17 213).

Free indirect speech is an economical mode: while providing the report of a speech, it may at the same time give vivid hints as to the speaker's idiolect; for instance it may accommodate elements of substandard language:

Susannah Sanders was then called, and examined by Serjeant Buzfuz, and cross-examined by Serjeant Snubbin. Had always said and believed that Pickwick would marry Mrs. Bardell; knew that Mrs. Bardell's being engaged to Pickwick was the current topic of conversation...; had been told it herself by Mrs. Mudbury which kept a mangle, and Mrs. Bunkin which clear-starched... (*PP* 34 482).

Most of the rendering of the witness's speech is in conventional English, but her own underlying idiolect is unmistakable.

It is characteristic of this mode that a number of verbs, many of them 'private' verbs, appear in it in a pregnant function. (Private verbs like *believe, fear, hope, remember, think,* and *wonder* are so called because it is only the speaker who makes a statement like *I fear so* who can decide whether that statement is true or false.) Typically *he feared* in its pregnant sense is synonymous with 'he said he feared'. Sometimes it is obvious from the context that a verb has been given such a pregnant function:

'... And we like 'em all the better for it, don't we?'
Mercury, with his hands in the pockets of his bright peach-blossom small-clothes, stretches his symmetrical silk legs with the air of a man of gallantry, and can't deny it. (*BH* 53 721).

In other cases verbs are given unconventional collocates that wrench them away from their basic meanings; thus *believe, hope,* and *wonder* are normally static verbs, but they may be made into dynamic ones in collocation with adverbials:

Pet laughingly believed he had been thinking of Miss Wade. (*LD* I 16 198).

And so he sat for half-an-hour at least, although Dolly, in the most endearing of manners, hoped, a dozen times, that he was not angry with her. (*BR* 78 603).

Ralph accompanied him to the street-door, and audibly wondering, for the edification of Newman, why it was fastened... (*NN* 56 746).

Similarly, the verbal phrases *be afraid* and *have no doubt* are basically static, referring to states of the mind, but they are both given unequivocal dynamic force, the former in conjunction with a manner adverbial, the latter by being made syntactically parallel with a preceding *said*, and by being preceded by the conjunction *whereupon* which initiates a new stage in the chain of events:

Mr. Blandois, in his most gentlemanly manner, was afraid he had disturbed her by unhappily presenting himself at such an unconscionable time. (*LD* I 30 353).

a gentleman ... said he was desirous of offering a few remarks to the company: whereupon the person in the cocked hat, had no doubt that the company would be very happy to hear any remarks that the man ... might wish to offer. (*PP* 37 525).

As is the case with indirect speech, we find items from direct speech cropping up in free indirect speech, for instance vocatives and imperatives:

'What time may you make it, Mr. Twemlow?' — Mr. Twemlow made it ten minutes past twelve, sir. (*OMF* III 13 568).

Where did he live now? hastily inquired Walter.
    He lived in the Company's own Buildings, second turning to the right, down the yard, cross over, and take the second on the right again. It was number eleven; they couldn't mistake it... (*DS* 15 219).

And the first-person pronoun of direct speech may be retained:

In spite of his seemingly retiring manner, a very intrusive person, this Secretary and lodger, in Miss Bella's opinion. Always a light in his office-room when we came home from the play or Opera... (*OMF* II 8 309).

the *we* having the function of establishing direct contact with Miss Bella's mind.
    As with indirect speech, a passage of free indirect speech may be abruptly cut off by the narrator obtruding his own comment:

In conclusion, he did hope that there wasn't a man with a beating heart who was capable of something that remained undescribed, in consequence of Miss Lavinia's stopping him as he reeled in his speech. (*OMF* IV 5 676).

The formal identity between narrative and free indirect speech can be exploited as a surprise effect, and it is sometimes only after he has considered an extended context that the reader becomes aware of a misinterpretation: what he at first took to be the narrator's voice is in fact something else:

He is borne into Mr. Tulkinghorn's great room, and deposited on the Turkey rug before the fire. Mr. Tulkinghorn is not within at the present moment, but will be back directly. The occupant of the pew in the hall, having said thus much, stirs the fire... (*BH* 27 376).

It has already been pointed out that free indirect speech is an economical mode. Many verbs are used pregnantly in it, and occasionally it lends itself to ellipsis. Thus, when the author alternates between direct and free indirect speech, he may content himself with implying an answer to a direct question, leaving the reader to supply the missing link for himself:

'I suppose you ain't in the habit of walking, yourself?' says Mr. Bucket. 'Not much time for it, I should say?'
    Besides which, Mercury don't like it. Prefers carriage exercise. (*BH* 53 722).

9. *Alternation between narrative modes.* We have now surveyed a number of examples illustrating the way in which the various modes are made to merge into each other, thus offending (if that is the word) against the conventional pure types. These mergers contribute substantially to the element of vividnes and unpredictability that is so characteristic of Dickens's style. But he also employs these modes in their pure form, and in that case they are often made to alternate rapidly. In *Little Dorrit* there occurs a passage in which Mr. Dorrit and his host are discussing life in the mountains. The account of this proceeds from (1) direct speech via (2) free indirect speech to (3) indirect speech:

    (1) 'But the space,' urged the grey-haired gentleman. 'So small. So — ha — very limited.'
    (2) Monsieur would recall to himself that there were the refuges to visit, and that tracks had to be made to them also.
    (3) Monsieur still urged, on the other hand, that the space was so — ha — hum — so very contracted. More than that, it was always the same, always the same. (II 1 441).

    The height of economy and artistry is achieved in a passage like the one quoted below, where free indirect speech is combined with telegraphese; it is an elliptical style that in several instances manages to do without subjects, finite verbs, and articles, but which at the same time incorporates direct speech and responds to a question that has evidently been put by one of the bystanders, so that an illusion of dialogue is conveyed; 'the Abbot' is the Night-Inspector, whose office has just been compared with a monastery:

... the merits of the case as summed up by the Abbot. No clue to how body came into river. Very often was no clue. Too late to know for certain, whether injuries received before or after death; one excellent surgical opinion said, before; other excellent surgical opinion said, after. Steward of ship in which gentleman came home passenger, had been round to view and could swear to identity. Likewise could swear to clothes. And then, you see, you had the papers, too. How was it he had totally disappeared on leaving ship, till found in river? Well! Probably had been upon some little game... (*OMF* I 3 24f.).

EPILOGUE

This study has focussed on the innovative aspects of Dickens's prose. It was my intention to show that those aspects — some of which are on the borderline of the nineteenth-century linguistic norm — were what offended a number of contemporary critics, and I hope I have succeeded in this. I have been onesided to the extent that I have been on the lookout for neologisms and for syntactic and stylistic oddities. If there is a balance to be redressed, let it be added here that such phenomena, though they *are* eye-catching, are after all not the statistically dominant features of Dickens's style. What strikes the reader with no axe to grind is no doubt his wonderful linguistic facility that is wielded with such ease, his care, his elegance, and his gift for turning out happy phrases. If we grant him these virtues, we must add that he has also made a substantial contribution to the English language: he is one of the makers of Modern English.

NOTES TO CHAPTER I

1. Cf. *DICKENS. The Critical Heritage,* edited by Philip Collins, London 1971, p. 21.
2. *An Autobiography* (written 1875-1876, published 1883), ch. XIII, p. 200 (the Fontana Library 1962).
3. *Dickens and His Readers,* 1955, p. 113.
4. 'Dickens and Interior Monologue', *PQ* 38 (1959), p. 65.
5. T. Yamamoto in a painstaking but somewhat unwieldy book, *Growth and System of the Language of Charles Dickens.* Revised edition, Kansai University Press 1952, points out some Dickensian neologisms. Jean McClure Kelty, in 'The Modern Tone of Charles Dickens' (*The Dickensian,* vol. 57 (1961), pp. 160-165), finds that Dickens foreshadowed the stream of consciousness type of writing. In *Dickens and the Suspended Quotation* (Yale University Press 1981) Mark Lambert devotes an interesting discussion to a stylistic device that Dickens favours in his early works to a greater extent than most of his contemporaries: the narrator's protracted interruption of his characters' speeches; this device, it is argued, was used by Dickens because he was jealous of the characters he had created and wanted to turn the attention of his readers to himself. See further IV.6.
6. Mark Lambert, *Dickens and the Suspended Quotation,* p. 4.
7. *Blackwood's Magazine,* Nov 1846, lx, pp. 590-605; quoted here from *The Critical Heritage,* p. 210.
8. Samuel Warren in *Blackwood's Magazine,* Dec. 1842; quoted from *The Critical Heritage,* p. 123.
9. Unsigned review of *Pictures from Italy* in *The Times,* 1 June 1846; *The Critical Heritage,* p. 140.
10. Thomas Cleghorn (?) in *The North British Review,* May 1856, iii, pp. 65-87; *The Critical Heritage,* p. 187f. See II.40ff.
11. See II.38.
12. Jan. 1843, lvi, pp. 212-237.
13. See *MEG* IV, pp. 210ff., and Albert C. Baugh/Thomas Cable, *A History of the English Language,* Prentice-Hall, Inc. 1978, pp. 291ff.
14. *MEG* II, p. 24f.
15. See for instance *The Watergate Hearings,* edited by the staff of *The New York Times,* Bantam Books 1973, p. 3 & p. 109.
16. *Catalogue of the Library of Charles Dickens from Gadshill...* edited by J. H. Stonehouse, London 1935.

NOTES TO CHAPTER II

1. K.M. Elisabeth Murray, *Caught in the Web of Words.* James A.H. Murray and the Oxford English Dictionary, Yale University Press 1977, p. 195.

2. *Op. cit.,* p. 196.
3. Susie I. Tucker, *Protean Shape,* London 1967, p. 157. — Very occasionally even more striking gaps may come to light. The *OED* dates the first appearance of *great-minded* to 1876, while I have found an example in *Nicholas Nickleby* (16 202). But according to the *OED*, the noun *greatmindedness* was first used *a* 1586. If the noun was used in the sixteenth century, it is barely possible to imagine that the adjective did not come into existence till 300 years later. In *Pope, Dickens, and Others* (Edinburgh 1969, p. 2) John Butt mentions deficiencies in the *OED* recording of Dryden's vocabulary, but adds that 'it was not surprising that omissions should be found, considering the field the editors undertook to cover'.
4. *Problems in the Origins and Development of the English Language,* Harcourt, Brace, Jovanovich, Inc. 1982, p. 19.
5. For a modern parallel compare the following passage from John Irving, *The World According to Garp* (Corgi Books 1981, p. 27f.): 'There were the usual elderly patients, hanging by the usual threads; there were the usual industrial accidents, and the automobile accidents, and the terrible accidents to children.' Here the first two occurrences of the word correspond to Dickens's usage, but not the third.
6. Cf. R.W. Zandvoort, *A Handbook of English Grammar,* Longman 1957, p. 342. I have noted the following examples in Dickens: *SB* 460; *PP* 43 606; *OT* 3 17; *NN* 3 27; *OCS* 38 288; *CS* 245 & 344; *DS* 56 781 & 794; *BH* 17 235 & 238; 30 411; 60 815; *UT* 292 & 545; *LD* II 42 499; *GE* 33 252; *OMF* III 15 597; *ED* 14 166.
7. Cf. A.P. Cowie & R. Mackin, *Oxford Dictionary of Current Idiomatic English,* Vol. l: Verbs with Prepositions & Particles, OUP 1975.
8. This idiom is in the *Concise Oxford Dictionary.*
9. Otto Jespersen, *Linguistica,* Copenhagen 1933, pp. 409ff.
10. This treatment of *decline and fall* as a regular verb may be compared with a modern example. In 'William Zeckendorf...wheeled and *dealed* his way into control of one of the world's largest real-estate empires' (*Time Magazine,* Jan. 1, 1973, p. 35) it is the compound *wheeler-dealer* that is the basis of a new, regularly conjugated verb.
11. We may compare the meanings of these words with the semantics of modern Australian colloquialisms like *killer* 'sheep that is to be killed' and *no-hoper* 'horse with no prospect of winning'.
12. See Knud Sørensen, 'From Postmodification to Premodification' (*Stockholm Studies in English* LII (1980), pp. 77-84); Krista Varantola, 'Premodification vs. Postmodification and Chain Compound Structures' (*Stockholm Studies in English* LVII (1983), pp. 75-82).
13. It is amusing to note how James Murray, battling with the problem of compounds in general, illustrated it in a letter through a string of *-less* adjectives: 'The other day I found myself *chairless* ..., and I am sometimes all but *bootless* and *shoeless,* before I can stir up the local shoemaker. ... The subject is endless & exhaustless, *boundless* and *bottomless*...' (*Caught in the Web of Words,* p. 192).
14. See Stephen C. Gill, ' "Pickwick Papers" and the "Chroniclers by the Line": A Note on Style'. *The Modern Language Review* 1968, pp. 33-36.

15. John Forster, *The Life of Charles Dickens,* edited by A.J. Hoppé, Everyman's Library 1980, Vol. One, p. 183.

16. *Ibid.,* p. 237.

17. In Louise Pound's formulation the hyphen serves the purpose of indicating 'the protraction of the initial syllable of trisyllabic words having penultimate accent, and sometimes of disyllabic words' ('The American Dialect of Charles Dickens', *American Speech* 1947, p. 128).

18. *Linguistica,* p. 437.

19. Samuel Warren in *Blackwood's Magazine,* December 1842; quoted from *DICK-ENS. The Critical Heritage,* edited by Philip Collins, London 1971, p. 122.

20. See Valerie Adams, *An Introduction to Modern English Word-Formation,* Longman 1973, p. 148.

21. *Linguistica,* p. 437.

22. Hans Aarsleff, *From Locke to Saussure,* University of Minnesota Press 1982, p. 311.

NOTES TO CHAPTER III

1. *MEG* VII, p. 528.

2. *MEG* VI, p. 154.

3. Cf. I.9.

4. *English Grammar,* p. 96.

5. But Dickens sometimes uses *neither* of three; see I.3.

6. Poutsma, II.882; *MEG* VII, p. 129.

7. Sylvère Monod, '"When the Battle's Lost and Won...' . Dickens *vs.* the Compositors of *Bleak House",* The Dickensian, vol. 69 (1973), p. 7.

8. In connexion with this passage Leech and Short ask the question whether Dickens is overstepping the limits of grammar here (*Style in Fiction,* Longman 1981, p.138).

9. An *icon* is 'a verbal sign which *somehow* shares the properties of, or resembles, the objects which it denotes' (W. K. Wimsatt, *The Verbal Icon,* 1967, p. x).

10. See Mary Lascelles, *Jane Austen and Her Art,* OUP 1965, p. 111.

11. Cf. *MEG* III, p. 313f., and Visser, III, Second Half, p. 2121. The construction is only sporadically documented in the *OED.*

12. Cf. K. Schibsbye, *A Modern English Grammar,* OUP 1970, p. 54f.

13. Cf. I.4.

14. *MEG* VII, p. 66.

15. Elsewhere Dickens refers to 'the opinions of this man or that man on Noodle or Doodle questions' (*The Uncollected Writings of CHARLES DICKENS. Household Words 1850-1859,* edited by Harry Stone, The Penguin Press, 1969, vol. II, p. 505). Harry Stone finds it probable that Dickens took these names from the burletta adaptation (1780) by Kane O'Hara of the burlesque *Tragedy of Trage-dies; or the Life and Death of Tom Thumb the Great* (1730-1731) by Henry Fielding.

16. Cf. J. C. Reid, *Dickens: Little Dorrit,* Studies in English Literature, No. 29 (1967), pp. 53ff.
17. See Charles J. Fillmore, 'The Case for Case', in Emmon Bach and Robert T. Harms (eds.), *Universals in Linguistic Theory,* New York 1968; Dwight Bolinger, *Aspects of Language,* Second Edition, Harcourt, Brace, Jovanovich, 1975.
18. *The Later Style of Henry James,* New York 1972, p. 35.

NOTES TO CHAPTER IV

1. Cf. Norman Page, *Speech in the English Novel,* Longman 1973, p. 97.
2. Ludwig Borinski, 'Dickens' Spätstil', *Die neueren Sprachen,* N. F. 6 (1957), pp. 405-428. In *The Uncollected Writings of CHARLES DICKENS. Household Words 1850-1859* (The Penguin Press 1969, p. 66) Harry Stone urges that Dickens has not been sufficiently recognized as a writer who foreshadows the twentieth-century novel.
3. *Speech in the English Novel,* p. 32.
4. *Style in Fiction,* Longman 1981, p. 349.
5. Wayne C. Booth, *The Rhetoric of Fiction,* Phoenix Books, Chicago 1967, p. 71. Cf. Wolfgang Iser's 'ein weiterer Erzähler' in *Der implicite Leser,* UTB, Munich 1972, p. 171.
6. *Dickens and the Suspended Quotation,* Yale University Press 1981, p. 58.
7. *Style in Fiction,* p. 322.

APPENDIX A: NEOLOGISMS

The entries are Dickensian neologisms, most of them established as such on the authority of the *OED*. I have included a batch of 176 words and phrases that have been overlooked by the *OED,* and another batch of 151 items not recorded in the Dictionary (cf. II.47). Quotations are given only for words and phrases that have not been discussed in Chapters I – IV. For the items that have been dealt with above there are references to the relevant passages.

The entries are alphabetized as follows:

Set phrases consisting of noun + noun, or of adjective (participle) + noun are listed under the first element: *c*asualty ward, *l*eaving shop, *ac*quired taste, *s*hort train.

Other kinds of phrases are listed under the first noun: a *c*reature of habit, *d*octor's orders, a *b*it of one's mind.

Idioms containing a verb and a noun (or a substantivized adjective) are listed under the noun: give it a *n*ame, go with a *r*oar, do the *c*ivil.

Other idioms containing a verb, but no noun, are listed under the verb: never *m*ind, I don't *t*hink, I *a*sk you.

Where it has been deemed necessary, definitions are given, often those of the *OED*. If a word is not in the *OED* or the Supplement, this is indicated. It is also indicated if an example antedates the first *OED* example (*'OED'* means either the main body of the Dictionary or the supplementary volumes).

Most of the entries are unmarked. Superscripts are, however, used to identify the following categories:

[1] : colloquialism, slang, humour

[2] : conversion

[3] : phrasal verb

[4] : idiom

Obsolete or archaic words are listed in APPENDIX B. Words that have been discussed above but which are not neologisms are listed in the INDEX.

[1] **A 1.** — 'He must be a first-rater,' said Sam. 'A 1,' replied Mr. Roker. (*PP* 41 575).

abolitionist. 'One who aims at or advocates the abolition of any institution or custom'. — The abolitionist of the national debt (*SB* 237).

abstractedly 'with absence of mind'. — 'Where indeed!' said Nicholas abstractedly. (*NN* 8 91).

accident 'victim of an accident'. Not in the *OED* — See II.5.

acidulated (drop) 'acid drop'. — Ma, in the openness of her heart, offered the governess an acidulated drop. (*SB* 106).

acidulation. First ex of technical use 1848; first ex of figurative use 1919. — Mrs. Pipchin ... was accustomed to rout the servants about, as she had routed her young Brighton boarders; to the everlasting acidulation of Master Bitherstone (*DS* 44 620).

[4] **acquired taste, an.** First *OED* ex 1858. — 'Chocolate, perhaps, you don't relish? Well, it *is* an acquired taste, no doubt.' (*BR* 75 575). — See II.12.

[3] **add up** 'make the correct total'. — the figures made her cry. They wouldn't add up, she said. (*DC* 41 605).

adjective euphemistically substituted for an expletive adjective. — See II.39.

admonitorial. — Miss Tox ... in her instruction of the Toddle family has acquired an admonitorial tone (*DS* 51 720).

aërial architecture 'building castles in the air'. — With such triumphs of aërial architecture did Mrs. Nickleby occupy the whole evening (*NN* 27 343).

again used in request for a repetition of what has previously been said: see II.29. A similar use is seen in: 'the young lady who was the daughter of the old lady ... — what was her name again?' (*NN* 21 263f.).

[1] **aged parent**, applied jocularly to a parent (whether elderly or not). — 'You don't object to an aged parent, I hope?' (*GE* 25 193).

aglitter. — Mr. Lammle, all a-glitter, produces his friend Fledgeby (*OMF* II 16 410).

allotment-garden. — Certain allotment-gardens by the roadside (*UT* in *All Year Round* 1 Aug. 1863 542/1).

[1] **all-overs** 'withdrawal symptoms' Not in the *OED*. — 'We've got the all-overs, haven't us, deary?' (*ED* 23 264).

[2] **allowance**, vb. — See II.14.

amiability used as a countable in the plural. Not in the *OED*. — See III.7.

[1] **amiable, do the.** — He used to ... flatter the vanity of mammas, do the amiable to their daughters. (*SB* 382).

[1] **amidships** 'on the solar plexus'. First *OED* ex 1937. — It struck him, as he said himself, amidships. (*CS* 137).

angular, of personal appearance. First *OED* ex 1850. — See II.37.

angularise, of personal appearance. Not in the *OED*. — A longer me — my shadow — walked before me, bending its back and drooping its arms, and angularising its elongated legs like drowsy compasses. (*HW* II 527, 1854).

angularity, of personal appearance: 'want of rounded outline'. — Miss Tox's dress ... had a certain character of angularity and scantiness. (*DS* 1 7).

angularly, of personal appearance. — Gashford ... was angularly made. (*BR* 35 267). — See II. 3.

[1] **animal**, noun, of a person. First *OED* ex 1922. — See II.41.

[4] **animal, go the extreme** 'go the whole hog'. — ... opposing all half-measures, and preferring to go the extreme animal. (*NN* 2 16).

ankle-jacks 'jack-boots reaching above the ankles'. the Captain ... put on an unparalleled pair of ankle-jacks (*DS* 15 214).

anyway 'in any case'. First *OED* ex 1859. — 'Any way,' said Sleary..., 'ith fourteen month ago' (*HT* III 8 292).

[1] **application** 'blow'. Not in the *OED*. — 'What!' exclaimed Mr. Snodgrass, ... rushing between the two, at the imminent hazard of receiving an application on the temple from each. (*PP* 15 197).

appointment book. — 'Would you take a seat ... while I look over our Appointment Book?' (*OMF* I 8 86).

[2] **apron**, vb., 'cover with, or as with, an apron'. — 'I mean to apron it [*sc.* a dress] and towel it

all over the front' (*OMF* III 4 451).

aquatic 'pertaining to pastime in or upon the water'. First *OED* ex 1866. — See II.32.

aquatically. First *OED* ex 1882. — Shall we go ... to Richmond, and stroll and dine aquatically? (*Pilgr.* 3 387, 1842; an editorial note explains: 'at the Star and Garter, whose garden ran down to the river').

area-bell. — [I] rang the area-bell. (*SB* 27).

area-door. — a piece of fat black water-pipe which trailed itself over the area door. (*OMF* I 5 45).

area-gate. — 'whenever area-gates is left open' (*BR* 35 271).

area-head — ... his daily occupation, which was to retail at the area-head above pennyworths of broth and soup (*BR* 8 68).

area-railing. — The hungry wayfarer ... plods wearily by the area railings. (*Bell's Life in London* 1836, 17 Jan. 1/1).

area-step. — The area and the area-steps ... were ... clean and bright. (*SB* 275).

arrival 'one who arrives or has arrived'. — See II.40.

artist 'one who practises a manual art in which there is much room for display of taste'. First *OED* ex 1849. — I therefore sent a message to an artist in boots (*AN* 18 250).

[4] **I ask you**, an exclamatory phrase indicating disgust or asseveration. — 'Now, I ask you,' said Mr. Meagles ... 'I ask you

simply, ... DID you ever hear of such damned nonsense as putting Pet in quarantine?' (*LD* I 2 16).
³ **ask down** 'invite (someone) to come and stay in the country'. — If I see him ... tomorrow, perhaps I'll ask him down. (*Monthly Magazine* 1834, 152).

asmear. — ... the shameful place [*sc.* Smithfield], being all asmear with filth and fat and blood and foam (*GE* 20 155).

aspirational. Not in the *OED* in this sense. — See II.32.

assassinatingly. Not in the *OED*. — See II.29.

astonisher. First *OED* ex 1871. — See II.17.

at about. First *OED* ex 1843. — We reached Washington at about half-past six that evening. (*AN* 8 115).

Athenæum, an 'a copy of —'. — I can't get an Athenæum, a Literary Gazette ... (*Pilgr.* 1 54, 1835).

ation 'process'. Not in the *OED*. — See II.5.

atomy (aphetic from *anatomy*), figuratively of things: 'skeleton'. — two withered atomies of teaspoons (*DS* 9 119).

auriferously, figuratively: 'yielding gold'. — Only one thing sat otherwise than auriferously ... on Mr. Dorrit's mind. (*LD* II 16 619).

baby-faced. — 'And now he's to bring home a new mistress, a baby-faced chit of a girl!' (*NN* 54 709).

bacchanalially. Not in the *OED*. — See II.46.

bachelor-apartment. — 'Ah, but he lived in a sweet bachelor-apartment' (*LD* II 30 781).

bachelor cottage. — They had taken a bachelor cottage near Hampton (*OMF* I 12 144).

² **Bah,** vb. — Mr. Richard ... is *Bah!'d* for his pains (*OCS* 7 54).

² **ball** 'give a ball in honour of'. Not in the *OED*. — See II.46.

ballast-heaver. First *OED* ex 1839. — the coal-whippers and ballast-heavers ... (*SB* 394).

balloon 'the outline enclosing words spoken or thought by a figure especially in a cartoon'. — See II.10.

¹ **the balmy** 'sleep'. — 'as it's rather late, I'll try and get a wink or two of the balmy.' (*OCS* 8 67).

bandbox 'a fragile or flimsy structure or one in which the accommodation is restricted'. First *OED* ex 1875. — 'Now,' said she, 'light my little lantern, and see me into my bandbox by the garden path;' for there was a communication between our cottages in that direction. (*DC* 44 639).

bandiness 'the quality of being bandy-legged or crooked'. — See II.19.

bar-counter. — He finishes by leaping gloriously upon the bar-counter, and calling for something to drink. (*AN* 6 91).

⁴ **bargain, drive a hard.** — I should be very sorry to appear anxious to drive a hard bargain. (*Pilgr.* 1 165, 1836).

² **Barlow,** vb., 'bore' (from the instructive monomaniac Mr. Bar-

low in Thomas Day's *Sandford and Merton* (1783)). Not in the *OED*. – ... with a further dread upon me of being Barlowed if I made inquiries, by bringing down upon myself a cold shower-bath of explanations and experiments, I forbore enlightenment in my youth (*UT* 340).

basket button 'button with a basket pattern'. – a blue coat and bright basket buttons (*SB* 254).

[4]**be: been and (gone and)** – : a vulgar or facetious expletive amplification of the past participle of a verb, used to express surprise or annoyance at the act specified. – 'Lauk, Mrs. Bardell, ... see what you've been and done!' (*PP* 26 361).

beadlehood. – Mr. Bumble ... was in the full bloom and pride of beadlehood. (*OT* 17 119; some editions read *beadledom* or *beadleism*).

beamer 'one who beams'. – the form of words which that benevolent beamer generally employed ... 'everything had been satisfactory to all parties' (*LD* II 32 796f.).

beamy, with Biblical allusion. Not in the *OED*. – Nevertheless, again I drank my cobbler...; full well knowing that, whatever little motes my beamy eyes may have descried in theirs, they belong to a kind, generous, large-hearted, and great people. (*CS* 115).

beckoner. Not in the *OED*. – 'Without the same queen beck-

oner too!' he added presently (*DS* 46 644).

bedside in attributive use. – a female servant came out into the lane to shake some bedside carpets. (*PP* 39 547).

beer-boy 'pot-boy'. – a beer-boy happened to pass... (*OCS* 34 254f.).

beer-chiller. – See II.10, 17.

[2]**bees'-wax**, vb. – the table-covers are never taken off, except when the leaves are turpentined and bees'-waxed (*SB* 9).

[4]**I believe you**, expressing emphatic agreement. – See II.12.

belligerent, noun, used of other hostile agents than fighters recognized by the law of nations. – See II.37.

belongings 'relatives'. – 'I have been trouble enough to my belongings in my day' (*BH* 21 299).

[1]**bender** 'a sixpence'. – 'Niver mind the loss of two bob and a bender!' (*SB* 112).

bepasture 'afford pasture for'. Not in the *OED*. – ... the bewildering amount of fleas, mosquitoes, bugs, and other Insects I have unwittingly bepastured ... (*Pilgr.* 4 311, 1845).

best-groomed, of a person. – ... his favourite original remark, that she is the best-groomed woman in the whole stud. (*BH* 28 391).

bewigment. Not in the *OED*. – he came down ... on his way to the bewigment of the Canterbury amateurs. (*Pilgr.* 5 138, 1847).

bibless. – she ... then sat down,

bibless and apronless. (*OMF* III 4 453).

[4] **a bit of one's mind, to give someone.** First *OED* ex 1864. — 'Old girl,' murmurs Mr. Bagnet, 'give him another bit of my mind.' (*BH* 34 477).

blacking-bottle. — 'his 'prentice ... sent 'em some medicine in a blacking-bottle.' (*OT* 5 34).

[3] **blaze away** 'work with enthusiastic vigour'. — I went at it again, and ... blazed away till 9 last night (letter quoted in Forster's *Life of Charles Dickens,* Everyman 1980, Vol. One, p. 291).

blind, adj., of a letter indistinctly or imperfectly addressed. First *OED* ex 1864. — The 'blind' letters have superscriptions which the sorters cannot decypher (*HW* I 76, 1850).

blisterous. Not in the *OED*. — ... an unctuous piece of roast beef and blisterous Yorkshire pudding (*LD* I 20 237).

Blondin rope 'tight-rope'. — An appalling accident happened at the People's Park near Birmingham, ... the enterprising Directors ... hanging the Blondin rope as high as they possibly could hang it. (*UT* 251, 1863).

bloomer trousers 'loose trousers reaching to the knee'. — ... a Corporal of his country's army, in the line of his shoulders, the line of his waist, the broadest line of his Bloomer trousers ... (*CS* 337, 1862).

[4] **boat, be in the same.** First *OED* ex 1845. — See II.12.

bodyguard, used of a single person. First *OED* ex 1861. — See III.8.

bog(e)y, Boguey 'a person much dreaded'. First *OED* ex 1857. — 'I am in the Downs. It's this unbearably dull, suicidal room — and old Boguey down-stairs, I suppose.' (*BH* 32 447).

boiling-over in attributive use. Not in the *OED*. — 'that boiling-over old Christian...' (*LD* I 35 412).

[2] **bolster,** vb., 'belabour with bolsters'. First *OED* ex 1871. — Then our fellows get nightmares, and are bolstered for calling out and waking other fellows. (*CS* 49, 1853).

bonded warehouse. — Goods brought in from foreign countries pay no duty until they are sold and taken out, as in a bonded warehouse in England. (*PI* 295).

[4] **bones, hear something in one's,** 'have a sure intuition of something'. — 'I seem to hear it, Muster Gashford, in my wery bones.' (*BR* 53 403).

[2] **bonnet,** vb., 'crush down a person's hat over his eyes'. — Two young men ... varied their amusements by 'bonneting' the proprietor of this itinerant coffee-house. (*SB* 390).

[2] **book** 'provide with books'. This sense is not in the *OED*. — 'At the delightful village of Dotheboys ... where youth are boarded, clothed, booked ...' (*NN* 4 32).

[3] **book through** 'obtain a ticket to cover a whole journey'. — The

other man, seating himself on the steps of the coach, remained in conversation with Slyme ... 'He's booked,' observed the man. 'Through,' said Slyme. (*MC* 51 794).

⁴books, keep in the good. — 'if you want to keep in the good books in that quarter, you had better not call her the old lady any more' (*NN* 31 404).

bother, used as a mild imprecation. — See II.31.

¹bottled lightning 'gin'. — 'bring in the bottled lightning, a clean tumbler, and a corkscrew.' (*NN* 49 648).

bounceably. — '... only there's no call to tell a man he is [*sc.* afraid], so bounceably.' (*OT* 28 205).

bow-windowed. First *OED* ex 1868. — ... when they reached the bow-windowed front room (*NN* 23 297).

¹bow-wows, go to the 'go to the dogs'. — 'it is all up with its handsome friend! He has gone to the demnition bow-wows.' (*NN* 64 821).

¹the boy 'the thing'. Not in the *OED*. — 'I have been thinking that the law is the boy for me.' (*BH* 17 232).

boy and girl in attributive use. — 'I have found it necessary to take some active steps towards setting this boy and girl attachment quite at rest' (*BR* 26 201).

¹boyslaughter. Not in the *OED*. — I felt he had done me an injury, not to say committed an act of boyslaughter, in running

over my childhood in this rough manner (*UT* 118, 1860).

²brandy, vb. – See II. 14.

¹brazen-faced, humorously of things. First *OED* ex 1864. — See II.37.

¹breach, noun, 'breach of promise'. — 'There's the chance of an action for breach' (*OCS* 8 61).

bread used as a countable. First *OED* ex 1865. — See III.7.

break, noun, 'chance, opportunity'. First *OED* ex 1911. — 'In point of fact, dear Mr. Fledgeby, ... not to affect concealment of Alfred's hopes..., there is a distant break in his horizon.' (*OMF* III 12 562).

breakage. — See II.45.

break-down 'a riotous dance'. — See II.34.

breaking-down, noun. — blowings-up in steamboats and breakings-down in coaches (*AN* 8 127).

brickmakeress. — carts, with brickmakers and brickmakeresses jolting up and down on planks (*CS* 747, 1857).

¹like bricks 'vigorously'. — See II.12.

³bring about 'restore to consciousness, or to health'. — 'That will bring him about or nothing will.' (*HT* I 8 52).

³bring round 'persuade, convert to an opinion'. First *OED* ex 1862. — 'I am not to be brought round in that way, always,' rejoined Madame, sulkily. (*NN* 17 206).

broody 'brooding'. Not in the *OED* in this sense. — See II.26.

bucellas 'Portuguese white wine'. — a bottle of sauterne, bucellas, and sherry (*SB* 282).

bulbous-shoed, with allusion to the wearer's gouty feet. — ... blue-nosed, bulbous-shoed old benchers, in select port-wine committee after dinner in hall (*BH* 1 4).

burst, noun, 'a great and sudden exertion of activity'. First *OED* ex 1862. — the upshot of Mr. Bounderby's investigations was, that he resolved to hazard a bold burst. (*HT* III 4 246).

business-looking. — a business-looking table, and several business-looking people (*NN* 2 11).

²**butler.** vb. — as nations are made to be taxed, so families are made to be butlered. (*LD* II 16 613).

¹**butterfingers.** — See II.13.

³**buy off** 'release from military service by payment', used figuratively. — If he could have bought him off, or provided a substitute, as in the case of an unlucky drawing for the militia, he would have been glad to do so on liberal terms. (*DS* 8 90).

buzzingly. — the pupils formed in line and buzzingly passed a ragged book from hand to hand. (*GE* 10 68).

by, prep., of a pub, etc: 'kept or managed by (as licensee).' — See II.30.

bygone 'belonging to past times'. — I hate the sight of the bygone assembly-rooms. (1869 *Lett.* (1880) II 413).

²**cab,** vb. — ... worth your while to walk or Cab so far East. (*Pilgr.* 1 84, 1835).

call 'call to the bar'. — A barrister? — he said he was not called. (*SB* 357).

candlestick-wards. Not in the *OED*. — Miss Volumnia rising with a look candlestick-wards, Sir Leicester politely performs the grand tour of the drawing-room, brings one, and lights it (*BH* 28 393).

cannibalic. — The fat youth gave a semi-cannibalic leer at Mr. Weller, as he thought of the roast legs and gravy. (*PP* 28 390).

capital (D), introducing the initial letter of a word, for emphasis. — See II.39.

¹**card** (1) with adj., indicating a person having some peculiarity. — Mr. Thomas Potter whose great aim it was to be considered as a 'knowing card'. (*SB* 269). — (2) without adj.: a 'character', an 'original'; a clever, audacious, etc., person. — 'You know what a card Krook was for buying all manner of old pieces of furniter.' (*BH* 62 840).

⁴**on the cards** 'within the range of probability', 'liable to turn up'. — 'If in short, if anything turns up.' By way of going in for anything that might be on the cards, I call to mind that Mr. Micawber ... composed a petition to the House of Commons. (*DC* 11 168).

carpentering. — Here he took to gardening, planting, fishing, carpentering, and various other pursuits (*OT* 53 413).

casualty ward. — we were conducted to the 'casualty ward' in which she was lying. (*SB* 242).

[1] catch-'em-alive-o 'fly-paper for catching flies'. — See I.7.

Cathedraly, adj. Not in the *OED*. — See II.45.

cellarous. — ... some underground way which emitted a cellarous smell. (*LD* I 20 236). — Cf. II.5.

cellary, adj. Not in the *OED*. — See II.5, 26.

[1] chaff, vb., 'rail at'. First *OED* ex 1850. — 'I have tasted your tripe, you know, and you can't "chaff" me' (*CB* 96f.).

[1] chaff, noun, 'badinage'. — 'I do,' said the 'prentice. 'Honour bright. No chaff, you know.' (*BR* 8 67).

chairman 'master of ceremonies'. — It requires no great exercise of imagination to identify ... the comic singer with the public-house chairman. (*SB* 110).

chance-child 'illegitimate child'. — No chance-child was he, for he could trace his genealogy all the way back to his parents (*OT* 5 31).

chanter : see horse-chaunter.

[1] the chap 'the thing'. Not in the *OED*. — 'Philosophy's the chap for me.' (*NN* 57 751).

[1] character 'person'. First *OED* ex 1931. — Mrs. Gradgrind was not a scientific character ... (*HT* I 4 17).

[2] charcoal, vb., 'suffocate with the fumes of charcoal'. — '... because she wouldn't shut herself up in an air-tight three-pair-of

stairs and charcoal herself to death' (*NN* 37 483).

charmed 'I am delighted'. — 'So delighted,' said Mrs. Merdle, 'to resume an acquaintance so inauspiciously begun at Martigny.' — 'At Martigny, of course,' said Fanny. 'Charmed, I am sure!' (*LD* II 7 512).

[1] chaw up 'do for, smash'. — See II.34.

[3] check off 'tick off'. — nearly every other member ... pulled a written paper from *his* pocket, to check Mr. Pugstyles off, as he read the questions. (*NN* 16 193).

[1] cheek 'impudent behaviour'. — See II.37.

cheekish. First *OED* ex 1851. — Yor'ne too cheekish by half Governor. (*Pilgr.* 3 503, 1843).

cheese 'a portion of cheese'. Not in the *OED*. — See III.7.

cheesemongery 'the commodities sold by a cheesemonger.' — Mr. Tuggs attended to the grocery department; Mrs. Tuggs to the cheesemongery (*SB* 335f.).

cheesiness 'cheesy quality'. — 'How's the cream of clerkship, eh?' — 'Why, rather sour, sir,' replied Mr. Swiveller. 'Beginning to border upon cheesiness, in fact.' (*OCS* 50 373).

cherubically. — See II.29.

Chesterfieldianity. Not in the *OED*. — See II.46.

cheval-glass. — the stranger surveyed himself ... in a cheval-glass (*PP* 2 18).

[3] chime with 'accord with'. First *OED* ex 1840. — See II.15.

chip, noun, 'fried piece of potato'. — husky chips of potato, fried with some reluctant drops of oil. (*TC* I 5 29).

choke, noun, 'the action and noise of choking'. — See II.14.

chop, vb. (1) 'to utter abruptly and disjointedly, with words or phrases cut short'. — 'Ah!' said Miss Wren thoughtfully, ... chopping the exclamation with that sharp little hatchet of hers (*OMF* III 2 435).

[1] **chop,** vb. (2) 'eat a chop'. First *OED* ex 1841. — ... unless you chop with me at 5. (*Pilgr.* 1 440, 1838).

Christian, like a 'like a (decent) person'. — See II.12.

[1] **chum,** vb., 'put as an occupant of the same room(s)'. — 'You'll be chummed on somebody to-morrow' (*PP* 40 572).

[1] **chummage** 'the quartering of two or more persons in one room. Hence **chummage-ticket**'. — 'You'll have a chummage-ticket upon twenty-seven in the third, and them as is in the room will be your chums.' (*PP* 42 588).

chump-end 'the thick blunt end of anything'. — three defaced Bibles (shaped as if they had been unskilfully cut off the chump-end of something)... (*GE* 10 68).

circuit 'a number of places of entertainment at which the same productions are presented successively'. — 'if he only acted like that, what a deal of money he'd draw! He should have kept upon this circuit.' (*NN* 30 398).

circular-visaged. — See II.21.

Circumlocutional 'representing the Circumlocution Office'. — I have found Circumlocutional champions disposed to be warm with me on the subject of my view of the Poor Law. (*OMF*, Postscript, 821f.).

Circumlocutionist 'one on the staff of the Circumlocution Office'. — ... this able Circumlocutionist (*LD* I 34 405).

[1] **civil, do the** 'act politely'. — 'There's Bill Sikes in the passage with nobody to do the civil to him.' (*OT* 22 158).

[1] **clap on** 'apply oneself with energy to a task'. First *OED* ex 1852. — 'and therefore if you can clap on a bit, I should take it kindly.' (*DS* 48 674).

class-grievance. — The turkey in the poultry-yard, always troubled with a class-grievance (probably Christmas)... (*BH* 7 82).

[3] **clear away** 'remove the remains of a meal'. — See I.7.

[3] **clear off** (1) 'get rid of (a debt or a claim) by settling it'. The extended sense illustrated below is not in the *OED*. — Said Mr. Podsnap to Mrs. Podsnap, 'Really I think we should have some people on Georgiana's birthday.' Said Mrs. Podsnap then to Mr. Podsnap, 'Which will enable us to clear off all those people who are due.' (*OMF* I 11 130).

[3] **clear off** (2) of intruders: 'be off, go away'. First *OED* ex 1888. — The wretched animal has not cleared off with the rest, but is here, under the window. (*CS* 757).

¹**clipper** 'first-rate person'. The *OED* lists another 1848 ex, from Thackeray's *Vanity Fair*. — 'Sol Gills, his uncle, is a man of science, and in science he may be considered a clipper' (*DS* 17 233).

⁴**cloak and dagger**, suggesting espionage and secrecy. — It was given him by a person then waiting at the door, the man replied. — 'With a cloak and dagger?' said Mr. Chester. — With nothing more threatening about him, it appeared, than a leather apron and a dirty face. (*BR* 24 183f.).

¹**closer** 'the last child born to a married couple'; probably from theatrical slang: 'a number or play that brings a programme to a close'. — See II.35.

coachfulness, coachlessness. — My purpose [*sc.* to look at a town in its degeneracy] was fitly inaugurated by the Dolphin's Head, which everywhere expressed past coachfulness and present coachlessness. (*UT* 242, 1860).

coal-whipper 'one who raises coal out of a ship's hold by means of a pulley'. — ... the appearance of the coal-whippers and ballast-heavers (*SB* 394).

⁴**cobbler's door, knocking at the.** 'A sort of fancy sliding in which the artist raps the ice in triplets with one foot while progressing swiftly on the other' (Farmer & Henley, *Slang and its Analogues*, s.v. *cobbler's knock*). — Sam Weller ... was displaying that beautiful feat of fancy sliding which is currently denominated 'knocking at the cobbler's door',

and which is achieved by skimming over the ice on one foot, and occasionally giving a two-penny postman's knock upon it, with the other. (*PP* 30 413). — Cf. **postman's knock** below.

cobbler's punch 'a warm drink of beer or ale with the addition of spirit, sugar, and spice'. — 'I mostly use it in cobblers' punch.' (*OMF* IV 14 780).

cocked hat 'a note, napkin, etc., folded in the form of a cocked hat'. First *OED* ex 1865 (*OMF*). — 'I beg to deliver this note to you,' said Watkins Tottle, producing the cocked-hat. (*SB* 463).

cocked-hat in attributive use. — The napkins are folded in cocked-hat fashion. (*PI* 267).

codger 'fellow, chap'. — 'I haven't been drinking your health, my codger,' replied Mr. Squeers. (*NN* 60 780).

coffee-shop. — Field Lane ... has its barber, its coffee-shop (*OT* 26 184).

cold, adj., of the person chosen to seek or guess, in children's games: 'distant from the object sought'. — 'That can't be the spot too?' said Venus. 'No,' said Wegg. 'He's getting cold.' (*OMF* III 6 487).

collapse 'lose courage suddenly'. First *OED* ex 1865 (*OMF*). — But I saw him collapse as his master rubbed me out with his hands (*GE* 19 144).

¹**collegian** 'a prison-inmate'. — 'they've been most infernally blown up by the collegians' [*sc.* in the Fleet]. (*PP* 44 621).

colloquially 'in colloquy'. Not in the *OED* in this sense. — See II. 29.

[1]**come** 'act the part of'. — 'That man, sir ... has comic powers that would do honour to Drury Lane Theatre... Hear him come the four cats in the wheelbarrow.' (*PP* 44 622).

come expensive. First *OED* ex 1862. — 'It must come expensive if they do.' (*OCS* 18 140).

[3]**come in** 'enter as a partner'. — See II.15.

[3]**come in for** 'incur punishment'. — See II.15.

[3]**come out** 'come out of curl'. Not in the *OED*. — See II.15.

[3]**come round** 'become reconciled'. First *OED* ex 1841. — See II. 15.

[3]**come up** 'win'. Not in the *OED*. — See II.6, 15.

[3]**come up** 'move!' (to a horse). First *OED* ex 1877. — See II.15.

[1]**command** 'a command performance'. — We are engaged to Macready ... at Covent Garden Theatre, on the night of the Queen's 'command'. (*Pilgr.* 1 497, 1839).

[2]**commercial** 'commercial traveller'. — 'The Commercials underneath sent up their compliments' (*GE* 13 99).

common, of persons and their behaviour: 'vulgar'. First *OED* ex 1866. — See II.38.

commoney 'a marble of a common sort'. — '... whether he had won any *alley tors* or *commoneys* lately' (*PP* 34 472).

companion in attributive use, of things. First *OED* ex 1844. — See II.14.

company-keeping, attributive adj. — See II.22.

composition-candle, one made of various ingredients. First *OED* ex 1861. — the figure of Venus on the first landing looked as if she were ashamed of the composition-candle in her right hand (*SB* 474).

compoundable 'capable of being commuted'. — a penalty of not less than forty shillings or more than five pounds, compoundable for a term of imprisonment. (*UT* 116, 1860).

[4]**concern, to whom it may.** — The Russia is a magnificent ship ... To whom it may concern, report the Russia in the highest terms. (*Let.* 26 Apr. (1960) 281, 1868).

condonatory. Not in the *OED*. — ... seeing condonatory smiles on the faces of those we loved (*HW* II 417, 1852).

conductorial. — On 17 Nov. 1853, while in Rome, [Dickens] sent Wills his 'Solemn and continual Conductorial Injunction' (*HW* I 34).

confide + object + *to*. — See II. 28.

congestively 'with abnormal accumulation of blood'. Not in the *OED*. — See II.32.

[1]**Conky,** a nickname given to a person with a prominent nose. — 'Conkey means Nosey, ma'am.' (*OT* 31 227).

connubiality. — 'why, I think

he's the wictim o' connubiality' (*PP* 20 273).

connubially. *OED* ex 1884. – Mrs. S., connubially considerate, carried him in that condition [*sc.* of intoxication] upstairs into his chamber (*SB* 684).

constabular. *OED* ex 1880. – The throwing of stones ... had become a crying evil, when the railway companies forced it on Police notice. Constabular contemplation had until then been the order of the day. (*UT* 305).

constabulary 'organized body of constables'. – See III.8.

[1] **constitutionally** 'by way of a "constitutional"'. – See II.32.

consularity. – See II.33.

conversationless. Not in the *OED*. – Conversationless at any time, he was now the victim of a weakness special to the occasion (*LD* I 17 208).

convulsionist 'a fanatic who falls into convulsions'. First *OED* ex 1865. – half of the half-dozen had become members of a fantastic sect of Convulsionists, and were even then considering within themselves whether they should foam, rage, roar, and turn cataleptic on the spot. (*TC* 2 7 101).

cool customer. First *OED* ex 1941. – 'that one is as cool a customer as ever I met with.' (*OMF* III 1 431).

coppice-topped. – ... the green rise, coppice-topped, that makes a background for the falling rain. (*BH* 2 9). Cf. II.20.

copy-slip 'a slip of paper on which a writing-copy is written'. First *OED* ex 1838. – ... the size and shape of the copy-slips which are used in schools (*SB* 206).

copying clerk. – See II.10.

[3] **cork down.** First *OED* ex 1860. – See II.43.

[2] **corkscrew,** vb., (1) 'cause to move or advance in a spiral manner'. – Mr. Bantam corkscrewed his way through the crowd (*PP* 35 501). – (2) 'draw out as with a corkscrew, elicit'. – ... 'from what we have corkscrewed out of him' (*BH* 55 757).

corkscrewism. Not in the *OED*. – See II.45.

round the corner 'nearby'. – the German-sausage shop round the corner (*PP* 32 441).

[4] **turn the corner** (1) 'start recovering from an illness'. – I hope to find on Monday at 12 o'Clock, that you have turned the corner, and come back again. (*Pilgr.* 1 229, 1837). – (2) 'overcome a critical financial difficulty'. First *OED* ex 1862. – 'if I could turn the corner, say of two hundred and fifty pounds, in one year..., Sophy and I should be united' (*DC* 59 827).

[2] **corner** 'take round a corner'. – 'he was taken down the Dover road and cornered out of it' (*GE* 45 352).

corporational 'belonging to a corporation'. – I sat pining under the imbecility of constitutional and corporational idiots. (*Lett.* 18 Jan. 1866).

cost price. – Every description

of goods ... fifty per cent. under cost price. (*SB* 369).

cottage 'a cottage piano'. First *OED* ex 1880. — she asked me if it were true that the girls at Shepherd's Bush 'had *Pianos*'. I shall always regret that I didn't answer yes — each girl a grand, downstairs — and a cottage in her bedroom (*Letters from Charles Dickens to Angela Burdett-Coutts,* 1850, p. 166).

cottage-room. — It was quite a cottage-room, with a lattice-window (*OT* 34 255).

[2] **counter** 'furnish with a counter'. — The offices were ... newly countered (*MC* 27 432).

counter-accusation. First *OED* ex 1917. — 'I make no counter-accusations' (*DC* 32 469).

counter-irritant. First *OED* ex 1854. — he maintained the Native about his person as a counter-irritant against the gout, and all other vexations (*DS* 26 374).

counter-irritation. First *OED* ex 1864. — the horse being troubled with a fly on his nose, the cabman humanely employed his leisure in lashing him about on the head, on the counter-irritation principle. (*PP* 46 646).

counterpray 'pray against'. — 'I might have made some money last week, instead of being counterprayed and countermined' (*TC* II 1 52).

coverture, used humorously of a man. — See II.40.

[1] **crack** 'a sharp, heavy, sounding blow'. — Green eid jist fetch him a crack over the head with the

telescope. (*Morning Chron.* 26 Oct. 1836, 3/5).

cramp-bone 'kneecap of a sheep, believed to be a charm against cramp'. — '[teeth] as was took by Mrs. Harris for a keepsake, and is carried in her pocket ... along with two cramp-bones' (*MC* 46 706).

creature of habit. Not in the *OED.* — See II.6.

[1] **the creeps** 'a sensation as of things creeping over one's body'. — She was constantly complaining of the cold, and of its occasioning a visitation in her back which she called 'the creeps'. (*DC* 3 38).

cross-firing. — This cross-firing of notes makes me smile. (*Pilgr.* 1 276, 1837).

cross-swell. — 'in the cross-swell of two steamers ... he over-balances' (*OMF* I 14 175).

[1] **crumb** 'plumpness'. — See I.7.

[1] **crusher.** — See II.17.

[4] **a good cry.** — See I.7.

[3] **cry off** 'announce one's withdrawal'. First *OED* ex 1857. — 'Whenever a person proclaims to you "In worldly matters I'm a child," you consider that that person is only a-crying off from being held accountable' (*BH* 57 775).

Cuba 'Cuba cigar'. — See II.14.

[4] **out of curl.** First *OED* ex 1924. — the pretty housemaid pushed Sam against the wall, declaring that he had ... put her hair quite out of curl. (*PP* 52 728).

current account. — a means of establishing a current account with Heaven, on which to draw ... for future bad actions. (*PI* 302).

cushioning 'throwing cushions'. Not in the *OED*. – Mr. George ... appears in two minds whether or no to shake all future power of cushioning out of him, and shake him into his grave. (*BH* 21 298).

customer 'opponent'. Not in the *OED*. – But if Miss Coutts ... had procured 'the Pet of the Fancy', or 'the Slashing Sailor Boy', or 'Young Sawdust' or some such gentleman to accomodate [sic] him with a customer as the sporting phrase is, I should have been still better pleased. (*Pilgr.* 2 207f., 1841).

[4] **cut it (too) fat** 'overdo something'. – Gentlemen in alarming waistcoats..., promenading about, three abreast, with surprising dignity (or as the gentleman in the next box facetiously observes, 'cutting it uncommon fat!') (*SB* 95).

[3] **cut off** 'run away, make off'. – The linen-draper cut off ... leaving the landlord his compliments and the key. (*SB* 61).

[3] **cut up** 'wound deeply'. – Scrooge was not so dreadfully cut up by the sad event. (*CB* 7).

[4] **cut up rough** 'become angry'. – 'p'raps I may say I von't pay, and cut up rough' (*PP* 43 609).

D 'damn'. – See II.39.

[1] **damp** 'a drink'. – 'We'll just give ourselves a damp, Sammy.' (*PP* 27 369).

any day 'without doubt'. – See II.29.

deadly-lively. – Even her black dress assumed something of a deadly-lively air from the jaunty style in which it was worn (*NN* 41 528).

declaration 'public official announcement of the numbers polled for each candidate'. – It will be unnecessary for me to remain here for the Declaration of the Poll on Monday. (*Pilgr.* 1 109, 1835).

declare oneself 'declare one's love for another person'. – See II.28.

dee 'damn'. – See II.39.

[4] **in a delicate state of health** 'pregnant'. – Mrs. Micawber, being in a delicate state of health, was overcome by it [*sc.* a surprising announcement] (*DC* 27 408).

Denmark satin 'a smooth worsted material used for ladies' slippers'. – ... a pair of Denmark satin shoes (*SB* 79).

depreciation 'writing off'. Not in the *OED*. – See II.6.

detainer 'a writ'. – 'unless the gen'lm'n means to go up afore the court, it's hardly worth while waiting for detainers...' (*SB* 445).

devil-may-care, adj. – 'he was a mighty free and easy, roving, devil-may-care sort of person, was my uncle...' (*PP* 49 691).

[4] **wish I may die**, as an asseveration of truth. – 'Wish I may die,' cried Mr. Riderhood... 'if I warn't a-going' to say the selfsame words to you' (*OMF* III 11 549).

[4] **never say die.** First *OED* ex *a* 1865. – See II.12.

dilapidative. Not in the *OED*. —
... dilapidative neglect (*HW* I
169, 1850).

dim 'somewhat stupid and dull'.
First *OED* ex 1892. — very dim,
indeed, he looks (*DS* 31 439).

diorama, used figuratively. First
OED ex 1876. — A RAPID DIO-
RAMA (*PI* 409).

[1] **discussion** 'consumption'. First
OED ex 1853. — Some fairy influence must surely have hovered
round the hands of Susan Nipper
when she made the tea, engen-
dering the tranquil air that reign-
ed in the back parlour during its
discussion. (*DS* 19 265).

disembarrass oneself of 'get rid
of'. — See II.6, 33.

dissective. — The three people
who write the narratives in these
proofs have a dissective property
in common. (1860 *Let.* (ed. 2) II
110).

distributionist 'one who advocates a system of distribution'. —
The distributionists trembled (*SB*
38).

ditchful 'full of ditches'. Not in
the *OED*. — the long white roads,
hedgeless, but, oh! so dismally
ditchful (*HW* II 527, 1854).

[1] **do** 'imposture'. — 'I thought it
was a do, to get me out of the
house.' (*SB* 29).

[1] **do: to have done it** 'to have
made a mess of things'. — 'Well,
young man, now you *have* done
it.' (*PP* 36 514).

doctor's orders. — I have been o-
bliged to make up my mind — on
the doctor's orders. — to stay
at home this evening. (*Pilgr.* 2
189, 1841).

dollarless. — a dollarless and unknown man (*MC* 17 291).

dollarous. Not in the *OED*. — the
greater, the more gorgeous, and
the more dollarous the establishment was, the less desirable it
was. (*CS* 115, 1855).

dolly 'like a doll'. — 'A dolly sort
of beauty, perhaps' (*BH* 28 392).

donkey 'stupid person'. First
OED ex 1840. — See II.41.

doormat 'a despised passive person'. — See II.1, 41.

double-barrelled. Not in the
OED in the Dickensian sense. —
Stations single and double-barrel-
led (*UT* 478).

double shuffle 'a dance in which
two movements of the same kind
are made by each foot alternate-
ly'. First *OED* ex 1837. — the
waterman ... is dancing the
'double shuffle' ... to keep his
feet warm. (*SB* 83).

dovetailedness. — 'The unities,
sir,' he said, 'are a completeness
— a kind of universal dovetailedness with regard to place and
time' (*NN* 24 311).

dowager 'an elderly lady of dig-
nified demeanour'. — ...rustling
through the room like the le-
gendary ghost of a dowager in
silken skirts (*ED* 3 25).

drag 'a heavy obstruction to progress'. First *OED* ex 1857. — See
II.10, 41.

draggle-haired. — See II.44.

[1] **drain** 'a drink'. — Two old men
who came in 'just to have a
drain.' (*SB* 186).

draught, of liquor: 'on draught'. — a pot of the real draught stout. (*SB* 267).

drawbridged 'having a drawbridge'. — See II.21.

[4]**out of drawing** 'incorrectly drawn'. First *OED* ex 1859, but not figuratively, as in Dickens. — resplendent creatures ..., who are sure to be stricken disgusted with the indifferent accommodation of our watering-place, and who, of an evening (particularly when it rains), may be seen very much out of drawing (*UT* 395).

dressing-gowned. — Mr. Dorrit, dressing-gowned and newspapered, was at his breakfast. (*LD* II 16 614).

[4]**drop it!** 'have done!' First *OED* ex 1872. — See II.31.

[1]**drop into** 'pitch into'. — 'He's welcome to drop into me, right and left.' (*BH* 24 353).

dry-saltery 'a shop selling drugs, dye-stuffs, gums, etc.' every thing ... was wet, and shining with soft soap and sand; the smell of which drysaltery impregnated the air. (*DS* 23 330).

Dundee marmalade. — Anchovy Paste, Dundee Marmalade, and the whole stock of luxurious helps to appetite... (*Household Words* 28 June 1856, 555/2).

earthfaring. Not in the *OED*. — the imaginary wearer [*sc.* of a nautical suit] ... with his seafaring and earthfaring troubles over (*UT* 221, 1860).

no earthly. — The fifty pounds ... makes no earthly difference. (*Pilgr.* 1 359, 1838).

earthquaky. — See II.26.

editorial we. — Every rotten-hearted pander who ... struts it in the Editorial We once a week. (*Pilgr.* 2 368, 1841).

effaceable. — by the time they had washed off all effaceable marks of the late accident, the room was warm and light ... (*NN* 6 54).

egg-box. — 'That was the cot of *my* infancy; an old egg-box' (*HT* I 4 16).

egg-cupful. '... There's nothin' so refreshin' as sleep, sir, as the servant-girl said afore she drank the egg-cupful o' laudanum.' (*PP* 16 211).

elastic, adj., applied to fabrics. — Elastic waistcoats, bosom friends, and warm stockings, poured in upon the curate. (*SB* 8).

election cry. — But I doubt if they [*sc.* the words 'Pip' and 'Property'] had more meaning in them than an election cry ... (*GE* 18 136).

embowerment. — these plants were of a kind peculiarly adapted to the embowerment of Mrs. Pipchin. (*DS* 8 99).

emetically 'in the manner of an emetic'. — See II.32.

emporium, pompously applied to a shop. — Emporiums of splendid dresses ... (*NN* 32 408).

[4]**how goes the enemy?** 'what is the time?' (*NN* 19 239).

engrossedly. — Bella's eyes drooped more engrossedly over her book (*OMF* III 5 463).

enjoinder 'injunction'. First *OED*

ex 1894. – his master ... gave him ... a note for Mrs. Dombey: merely nodding his head as an enjoinder to be careful (*DS* 46 641).

enthoosemoosy 'gushing enthusiasm'. Not in the *OED*. – I was quite self-possessed however, and, notwithstanding the enthoosemoosy, which was very startling, as cool as a cucumber. (*Pilgr.* 2 311, 1841).

[2] **errand**, vb. Not in the *OED*. – 'Upon that there stool ... sets that there boy of mine ... wot will errand you' (*TC* III 9 292).

escape 'mental or emotional distraction from the realities of life'. – Labouring people ... in need of mental refreshment and recreation ... Come! Amuse me harmlessly, show me something, give me an escape! (*Household Words* 1853, extra Christmas number, 35/2).

et cetera, used with *Yours* as an ending in letters. – Cheaper in comparison than a Leg. Yours &c C Dickens. (*Pilgr.* 1 1, 1825-1826).

[1] **ever so**, used in affirmative contexts as a vague intensive. First *OED* ex 1858. – See II.29.

everbrowns. – See III.28.

evil-adverbiously. Not in the *OED*. – See II.45.

excitableness. First *OED* ex 1875. – 'the known excitableness of my little woman' (*BH* 42 584).

exclusion 'exclusivity'. Not in the *OED*. – 'Oh! Exclusion itself!' said Miss Tox. (*DS* 8 98).

excursional. – Pray let me divide the little excursional excesses of the journey, among the gentlemen, as I have always done before. (*Pilgr.* 5 374, 1848).

[4] **make an exhibition of oneself** 'behave in a laughable manner'. First *OED* ex 1853. – Miss P., by-the-bye, had only the week before made 'an exhibition' of herself (*SB* 423).

extollable. Not in the *OED*. – the Circumlocution Office not only was blameless in this matter, but was commendable in this matter, was extollable to the skies in this matter. (*LD* I 10 106).

[1] **clap eyes on.** – 'you might never have clapped eyes upon the boy' (*OT* 26 193).

[4] **facts and figures** 'precise information'. First *OED* ex 1845 (*The Chimes*). – Several other members, too, dwelt upon the immense and urgent necessity of storing the minds of children with nothing but facts and figures ... (*SB* 641).

fadedly. – ... a dull room, fadedly furnished. (*BH* 51 692).

faint 'not fresh'. – A man ... chewing a faint apple (*DS* 57 807).

fairy story. – life was more like a great fairy story, which I was just about to begin to read, than anything else. (*DC* 19 273).

[4] **break somebody's fall.** First *OED* ex 1848. – If you make the driver alight first, and then throw yourself upon him, you will find

that he breaks your fall material-ly. (*SB* 143).

³**fall back on** 'have recourse to'. First *OED* ex 1841. – Abandon-ed by the world, having nothing to fall back upon..., they turn their eyes and not their thoughts to Heaven. (*UT* 655, 1836).

falling in 'reconciliation'. – It al-most seems as if we had had a mortal falling out. I hope we shall have a lasting falling in a-gain, soon. (*Pilgr.* 1 355, 1838).

fancy fair (where fancy goods are sold). – Flaming accounts of some 'fancy fair in high life'. (*SB* 92).

fascinator. – 'Had I not seen ... the demdest little fascinator in all the world...' (*NN* 17 207).

fast-goer. – His great aim ... was to be considered as a 'knowing card', a 'fast-goer' (*SB* 269).

father, used colloquially by a wife addressing or referring to her husband. – 'Never mind, Father, never mind!' said Mrs. Meagles. (*LD* I 2 16).

fearfully, intensifier. – This place is fearfully dull ... (*Pilgr.* I 106, 1835).

featherweight 'a very small thing'. – He turned ... to observe the effect of the slightest feather-weight in his favour. (*OT* 52 404).

fellow (1) of a woman. – See II. 40. – (2) 'one', vaguely indicat-ing the speaker himself. First *OED* ex 1861. – 'I hate her. So I do that white chap; he's always got his blinking eyes upon a fel-low.' (*HT* 3 2 227).

³**fill out** 'put on weight'. First *OED* ex 1851. – nurse says he [*sc.* a baby] is filling out every day. (*SB* 470).

fill-out 'meal'. – See II.16.

filter-shop. – I have seen water like it at the Filter-shops, but nowhere else. (*AN* 12 172).

⁴**finger, turn (somebody) round one's.** First *OED* ex 1855. – 'I may tell you ... that I can turn them round my finger.' (*BH* 2 12).

finishing-school. – 'I'll bring in a bill for the abolition of finishing-schools.' (*SB* 333).

fireworkless. – Whom I found with some fireworkless little boys in a desolate condition. (*Lett.* 1856 (1880) I 437).

¹**fix** 'deal with, do for'. First *OED* ex 1874. – But he sat turn-ing it over in his mind, with such an obvious intention of fixing Mrs. Pipchin presently, that even that hardy old lady deemed it prudent to retreat... (*DS* 8 104).

fix oneself on 'concentrate on'. – a mind unable ... to detach it-self from old ... associations, though enabled to fix itself steadily on one object (*OT* 44 337).

flare, noun and vb. – See II.46.

flint 'skinflint'. First *OED* ex 1840. – 'He was the cruellest, wickedest, out-and-outerest old flint that ever drawed breath' (*NN* 41 539).

fluey 'covered with flue'. – I went upon 'Change, and I saw fluey men sitting there under the bills about shipping... (*GE* 22 175).

fluffy 'covered with fluff'. — fluffy and snuffy strangers (*DS* 59 833).

[1] **flummox** 'bring to confusion'. — 'He'll be what the Italians call reg'larly flummoxed' (*PP* 33 455).

foggy 'not clear to one's mind'. First *OED* ex 1840 (*BR*). — ... the mottle-faced man, whose apprehension of matters in general was of a foggy nature (*PP* 55 772).

[3] **follow up** 'go after, pursue'. First *OED* ex 1847. — 'If you seriously want to follow up the niece, tell the uncle that you must know where she lives' (*NN* 26 333).

for, prep., 'in preparation for or anticipation of (the stated time of a dinner, etc.)'. First *OED* ex 1900. — See II.30.

[1] **in amazing force** 'displaying readiness and vivacity in conversation'. First *OED* ex 1849. — John Willet was in amazing force to-night, and fit to tackle a Chief Justice (*BR* 1 10).

forewoman (in a shop or department). — 'Miss Knag the forewoman shall then have directions to try you with some easy work' (*NN* 10 126f.).

forget-me-not in attributive use. — a small gold chain and a 'Forget me not' ring: the girl's property. (*SB* 194).

[3] **fork out** in absolute use: 'pay'. First *OED* ex 1856. — 'he declines to fork out with that

cheerfulness which is always so agreeable and pleasant in a gentleman of his time of life...' (*OCS* 2 20).

fraud 'fraudulent person'. — See II.40.

[4] **free gratis for nothing.** — See II. 12.

[2] **French-polish,** vb. — You could ... French-polish yourself on any one of the chairs (*SB* 275).

freshener 'something that freshens'. First *OED* ex 1884. — This was a good freshener to my presence of mind (*DC* 4 57).

fried-fish warehouse. — Field Lane ... has its barber, its coffee-shop ... and its fried-fish warehouse. (*OT* 26 184).

frivolity 'a frivolous act or thing'. — See III.7.

frog-eater 'Frenchman'. First *OED* ex 1863. — One of these benighted frog-eaters would scarcely understand your meaning (*UT* 590).

[3] **frown down** 'force with a frown'. First *OED* ex 1870. — See II.15.

fruity, of wine: 'having the taste of the grape'. — the head waiter inquired ... whether he would wish to try a fruity port with greater body. (*MC* 12 198).

fumigator. First *OED* ex 1872. — '... if I am not first tempted to break the head of Mr. Dolls with the fumigator.' (*OMF* III 10 539).

[4] **the fun of the fair.** — 'You're half the fun of the fair, in the Court of Chancery' (*BH* 24 353).

furniture-broker. — ... the small

shops ... occupied by furniture-brokers (*AN* 8 115).

gag 'introduce improvised remarks into a piece'. − the same vocalist 'gags' in the regular business like a man inspired. (*BH* 39 558). − Cf. **ponging**.

galley, used with allusion to Molière, *Scapin* II, xi. − 'What the devil do *you* do in that galley there?' (*TC* I 5 32).

galley slavery. Not in the *OED*. − Galley slavery has preceded merry making ... (*Pilgr*. 5 604, 1849; with allusion to galley-proof?).

galvanically. First *OED* ex 1848. − Clemency hovered galvanically about the table, as waitress (*CB* 249, 1846).

[1] **gammoning** 'hoaxical'. − ... the gammoning nature of the introductory speech (*NN* 16 194).

gardenful, noun, 'as many as a garden will contain'. − ... like a great sunflower pushing its way at the sun from among a rank gardenfull of flaring companions. (*TC* II 5 80).

garter 'tape held up for a circus-performer to leap over' − 'Offered at the Garters four times last night, and never done 'em once' (*HT* I 6 31).

[4] **gas and gaiters, all is** 'everything is very satisfactory'. − 'She is come at last − at last − and all is gas and gaiters!' (*NN* 49 648).

gashliness 'dismalness'. − ... the general dulness ('gashliness' was Mrs. Wickam's strong expression) of her present life (*DS* 8 104).

[1] **gasper,** a vaguely derogatory term. First *OED* ex 1868. −

When I think of the possible consequences − of little gaspers like Papa − ... a chill runs through my blood. (*Pilgr*. 4 389, 1845).

gentility 'genteel people'. − See II.40.

German 'German sausage'. First *OED* ex 1883. − 'Circumstances ... interpose obstacles between yourself and Small Germans' (*OMF* II 8 315).

[4] **I wish you may get it,** ironical phrase implying the speaker's doubt of, or lack of desire for, another's success. − ... an 'I wish you may get it' sort of expression in his eye... (*SB* 22).

[2] **gimlet** 'pierce with or as with a gimlet'. − See III.26.

ginger-beery. − Our honourable friend ... made them a brisk, ginger-beery sort of speech (*UT* 562f., 1852).

gingerous. − See II.25.

[1] **gingham** 'umbrella'. First *OED* ex 1861. − It [*sc.* the soup] an't so thick, but wot you'll find three and sixpence worth of ginghum among the ox heads as you pave your garden with. (*Pilgr*. 3 503, 1843).

girl-driving. Not in the *OED*. − See II.45.

give 'allow a specified period of time'. − I give Cruikshank 'till Saturday: − I hope we shall have something to look at by that time. (*Pilgr*. 1 114, 1835).

[3] **give on** 'afford a view of'. − See II.33.

given-out 'assigned'. − It come to her through two hands ... The second hand took the risk of the given-out work. (*All Year Round* 19 Dec. 1868, 63/2).

giver up. Not in the *OED.* − 'but anyways I'm not a giver up, I hope'. (*DS* 23 324).

[3]**go off** 'lose consciousness'. First *OED* ex 1844. − 'She's a-goin' off,' soliloquised Sam ... 'Wot a thing it is, as these here young creeturs *will* go a-faintin' avay' (*PP* 39 551).

[4]**going on for** 'nearly'. First *OED* ex 1848. − See II.12.

[2]**God-bless** 'say "God bless" to'. Not in the *OED.* − 'I commend your prudence highly. Thank you. God bless you. Good-night.' − To be commended, thanked, God-blessed, and bade good-night by one who carried 'Sir' before his name... (*BR* 40 302).

gold-dusty. First *OED* ex *a* 1907. − the coaly (but to him gold-dusty) little steamboat (*OMF* IV 4 664).

gonoph 'pickpocket'. − 'He's as obstinate a young gonoph as I know' (*BH* 19 265).

gonophing 'picking pockets'. Not in the *OED.* − ... designing young people who go out 'gonophing' (*UT* 488, 1857).

good for 'safe to live or last so long'. First *OED* ex 1859. − 'I am sure, on the day of your marriage, I thought she was good for another twenty years' (*DS* 41 585).

goose-skinned 'affected with goose-skin'. − And a breezy, goose-skinned, blue-nosed, red-eyed, stony-toed, tooth-chattering place it was... (*CB* 83).

[1]**gorm** '(God) damn'. − See II. 39.

gossamer 'light silk hat; any hat'. − See II.13.

[1]**governor,** vulgar form of address to a man. − See II.13.

grampus 'a person given to puffing and blowing'. − See II.41.

[1]**gran,** a childish or familiar shortening of *granny.* − And now dear Gran let me kneel down here where I have been used to say my prayers. (*All Year Round* 3 Dec. 1863, 11/2).

great-minded. First *OED* ex 1876. − ... coolness and great-minded selfishness (*NN* 16 202). − See II.3, note 3.

green, noun, short for *green man* or *Jack-in-the-Green.* − For some few years the dancing on May-day began to decline; small sweeps were observed to congregate..., unsupported by a 'green'. (*SB* 172).

green-hearted. − 'No worldliness about him. Fresh and green-hearted!' (*BH* 37 521).

[1]**Greenland** 'the country of greenhorns'. − See II.12.

grimy 'unpleasant, mean'. − The machinery is finished, ... the Orchestra complete − and the manager *grimy*. (*Pilgr.* 1 19, 1833).

[4]**grinder, take a.** − Here Mr. Jackson smiled once more upon the company, and, applying his left thumb to the tip of his nose, worked a visionary coffee-mill with his right hand, thereby performing a very graceful piece of pantomime (then much in vogue, but now, unhappily, almost ob-

solete) which was familiarly denominated 'taking a grinder'. (*PP* 31 421).

[3] **groan down** 'silence by means of groans'. — 'And whether you did not submit to be coughed and groaned down...?' (*NN* 16 193).

groove 'slide'. First *OED* ex 1866. — See II.35.

growlery 'a place to growl in'. — 'Sit down, my dear,' said Mr. Jarndyce. 'This, you must know, is the Growlery. When I am out of humour, I come and growl here.' (*BH* 8 94).

guard, noun, used with reference to a railway train. — The conductor or check-taker, or guard ... wears no uniform. (*AN* 4 63).

Guinness. — a large hamper of Guinness's stout. ... taking a draught of Guinness. (*SB* 295).

gunpowderous. — See II.25.

gymnastic, adj., 'exhibiting positions of the body assumed in gymnastics'. First *OED* ex 1850. — See II.42.

half-baptize 'baptize privately or without full rites'. — He got out of bed ... to half-baptize a washerwoman's child in a slop-basin. (*SB* 8).

half-price (1) adj. — their last half-price visit to the Victoria gallery. (*SB* 55). — (2) adv. — 'He takes me halfprice to the play.' (*MC* 32 507). — (3) 'people who have paid half price', not in the *OED*. — See II.40.

[4] **get a hand** 'receive applause'. — 'So he has gone on night after night, never getting a hand, and you getting a couple of rounds at least' (*NN* 29 378).

hard-worked. First *OED* ex 1894. — I entertain a weak idea that the English people are as hard-worked as any people upon whom the sun shines. (*HT* 1 10 63).

hartshorning 'applying hartshorn or smelling salts'. Not in the *OED*. — after ... much damping of foreheads, and vinegaring of temples, and hartshorning of noses (*BR* 19 147).

[4] **eat one's hat,** colloquial asseveration. — 'If I knew as little of life as that, I'd eat my hat and swallow the buckle whole.' (*PP* 42 592).

[4] **his hat covers his family,** said of one who has to provide only for himself. — They would say, 'While my hat covers my family ... I have only one to feed' (*HT* 2 1 118).

[4] **go round with the hat** 'collect money'. First *OED* ex 1857. — Any new going round with the Hat, I abhor the idea of... (*Pilgr.* 5 190, 1847).

headwork 'mental work'. — 'how the blazes you can stand the head-work you do, is a mystery to me.' (*PP* 55 772).

hearth-broomy. Not in the *OED*. — It [*sc.* his brushed-up hair] gave him a surprised look — not to say a hearth-broomy kind of expression (*DC* 41 591).

hearth-stoning 'whitening with hearthstone'. Not in the *OED*, which, however, has the vb. *hearthstone,* 1840. — The area and the area-steps, and the street-door and the street-door steps, and the brass handle ... were all as clean and bright, as indefatigable whitewashing, and hearthstoning ... could make them. (*SB* 275).

[1] **heavens,** used adverbially as intensifier. − ... when we had played the last company out, which was a shy company, through its raining Heavens hard ... (*CS* 218, 1858).

can help, idiomatically with negative omitted (*can* for *cannot*), after a negative. First *OED* ex 1862. − 'hoping ... that you'll not permit yourself to be more reduced in mind than you can help' (*DS* 53 741).

[1] **help oneself** 'steal'. First *OED* ex 1868. − See II.39.

henbane, as the name of a narcotic. First *OED* ex 1840 (*BR*). − I ... was obliged last night to take a dose of henbane. (*Pilgr.* 1 448, 1838).

herewith, adj., 'accompanying'. *OED* ex 1917. − ... the herewith invitation (*PP* 37 517).

high chair 'a child's chair with high legs'. First *OED* ex 1848. − ... a little boy who was sitting up to supper in a high chair (*SB* 529f.).

hint, vb., with sentence as object. − 'I'm sure he is very rich, Fred,' hinted Scrooge's niece. (*CB* 52).

[4] **make a hole in the water** 'drown oneself'. − 'I don't know why I don't go and make a hole in the water.' (*BH* 46 631).

home, in games: 'the place in which one is free from attack'. − the keeping up of a 'home' at rounders. (*Let.* 1854 (1938, II 566)).

homoeopathic 'very small'. − Mr. Claypole taking cold beef from the dish, and porter from the pot, and administering homoeopathic doses of both to Charlotte (*OT* 42 321).

[2] **hook and crook,** verbal phrase. Not in the *OED*. − 'those who hooked and crooked themselves into this family' (*MC* 4 60).

horse chaunter 'one who sells horses fraudulently'. − 'He *was* a horse chaunter...' (*PP* 42 589).

hospitalities 'instances of hospitality'. First *OED* ex 1856. − I am stopped in my original intention by the hospitalities of the Americans. (Fielding, p. 35, 1842).

hothouse, figuratively in attributive use. − 'Mrs. Wititterly is of a very excitable nature; very delicate, very fragile; a hothouse plant' (*NN* 21 267).

the House 'the workhouse'. − I suppose you must have an order into the house. (*SB* 2).

[1] **hulker.** Not in the *OED* (but formed from *hulk* 'hang about'). − See II.17.

hunchy 'hunchbacked'. − 'I'm a little hunchy villain and a monster, am I?' (*OCS* 5 40).

hurry 'a tremolo passage on the violin or other instrument to accompany an exciting scene'. − then the wrongful heir comes in to two bars of quick music (technically called 'a hurry'). (*SB* 116).

[1] **Ikey,** familiar abbreviated form of *Isaac,* used typically for a Jew. — 'Let me alone,' replied Ikey (*SB* 450).

ill-to-do 'poor'. First *OED* ex 1853. — See II.45.

imitative 'sham'. — the other ladies displayed several dazzling articles of imitative jewellery (*NN* 25 326).

impenetrability, used as a countable in the plural. Not in the *OED*. — See III.7.

impossibly 'to a preposterous degree'. Not in the *OED*. — See II. 6.

inappeasably. Not in the *OED*. — Inappeasably indignant with her for her triumphant discovery of Mrs. Pegler, he turned this presumption ... over and over in his mind... (*HT* 3 9 294).

inch-rule. — 'Neither will you find him measuring all human interests ... with his one poor little inch-rule now.' (*DC* 60 837).

incidental music. First *OED* ex 1864. — you have a melo-drama ..., a pantomime, a comic song, an overture, and some incidental music... (*SB* 115).

inexplicables 'trousers'. — He usually wore a brown frock coat without a wrinkle, light inexplicables without a spot. (*SB* 312).

inflammatorily. — Yours inflammatorily and despondingly Charles Dickens. (*Pilgr.* 2 131, 1840).

innings in figurative use. — 'It's my innings now...' (*PP* 23 315).

[2] **intended,** converted into a noun. — See II.14.

invalid, noun, 'anything damaged, dilapidated, or the worse for wear'. First *OED* ex 1860. — See II.42.

iron-headed 'very hard-headed or determined'. First *OED* ex 1852. — ...'my iron-headed friend —' (*CB* 263, 1846).

irons 'iron supports to correct bow-legs, etc.'. — ... deformities [i.e. deformed children] with irons upon their limbs... (*NN* 8 88).

[2] **irrepressible,** converted into a noun. First *OED* ex 1890. — See II.14.

ization. — See II.5.

Jack-in-the-water 'an attendant at the watermen's stairs'. — 'Would you prefer a wessel, sir?' inquired another waterman, to the infinite delight of the 'Jack-in-the-water'. (*SB* 390).

[1] **Jeff** 'a rope'. — 'Tight-Jeff or Slack-Jeff, it don't much signify; it's only tight-rope and slack-rope.' (*HT* 1 6 31).

Jehuicular 'vehicular' (in allusion to 2 Kings 9:20). Not in the *OED*. — A sensible Belgravian has put forth his might in the "Times" newspaper, towards effecting Jehuicular reform. (*HW* I 224, 1851).

jemmy (1) 'a great-coat'. — 'your friend in the green jemmy.' (*PP* 2 10). — (2) 'a sheep's head as a dish'. — The man in the shop, perhaps, is in the baked 'jemmy' line... (*SB* 72).

jog-trotty 'monotonous'. — See II.1, 26.

[4] **a joke is a joke** 'a joke is not to be taken seriously'. — A joke's a joke: and even practical jests are very capital in their way, if you can only get the other party to see the fun. (*SB* 43).

jostlement. — ... bursting in his full-blown way along the pavement, to the jostlement of all weaker people (*TC* 2 12 135).

jungled, adj. — primeval forests ... where the jungled ground was never trodden by a human foot. (*AN* 11 161).

kennel 'a small and mean dwelling'. — 'He got us a room — we were in a kennel before —' (*PP* 45 642).

Kensal Green, a London cemetery, used allusively as the type of a cemetery or as a symbol of death and burial. — What would I give if the dear girl whose ashes lie in Kensal-Green, had lived. (*Pilgr.* 3 211, 1842).

[4] **put the kibosh on somebody.** — See II.12.

kick-up 'lifting the legs in kicking'. — See II.16.

kill, vb., 'represent as killed or dead'. The first *OED* ex of *kill off* = 'remove the names of dead officers from the navy-list' is from 1867. — Any one of these scouts used to think nothing of politely assisting an old lady in black out of a vehicle, killing any proctor whom she inquired for, representing his employer as the lawful successor and represen-tative of that proctor... (*DC* 39 563).

[1] **kinchin-lay** 'the practice of stealing money from children sent on errands'. — 'Ain't there any other line open?' — 'Stop,' said the Jew... 'the kinchin lay.' (*OT* 42 325).

[4] **King Charles's head** 'an obsession'. — See II.36.

kitchen-pokerness 'a stiffness like that of a kitchen-poker'. — See II.19.

knifer 'one who carries or uses a knife as a weapon'. — 'Jacks, and Chayner men. And hother Knifers.' (*ED* 23 275).

[3] **knock over** 'dumbfound'. — 'I found ... such a resemblance between Miss Esther Summerson and your ladyship's own portrait, that it completely knocked me over...' (*BH* 29 406).

[3] **knock up** 'prepare (food) quickly'. First *OED* ex 1869. — 'I'll tell you what I knocked up for my Christmas-eve dinner...' (*CS* 471, 1865).

[3] **knock up against** 'encounter'. First *OED* ex 1887. — 'one never knows, when one gets into the City, what people one may knock up against...' (*OMF* III 13 567).

knock-kneed 'feeble'. — See II. 42.

lady wife. — I wish I could send you some autographs ... but I find ... that my lady wife has been bestowing them upon her friends. (*Pilgr.* 2 7, 1840).

language 'bad language'. First *OED* ex 1886. — See II.38.

languish, of a non-person. Not in the *OED*. — See II.42.

²laundress 'serve (a person) as a laundress'. — 'Sir,' said Mrs. Crupp, in a tone approaching to severity, 'I've laundressed other young gentlemen besides yourself...' (*DC* 26, 399).

⁴the law is a ass. — See II.36.

law-stationering, adj. Not in the *OED*. — the same law-stationering premises (*BH* 10 127).

³lay down 'store (wine) by putting it away in cellars'. — 'That was laid down, when Mr. Linkinwater first come, that wine was.' (*NN* 37 476).

³lay on 'provide for the supply of water, gas, etc. through pipes'. First *OED* ex 1845. — Fresh water is laid on in every cell... (*AN* 7 101).

²lead 'example, precedent'. First *OED* ex 1863. — she ... turned aside and suffered the tears to gush from her eyes, without waiting for a lead from that wise matron. (*DS* 18 244).

³lead up to 'prepare gradually for'. First *OED* ex 1861. — 'But for my great respect for your sister, I might not have led up so pleasantly to a little proposal that I wish to make...' (*TC* 3 8 283).

leader 'leading article'. There is an *OED* ex from 1837. — ... this manifesto (which formed a portion of his last week's leader) (*PP* 51 718).

at least 'or rather'. Not in the *OED*. — See II.6.

³leather away 'work hard'. First

OED ex 1869. — the Drum was on the very brink of leathering away with all his power... (*CB* 153).

¹leathers, a name for one who wears leather breeches or leggings. — 'Out of the vay, young leathers.' (*PP* 19 254).

⁴take leave of one's senses. First *OED* ex 1893. — 'The child has taken leave of her senses...' (*DC* 45 657).

¹leaving shop 'an unlicensed pawnshop'. — Upon the smallest of small scales she was an unlicensed pawnbroker, keeping what was popularly called a Leaving Shop, by lending insignificant sums on insignificant articles of property deposited with her as security. (*OMF* II 12 350).

³let off 'lease in portions'. — It [*sc.* a large house] is let off in sets of chambers now... (*BH* 10 130).

³let out 'use strong language'. First *OED* ex 1840. — See II.39.

⁴life or death, a matter of. — It is a matter of life or death to us, to know whether you have got Ainsworth's MS yet. (*Pilgr.* 1 249, 1837).

³lift down. — Sikes dismounted..., holding Oliver by the hand ... and, lifting him down directly, bestowed a furious look upon him... (*OT* 21 154).

light porter 'one who carries only light packages'. — A deaf serving-woman and the light porter completed Mrs. Sparsit's empire. (*HT* 2 1 113).

⁴in one's line 'suited to one's

taste'. 'Have you got anything in my line to-night?' (*OT* 26 185).

[3]line out 'delete'. First *OED* ex 1963. — 'Well!' says Watt, 'it's to be hoped they line out of their Prayer-Books a certain passage for the common people about pride and vainglory...' (*BH* 12 157f.).

lion-inspecting 'sight-seeing'. Not in the *OED*. — I should be glad to plan some lion-inspecting expedition... (*Pilgr.* 3 106, 1842).

[1]live 'actual, real', in jocular use. First *OED* ex 1887. — in came Sir Matthew Pupker, attended by two live members of Parliament (*NN* 2 12).

living-dead. First *OED* ex 1917. — the living-dead man (*OMF* II 13 373).

[4]a load off one's mind. First *OED* ex 1852. — 'It's a load off my mind, Trotwood, to have such a partner.' (*DC* 35 518).

lock 'lock-keeper'. — 'I am the Lock,' said the man. (*OMF* III 8 508).

lock-up in attributive use. — choice stabling, and a lock-up coach-house (*BR* 35 264).

locomotively 'with regard to locomotion'. — He always slouched, locomotively, with his eyes on the ground... (*GE* 15 105).

[4]not look at 'not consider (as a business partner)'. Not in the *OED* in this sense. — 'Now, what name have you got? Have you got Merdle?' And, the reply being in the negative, the weightiest of men had said, 'Then I won't look at you.' (*LD* I 21 247).

look-in 'a short visit'. First *OED* ex 1865 (*OMF*). — See II. 16.

looking-forward 'an anticipation of future events'. — Anxious lookings-forward to the pleasure of your society. (*Pilgr.* 1 328, 1837).

[3]look out 'field, scout (at cricket)'. — Several players were stationed, to 'look out', in different parts of the field... (*PP* 7 90).

[4]look-out: that is his look-out, i.e. his 'headache'. — See II.16.

[1]look (somebody) up (1) 'go to see (a person)'. — 'George will look us up ... at half-after four.' (*BH* 49 668). — (2) 'direct vigilance to'. First *OED* ex 1855. — 'I don't know but what it might be worth a fellow's while to look him up a bit.' (*BH* 20 280).

love-making, adj. in attributive use. *OED* ex 1868. — See II.22.

L.S.D.-ically. Not in the *OED*. — See II.45.

[1]lummy 'first-rate'. — 'Jack Dawkins — lummy Jack.' (*OT* 43 329).

[1]lush, vb., 'drink'. — 'some of the richest sort you ever lushed.' (*OT* 39 290).

lust, used as a countable in the plural. Not in the *OED*. — See III. 7.

[2]mace 'strike as with a mace'. — See II.44.

[1]magpie 'a halfpenny'. — See II. 13.

[1]mahogany 'a table'. — See II.3.

[2]make up (intransitive for reflexive construction) 'prepare one's face, etc. for a performance'. —

Mr. Crummles ... had ... 'made up' for the part by arraying himself in a theatrical wig (*NN* 25 326).

⁴go the odd man: a mode of tossing for drinks, etc. — He imparted to her the mystery of going the odd man or plain Newmarket for fruit, ginger-beer, baked potatoes, or even a modest quencher (*OCS* 36 271).

Manchesterially. Not in the *OED*. — See II.46.

²manslaughter, vb. First *OED* ex 1920. — ... those who hooked and crooked themselves into this family by getting on the blind side of some of its members before marriage, and manslaughtering them afterwards by crowing over them to that strong pitch that they were glad to die... (*MC* 4 60).

the many-headed 'the many-headed multitude'. — the playful disposition of the many-headed (*PP* 19 260).

many-thoughted. Not in the *OED*. — they had laid a moral foundation calculated to promote the best uses amongst what was styled the 'many-headed', but which by the aid of such institutions would soon be designated the 'many-thoughted, monster'. (Fielding, p. 5, 1840).

marine store in attributive use. — the marine-store dealer at the corner of the street. (*SB* 60).

marshy used figuratively. Not in the *OED*. — his old eyes will glimmer with a moist and marshy light. Then the little old man is drunk. (*LD* I 31 363).

mash one's way 'stamp one's way'. — With drooping heads and tremulous tails, they mashed their way through the thick mud (*TC* 1 2 4).

matter-of-course in attributive use. — See III.4.

maudlinism. — At this precise period of his existence, Mr. Benjamin Allen had perhaps a greater predisposition to maudlinism than he had ever known before (*PP* 38 535).

the mazy 'the mazy dance'. — '... in remembrance of her with whom I shall never again thread the windings of the mazy...' (*OCS* 56 414).

meltability. — the brittleness and meltability of wax (*OMF* IV 8 714).

merry-go-rounder (1) 'a cause of astonishment'. — 'Oh, my eye! here's a merry-go-rounder! — Tommy Chitling's in love!' (*OT* 25 180). — (2) Not in the *OED*. — '... so we make it quite a merry-go-rounder.' — I was obliged to consider a little before I understood what Mr. Peggotty meant by this figure, expressive of a complete circle of intelligence. (*DC* 7 103).

²message 'carry a message'. — 'our people go backwards and forwards ... lettering and messaging, and fetching and carrying' (*BR* 24 186).

²mildew, vb., used figuratively. First *OED* ex 1864. — In Belgrave Square I met the last man ... sitting on a post in a ragged red waistcoat, eating straw, and mildewing away. (*UT* 446, 1855).

mildewy. – the damp mildewy smell which pervades the place. (*SB* 123).

[2] **milk-and-water,** vb. – See II.14.

mill 'treadmill'. – 'The mill's a deal better than the Sessions.' (*SB* 273).

[2] **mill** 'send to the treadmill; send to prison'. – 'I shouldn't have been milled, if it hadn't been for her advice. But ... what's six weeks of it?' (*OT* 25 180).

millinerial. First *OED* ex 1888. – Let it [*sc.* a dress] never ... undergo millinerial alteration (*Pilgr.* 4 89, 1844).

[4] **(one) in a million (million).** – See II.12.

Miltonian 'an admirer or imitator of Milton'. – I have been *going,* every day, to write to you about the Miltonians. (*Pilgr.* 3 352, 1842).

[1] **never mind** 'it is none of your business'. – See I.8.

minder 'a child who is taken care of at a minding school'. – '... Those are Minders.' – 'Minders?' the Secretary repeated. – 'Left to be Minded, sir.' (*OMF* I 16 199). Cf. II.17.

minus 'absent'. – Being, when called upon to answer for the assault, what Waterloo described as 'Minus', or, as I humbly conceived it, not to be found. (*UT* 533, 1853).

minuting 'writing minutes'. – the work of form-filling, corresponding, minuting, memorandum-making... (*LD* II 8 517).

mirthfulness. First *OED* ex 1867. – the blood quickened its pace, and whirled through one's veins on that clear frosty morning with involuntary mirthfulness. (*AN* 1 5).

misery-making, attributive adj. – See II.22.

[1] **missis, missus,** dialectal or vulgar forms. – Hint this delicately to your *Missus.* (*Pilgr.* 1 34, 1833).

[2] **Missis** 'address as "Mrs."'. – 'Don't *Missis* me, ma'am...' (*NN* 42 549).

[4] **the mixture as before,** set phrase often found on medicine bottles. – I have taken a wineglass full of 'the mixture as before' twice a day... (*Pilgr.* 1 40, 1834).

[3] **mole out** 'find by groping'. – he had felt his way inch by inch and 'Moled it out, sir' (that was Mr. Pancks's expression), grain by grain (*LD* I 35 410).

[4] **coin money** 'make money rapidly'. First *OED* ex 1863. – nobody knew with the least precision what Mr. Merdle's business was, except that it was to coin money... (*LD* I 33 394).

monomaniacally. – ... young Sparkler hovering about the rooms, monomaniacally seeking any sufficiently ineligible young lady (*LD* I 21 253f.).

mortary 'having mortar obtrusively present'. – We are a little mortary and limey at present, but we are getting on capitally. (*UT* 447).

[1] **mother,** used colloquially by a

husband addressing or referring to his wife. — 'Mother (my usual name for Mrs. Meagles) began to cry so, that it was necessary to take her out. 'What's the matter, Mother?' said I...' (*LD* I 2 17).

²**mother-in-law** 'rule as a mother-in-law' (i.e. a stepmother). — 'I will not ... submit to be mother-in-lawed by Mrs. General' (*LD* II 14 590).

⁴**give it mouth** 'express it with vehemence'. — 'What I say in respect to the speeches always is, "Give it mouth".' (*BR* 65 502).

on the move 'dying'. First figurative *OED* ex 1881. — See II.43.

¹**muff** 'clumsy fellow'. — See II. 13.

mug 'make a face'. — the low comedian had 'mugged' at him in his richest manner... (*LD* I 20 236).

mugful. — ... a glassful of spirits and water for Nicholas, and a cracked mug-full for the joint accommodation of himself and Smike (*NN* 15 177).

mugless. Not in the *OED*. — Henry the Eighth had melted down their [*sc.* the bells'] mugs; and they now hung, nameless and mugless, in the church-tower. (*CB* 82).

mumbly, adj. Not in the *OED*. — 'And when I'm too deaf, and too lame, and too blind, and too mumbly for want of teeth, to be of any use at all..., then I shall go to my Davy' (*DC* 8 111).

³**murmur out.** — Gabriel murmured out something about its being very pretty... (*PP* 29 403).

⁴**call out of one's name** 'address by a name other than the true one'. — perhaps if she was to be called out of her name, it would be considered in the wages. (*DS* 2 16).

⁴**give it a name** 'what would you like to drink?' First *OED* ex 1854 (*HT*). — See II.12.

name-calling 'abusive language'. — such name-calling and dirt-throwing (*CS* 63, 1853).

National Participled 'damned'. Not in the *OED*. — See II.39.

Nellicide. Not in the *OED*. — See II.46.

nephewless. Not in the *OED*. — 'poor, nevyless Old Sol, where are *you* got to?' (*DS* 32 463).

never, used for emphatic denial. — See II.29.

¹**nevvy, nevy** 'nephew'. — 'he might die a little sooner for the loss of—' 'Of his Nevy,' interposed the Captain. (*DS* 15 209).

⁴**new boy.** — Here is the table upon which he sat forlorn and strange, the 'new boy' of the school. (*DS* 41 579).

Newmarket, a card-game. — going the odd man or plain Newmarket for fruit... (*OCS* 36 271).

next door 'the occupant of the adjoining house'. — One answered, 'I will if next door will;' and another, 'I won't if over the way does.' (*UT* 548, 1855).

nice, used ironically. — I have been clearing off all the rejected articles to-day, and nice work I have had. (*Pilgr.* 1 217, 1836).

⁴**as nice as nice could be.** — ... a capital bed, and all as nice as nice

145

could be. (*Pilgr.* 1 521, 1839).

²**niche** 'place in a niche'. Dickens seems to be the first to have used the verb figuratively. – ... a family so conspicuously niched in the social temple as the family of Dorrit. (*LD* II 5 482).

no-coated. – He was a brown-whiskered, white-hatted, no-coated cabman. (*SB* 142).

nomadically, used figuratively. Not in the *OED*. – See II.29.

non-market in attributive function. First *OED* ex 1884. – ... on non-market days (*CS* 335, 1862).

non-political. – If the prisoner ... had committed every non-political crime in the Newgate Calendar..., nothing would have been easier than ... to obtain his release. (*UT* 172).

notice 'a review of a play'. – If I take a cab and put off writing my notice 'till we return, I can easily manage it. (*Pilgr.* 1 97, 1835).

at – minutes' notice. – There is *always* a bed for you at five minutes' notice. (*Pilgr.* 1 569, 1839).

⁴**get someone's number** 'size someone up'. – 'Whenever a person proclaims to you "In worldly matters I'm a child," you consider that that person is only a-crying off from being held accountable, and that you have got that person's number, and it's Number One.' (*BH* 57 775).

nurse 'clasp (one's knee)'. – he ... nursed his left leg, and waited to be spoken to (*PP* 31 429).

²**nutcracker,** vb. – 'Are infants to be nutcrackered into their tombs, and is nobody to save them?' (*GE* 23 183; a baby has been given the nutcrackers to play with).

¹**ochre** 'money'. – 'pay your ochre at the doors and take it out.' (*HT* 1 6 30).

²**odd-job** in attributive function. – See III.4.

²**odd job,** transitive verb. – 'a gentleman like yourself wot I've had the honour of odd jobbing till I'm gray at it...' (*TC* 3 9 291).

odour 'repute'. – As the Tories are the principal party here, *I* am in no very good odour in the town. (*Pilgr.* 1 106, 1835).

²**officer** 'direct'. – some great lady ... upon whom Kate was deputed to wait, accompanied by Miss Knag, and officered of course by Madame Mantalini. (*NN* 17 213).

off-minutes 'period when one is off work'. Not in the *OED*. – The same dogs must encounter them over and over again, as they trudge along in their off-minutes... (*UT* 99).

off-time 'a time when one is off duty'. – The answer to this inquiry, 'Where's Lamps?' was ... that it was his off-time. (*CS* 488, 1866).

¹**the old one** 'one's father or mother'. – 'It's the old 'un.' – 'Old one,' said Mr. Pickwick. 'What old one?' – 'My father, Sir,' replied Mr. Weller. (*PP* 20 270).

oldster. – See II.45.

ological. – 'and I hope you may

now turn all your ological studies to good account' (*HT* 1 15 102).

[1] **oner** 'a unique person'. — See II.13.

[2] **opium-smoke,** transitive vb. — The woman has opium-smoked herself into a strange likeness of the Chinaman. (*ED* 1 2).

order 'a request for refreshments or food'. — 'Pray give me your orders gen'lm'n — pray give me your orders' (*Bell's Life in London,* 17 Jan. 1836, I/1).

under orders. — I regret to say that my being under orders from The Chronicle will prevent my enjoying the pleasure of seeing you tomorrow. (*Pilgr.* 1 113, 1835).

[3] **order about.** First *OED* ex 1853. — 'He never could come into the office, without ordering and shoving me about,' said Uriah. (*DC* 42 608).

orphan-in-law. Not in the *OED*. — 'I mean to say, Dombey,' returned the Major, 'that you'll soon be an orphan-in-law.' (*DS* 40 572; a jocular reference to the likelihood that Dombey's mother-in-law is not long for this world).

out-at-elbowed, used figuratively. — a ragged, white-seamed, out-at-elbowed bagatelle board. (*UT* 89).

[1] **outdacious** 'audacious'. 'That out-dacious Oliver' (*OT* 17 122).

outpush. — See II.45.

outspeaking 'outspoken'. — 'you are for ever telling her the same thing yourself in fifty plain, out-speaking ways' (*MC* 36 574).

[2] **over** 'leap over'. — ... playing at leap-frog with the tombstones: ... 'overing' the highest among them (*PP* 29 400).

[4] **over the left,** implying that the words to which this phrase is appended express the reverse of what is really meant. — each gentleman pointed with his right thumb over his left shoulder. This action, imperfectly described in words by the very feeble expression of 'over the left', when performed by any number of ladies or gentlemen who are accustomed to act in unison, has a very graceful and airy effect; its expression is one of light and playful sarcasm. (*PP* 42 592).

overcarefully. — 'The sister,' said Bradley, separating his words over-carefully, and speaking as if he were repeating them from a book, 'suffers under no reproach.' (*OMF* II 14 388).

overhand 'with the hand over the object which it grasps'. First *OED* ex 1861 (*GE*). — he stood the pudding on the bare table, and ... stabbed it, overhand, with the knife (*UT* 134, 1860).

over-proof 'over-proof spirit'. — 'Show us the best — the very best — the over-proof that you keep for your own drinking, Jack!' (*BR* 54 413).

overswinging, adj. — the feeble over-swinging lamps (*TC* 1 6 47).

Oxford-mixture 'pepper and salt'. — His legs ... graced a pair of Oxford-mixture trousers (*PP* 41 581).

oystery. — Seeing your hand upon the cover of a letter ... I ... opened the despatch, with a moist and oystery twinkle in my eye. (*Pilgr.* 4 2, 1844).

Pagodian. Not in the *OED*. − See II.45.

another pair of shoes. − See II. 12.

palmy days. − I hope you will meet with every happiness that you picture to yourself in these palmy days. (*Pilgr.* 1 232, 1837).

paper-hanging 'the affixing of bills, advertisements, etc., on a bill-board or hoarding'. − [I] Hired a large one [*sc.* hoarding] ... let out places on it, and called it 'The External Paper-Hanging Station'. (*Household Words* 22 March 1851, 604/2).

parenthetical 'bandy'. *OED* ex from 1856. − town-made children, with parenthetical legs (*SB* 382).

[2] **parliamentary** 'parliamentary train' (carrying passengers at a rate not exceeding one penny a mile). First *OED* ex 1864. − 'I came forty mile by Parliamentary this morning' (*HT* 1 12 78).

parlour-maid. − Miss Monflather's parlour-maid inspected all visitors before admitting them (*OCS* 31 234).

participled, a euphemism for 'damned'. Now obsolete. First *OED* ex 1887. − 'they are so' − Participled − 'sentimental!' (*CS* 341, 1862).

[1] **partickler,** noun, adj., and adv., a spelling used to suggest an uneducated pronunciation. − I am so very anxious to hear the *par-*

ticklers. (*Pilgr.* 1 14, 1833). − 'which is your partickler wanity?' (*PP* 45 634). − 'He wants you partickler; and no one else'll do' (*PP* 15 193).

[1] **particular** 'fog'. − 'This is a London particular... A fog, miss.' (*BH* 3 28).

[4] **go partners.** This idiom is listed in the *OED* s.v. *go,* 35.c., but no example is given. − Isabella Wardle and Mr. Trundle 'went partners' [at cards] (*PP* 6 70).

pastoral 'resembling a shepherd'. Not in the *OED*. − Another man in a sheepskin, who always lies asleep in the sun ... is the Pastorial Model. (*Letters from Charles Dickens to Angela Burdett-Coutts,* p. 66, March 18, 1845).

pastureless. Not in the *OED*. − the circumjacent region of sitting-room was of a comparatively pastureless and shifty character (*GE* 22 169).

patent theatre 'a theatre established by Royal patent'. − Why were they not engaged at one of the patent theatres? (*SB* 252).

[2] **patten** 'walk about on pattens'. − These household cares involve much pattening and counter-pattening in the backyard (*BH* 27 386).

patter-allusion. − See II.35.

pending, preposition. − See II. 30.

penitentials 'black clothes'. − he emerged ... in a full suit of Sunday penitentials. (*GE* 4 20).

peppercorny. − Mr. Pumblechook's premises ... were of a

peppercorny and farinaceous character (*GE* 8 49).

performing, adj., of an animal trained to perform tricks. — Signor Jupe was that afternoon to 'elucidate the diverting accomplishments of his highly trained performing dog Merrylegs'. (*HT* 1 3 11).

perpendicular, noun, 'upright position'. First *OED* ex 1859. — ... several ineffectual attempts to preserve his perpendicular (*SB* 401).

[1] **perpetrate**, used humorously of doing anything which the speaker affects to treat as outrageous. First *OED* ex 1849. — He ... bribed a cheap miniature-painter to perpetrate a faint resemblance to a youthful face (*SB* 248).

perspirational. Not in the *OED*. — M'Ian was in a frightful state of perspirational excitement. (*Pilgr.* 5 556, 1849).

pet 'a sweet or obliging person'. — 'The Pet of the Fancy', or 'the Slashing Sailor Boy'... (*Pilgr.* 2 208, 1841).

[3] **pick up** 'cause (a person) to revive'. — Several of both kinds look in at the chemist's ... to be 'picked up'. (*CS* 749, 1857).

pickle-bottle. — Pickle bottles, wine bottles, ink bottles ... (*BH* 5 49).

pickle-jar. — Some pickle-jars ... (*SB* 178).

Pickwickian 'idiosyncratic, esoteric'. — he had used the word in its Pickwickian sense. (*PP* 1 5). Cf. I.7, II.36.

pigeon-breast 'a deformed human chest'. — That valiant general ... is an old, old man with ... the remains of a pigeon-breast in his military surtout. (*Pilgr.* 3 180, 1842).

pill-box 'carriage'. — a one-horse carriage, irreverently called, at that period of English history, a pill-box. (*LD* I 33 390).

pint 'point'. — 'Upon all little pints o' breedin', I know I may trust you as vell as if it was my own self' (*PP* 23 315).

pipe-bowl. — the pipe-bowl ... is burning low (*BH* 21 301).

pipe-smoke. — a cloud of pipe-smoke ... pervades the parlour (*BH* 11 149).

pipe-smoking. — 'I'll have no more of your pipe-smokings and swaggerings' (*BH* 34 481).

[3] **pipe up** 'speak in a piping voice'. First *OED* ex 1889. — Mrs. Smallweed instantly begins to shake her head, and pipe up, 'Seventy-six pound seven and sevenpence! ...' (*BH* 33 466).

[2] **pistol**, transitive and intransitive vb. Not in the *OED*. — 'If he was to talk of pistolling 'em all, I should be obliged to say, "Certainly. Serve 'em right."' (*NN* 31 406). — should we not know that they who among their equals stab and pistol in the legislative halls ... must be to their dependants ... so many merciless and unrelenting tyrants? (*AN* 17 242).

[4] **put a pistol to somebody's head** 'coerce somebody'. — Put a pistol to Chapman's head, and de-

mand the blocks of him. (*Pilgr.* 2 220, 1841).

[4] **pitch it strong** 'express oneself forcefully'. — 'I'm going to write to my father, and I must have a stimulant, or I shan't be able to pitch it strong enough into the old boy.' (*PP* 40 564f.).

pledge oneself 'bind oneself by a pledge'. — He could not ... pledge himself whether it would appear this season ... (*Pilgr.* 1 198, 1836).

[3] **pluck up** 'recover strength'. First *OED* ex 1842 (*AN*). — the worthy Mr. Lillyvick ... plucked up amazingly (*NN* 14 167).

[4] **make the plunge** 'take a decisive first step'. — The venture is quite decided on; and I have made the Plunge. (*Pilgr.* 4 412, 1845).

Podsnappery. — See II.36.

point of departure. — he passed on to both [*sc.* subjects], and both brought him round again ... to his point of departure. (*LD* II 13 583).

[4] **not to put too fine a point upon it** 'bluntly'. — See II.12.

poison bottle. — 'It were the Poison-bottle on table' (*HT* 1 13 88f.).

police station. — the hall ... is as dirty as a police-station in London (*PI* 293).

pollard 'bald-headed'. — On his 'days out', those flecks of light in his flat vista of pollard old men, it was at once Mrs. Plornish's delight and sorrow ... to say, 'Sing us a song, Father.' (*LD* I 31 364).

[2] **poll-parrot**, transitive and in-transitive vb. — 'What are you Poll Parroting at now? ... But don't Poll Parrot me.' (*OMF* II 12 356).

[1] **Polly** 'a bottle of Apollinaris water'. — 'four small rums is eight and three, and three Pollys is eight and six' (*BH* 20 282).

polygamically. — To suppose the family groups of whom the majority of emigrants were composed, polygamically possessed, would be to suppose an absurdity. (*UT* 230, 1863).

ponging, of an actor: amplifying the text of his part. The word is not in the *OED*; the first example of the vb. *pong* is from 1893. — 'Missed his tip at the banners, too, and was loose in his ponging.' (*HT* 1 6 31). Cf. **gag.**

pony power, formed on the analogy of *horse power.* Not in the *OED*. — It certainly was not called a small steamboat without reason ... I should think it must have been of about half a pony power. (*AN* 5 72).

pooh-pooher. — The pooh-poohers and Lord Burleighs have it hollow, all the world through (*Pilgr.* 2 249, 1841; the letter concerns Thomas Hill, and the editor points out that one of Hill's catch-phrases was 'Pooh! pooh! I happen to know', which probably accounts for the neologism).

[2] **poor**, vb. — Miss Lavinia ... put in that she didn't want to be 'poored by pa', or anybody else. (*OMF* I 4 36).

⁴all porter and skittles 'unmixed enjoyment'. – See II.12.

postman's knock, used in allusion to a parlour game in which the participants in turn take the role of postman and deliver letters which are paid for by kisses. – ... skimming over the ice on one foot, and occasionally giving a twopenny postman's knock upon it, with the other (*PP* 30 413).

postscript 'an additional or conclusory remark'. First *OED* ex 1926. – 'I have taken the liberty of calling upon you, Mr. Twemlow, to add a sort of postscript to what I said that day.' (*OMF* III 17 620).

practicable, adj. – See II.35.

prawn, used of a person. – You never saw such a human Prawn as he looked, in your life. (*Pilgr.* 4 253, 1845).

precipitate, noun, in chemistry used of a substance separated from a solution. First *OED* ex 1851; here used figuratively. – ... a heap of minute wax dolls ... in the direst confusion, with their feet on one another's heads, and a precipitate of broken arms and legs at the bottom. (*CB* 341, 1848).

prejoction. Not in the *OED*. – I suppose, 'under the circumstances' there is no prejoction? (*Pilgr.* 1 563, 1839; the editor comments: 'Perhaps a fusion of "prejudice" and "objection" – an early Gampism').

a present from: an inscription on a piece of souvenir pottery. – ...

we found a mug, with 'A Present from Tunbridge Wells' on it (*BH* 4 40).

preventible. – ... preventible sickness and death (*UT* 385, 1850).

²price 'assess the price of'. This sense is not in the *OED*. – Mrs. Perch ... has made the tour of the establishment, and priced the silks and damasks by the yard (*DS* 35 497).

the price of 'money enough to pay for'. Not in the *OED*. – See II.6.

primeness, used in a special, contextually conditioned sense. – See II.19.

⁴as plain as print. First *OED* ex 1895. – 'if you have put us in danger of being sold up – and I see sold up in your face ... as plain as print' (*BH* 34 475).

prisonous. – His son began ... to be of the prison prisonous and of the streets streety. (*LD* I 6 64; cf. 1 Cor. 15:47).

proctorial 'relating to a proctor in the ecclesiastical courts'. First *OED* ex 1883. – I observed, however, that Mr. Spenlow's proctorial gown and stiff cravat took Peggotty down a little (*DC* 33 475).

produce 'bring (a performance) before the public'. – A farce in two acts ... to be produced at the Saint James's Theatre (*Pilgr.* 1 171, 1836).

professional 'a professional man'. – the family practitioner opening the room door for that distinguished professional (*DS* 1 5).

projectress. First *OED* ex 1880. – ... on the authority of the projectress (*HW* I 86, 1850).

[1] **promiscuous** 'casual'. – 'I walked in ... just to say good mornin', and went, in a permiscuous manner, upstairs' (*PP* 34 476).

promise-breaking, adj. – See II. 22.

prompterian. Not in the *OED*. – See II.46.

proprietorship 'owners collectively'. – See II.40.

[1] **prose** 'dull person'. – See II.40.

proud-stomached. – See II.21.

[4] **prunes and prism(s)** 'affected speech or behaviour'. – See II. 36.

Prussian blue, in Dickens probably a variant or intensive of 'true blue' (*OED*). – 'Vell, Sammy,' said the father. 'Vell, my Prooshun Blue,' responded the son. (*PP* 33 450).

puddled 'filled with puddles'. – one ... let the fragment of his torch fall hissing on the puddled ground. (*BR* 16 123).

pull 'a rough proof'. – The carriage ... is to call for a pull of the first part of the *Cricket.* (*Pilgr.* 4 423, 1845).

[3] **pull through** 'get through sickness, a trial, etc.'. – 'Bless your heart ... I shall be all right! I shall pull through, my dear!' (*BH* 37 529).

[3] **pull up** 'bring a vehicle to a stop'. First *OED* ex 1844. – the moment there is the slightest indication of 'pulling up' at the corner of Regent Street (*SB* 140).

[2] **pull-up** 'sudden stop', used figuratively. First *OED* ex 1854. – See II.16.

pulverization 'moral defeat'. First *OED* ex 1873. – I waited only for what Mr. Micawber called the 'final pulverization of Heep' (*DC* 54 770).

punish 'sing (a tune) too vigorously, or badly'. – But he punished the Amens tremendously (*GE* 4 21; of a singer who 'had a deep voice which he was uncommonly proud of').

pupil-less. – 'I perceive the schoolmaster on the watch; sometimes accompanied by his hopeful pupil; oftener pupil-less.' (*OMF* III 10 542).

[3] **put back** 'defer, put off'. First *OED* ex 1885. – The dinner was put back an hour... (*BH* 9 116).

[3] **put up** 'bring (a play) on the stage for performance'. – I don't know what they put up at the Theatre for that night. (*Pilgr.* 1 465, 1838).

putter-in. There is an *OED* example of technical use from 1881; **taker-out** is not in the *OED*. – It is because my cut-out way in life obliges me to be so much upon the strain, that I think it [i.e. a shower bath] is of service to me as a refresher – not as a taker out, but as a putter in of energy. (*Letters from Charles Dickens to Angela Burdett-Coutts,* 1852, p. 193).

quencher 'a drink'. – See II.17.

race-horse, used attributively. – Barnaby moves – not at race-horse speed. (*Pilgr.* 1 605, 1839).

racket-ground. – This area ... was the racket-ground. (*PP* 41, 574).

rampacious. – ... a stone statue of some rampacious animal with flowing mane and tail (*PP* 22 303).

[4]**on the rampage.** – 'she's been on the Ram-page, this last spell, about five minutes, Pip' (*GE* 2 7).

ramshacklement. Not in the *OED*. – See II.18.

rasper 'an unpleasant person'. – See II.17.

raspish 'irritating, irritable'. – 'You are such a waspish, raspish, ill-conditioned chap, you see,' said Mr. Bounderby (*HT* 2 5 152).

[1]**rattle** 'ride (in a rattletrap?)'. Not in the *OED*. – 'if I have a good rattle to London and back in a post-chaise, and put that down at four pounds, I shall have saved one...' (*BH* 9 114).

ravenless. Not in the *OED*. – See II.24.

reason 'say by way of argument'. – What *have* I done?' reasoned poor Joe. (*BR* 1 8).

reception 'an ovation granted a popular actor on taking the stage'. First *OED* ex 1847. – 'What do you mean by a reception?' asked Nicholas. 'Jupiter!' exclaimed Mr. Folair, 'what an unsophisticated shepherd you are, Johnson! Why, applause from the house when you first come on...' (*NN* 29 378).

[3]**reckon up** 'estimate the character of (a person)'. – 'the deceased Mr. Tulkinghorn employ-ed me to reckon up her Ladyship – if you'll excuse my making use of the term we commonly employ – and I reckoned her up, so far, completely.' (*BH* 54 727f.).

reconsignment. – she is admonished ..., on point of instant reconsignment to her patron saint, not to omit the ceremony of announcement. (*BH* 19 261).

red-eyed 'having the eyelids reddened by tears, want of sleep, or the like'. – It was as heavy on him in his scanty sleep, as in his red-eyed waking hours. (*OMF* IV 15 791).

refresher 'reminder'. – His memory had received a very disagreeable refresher on the subject of Mrs. Bardell's action. (*PP* 31 422).

refreshment bar. – Crowds of us had sandwiches and ginger-beer at the refreshment-bars ... in the Theatre. (*UT* 34, 1860).

refreshmenter 'staff member of a refreshment room'. Not in the *OED*. – I look upon us Refreshmenters as ockipying the only proudly independent footing on the Line. (*CS* 516, 1866).

reg'lar, indicating a colloquial pronunciation of *regular*. – The Newhaven serenade was not so good; though there were a great many voices, and a 'reg'lar' band. (*Pilgr*. 3 69, 1842).

regular, adj., of a long-standing client or customer. – the regular Maypole customers ... each ... in his allotted seat... (*BR* 11 85).

regulation, used attributively. –

See II.14.

resurrectionary. — old men and women, ugly and blind, who always seemed by resurrectionary process to be recalled out of the elements for the sudden peopling of the solitude! (*UT* 63, 1860).

[2]**revise** 'a revised version'. — Mr. Dickens will be glad if Mr. Newby will send a complete revise of the whole book (*Pilgr.* 4 153, 1844).

revive 'treat (faded clothing, etc.) with a reviver' (see below). — It [*sc.* a hat] was as black as the coat. The truth flashed suddenly upon us — they had been 're-vived'. (*SB* 264).

reviver 'a preparation for restoring a faded colour'. — It is a deceitful liquid that black and blue reviver. (*SB* 264).

[4]**good riddance of bad rubbish.** — A good riddance of bad rubbish! ... Get along with you, or I'll have you carried out!' (*DS* 44 617).

ridgy 'producing ridges'. This sense is not in the *OED*. — See II. 26.

right-hander 'a blow struck with the right hand'. First *OED* ex 1857. — I have endeavoured to plant an indignant right-hander on the eye of certain Wicked Cant that makes my blood boil... (*Pilgr.* 4 232, 1844).

[3]**rile up** 'get angry'. — See II.34.

rim 'that part of the frame of a pair of spectacles which surrounds the lens'. — Mr. Wegg, in fitting on his spectacles, opened his eyes wide, over their rims...

(*OMF* III 6 480).

ring 'accompany with the ringing of a bell'. — The muffin boy rings his way down the little street, much more slowly than he is wont to do. (*SB* 53).

[3]**ring up** 'direct (a theatre-curtain) to be drawn up'. — 'Look sharp below there, gents ... they're a-going to ring up...' (*SB* 124).

ringing-up, noun; see preceding entry. — Let us take a peep 'behind', previous to the ringing up. (*SB* 123).

[2]**rinse** 'a wash'. — See II.14.

on the road, of a person travelling as a salesman. — I am both a town traveller and a country traveller, and am always on the road. (*UT* 1).

[4]**go with a roar** 'be a conspicuous success'. — It was a most prodigious success; and went, with a roar, all through. (*Pilgr.* 4 347, 1845).

robe 'a dressing-gown'. — she arose, put on a loose robe, and went out of her room (*HT* 2 8 189).

roll 'make (a cigarette) by rolling paper round loose tobacco'. — he was now rolling his tobacco into cigarettes, by the aid of little squares of paper (*LD* I 1 7).

roll-collar 'a turned-over collar on a garment'. — embroidered waistcoats with large flaps have yielded to double-breasted checks with roll-collars. (*SB* 74).

[4]**rolled into one.** — See II.3.

[2]**roman** 'a roman nose'. — 'Snubs and romans are plentiful e-

nough...' (*NN* 5 43).

Rooshan 'Russian'. — 'Some people ... may be Rooshans, and others may be Prooshans; they are born so, and will please themselves...' (*MC* 19 317).

²**rose-pink**, vb., 'colour with rose-pink'. — 'Where's the bleeding officer?' — 'Here!' replies the officer, who has been rose-pinking for the character. (*SB* 124f.).

¹**the rosy** 'wine'. — Richard Swiveller finished the rosy, and applied himself to the composition of another glassful... (*OCS* 7 54).

rough 'unrefined (but kindly or friendly)'. — See II.37.

roundaboutedly 'in a roundabout way'. — the schoolroom ... was euphuistically, not to say roundaboutedly, denominated 'the apartment allotted to study'... (*ED* 9 83).

round-elbowed. Not in the *OED*. — he stood poised on one leg, in a high-shouldered, round-elbowed state of elegance. (*BH* 14 190).

⁴**what's the row?** 'what's the matter?' — See II.12.

²**ruler** 'beat with a ruler'. — I think he was caned every day that half-year, except one holiday Monday when he was only ruler'd on both hands (*DC* 7 91).

rulering 'a beating with a ruler'. — See II.44.

rumness. — 'But what you may call the Fates ordered him into it [*sc.* the house] again. Which is rumness: ain't it?' (*OMF* III 3 447).

run 'a running away'. — 'If I didn't know he was too fond of me to make a run of it..., I should begin to be fidgety,' said Mr. Gills (*DS* 4 34).

³**run down**, used figuratively. First *OED* ex 1869. — That engaging old gentleman is still murmuring, like some wound-up instrument running down, 'How de do, sir...' And then having run down, he lapses into grinning silence... (*BH* 39 559).

³**run in upon**. Not in the *OED*. — 'I shall not be run in upon and worried like a rat.' (*DS* 55 768).

runaway, used attributively. First *OED* ex 1844 (*MC*). — We were about to remark that it was surely beyond post-time, and must have been a runaway knock... (*SB* 527).

¹**sad dog**, used in humorous reproof. — he had been a sad dog in his time... (*SB* 246).

Sahara, used figuratively. — the bleak wild solitude ... was a snowy Sahara. (*CS* 101, 1855).

⁴**as plain as Salisbury**. — See II. 12.

sandwich 'a person carrying two advertisement boards'. — See II. 41.

Saracenic 'barbaric, heathenish'. — so surely did old Lobbs commence swearing at him in a most Saracenic and ferocious manner... (*PP* 17 233).

sassagerial 'connected with sausages'. Not in the *OED*. — the sassagerial disturbance in him must have been so immense, that I thought he was gone. (*CS* 220,

1858).

saucepanful. − the other Princes and Princesses were squeezed into a ... corner to look at the Princess Alicia turning out the saucepanful of broth (*UT* 704, 1868).

saveloy 'sausage'. − Mr. Solomon Pell ... regaling himself ... with a cold collation of an Abernethy biscuit and a saveloy. (*PP* 55 771).

[1] **sawbones** 'surgeon'. − 'What, don't you know what a Sawbones is, Sir,' enquired Mr. Weller; 'I thought everybody know'd as a Sawbones was a Surgeon.' (*PP* 30 406).

sawdusty. First *OED* ex 1861 (*GE*). − that smell of sawdusty horses [*sc.* at Astley's] (*Pilgr.* 4 185, 1844).

Scheherazade, used allusively to suggest a type of storyteller. − My dear Scheherazade, − For I am sure your powers of narrative ... must be good for at least a thousand nights and one. (*Let.* 25 Oct. 1851, in W. Gérin, *E. Gaskell* (1976) xii 123).

score 'count, be reckoned in a score'. First *OED* ex 1885. − A gentleman or lady receiving visitors from without, or going out to tea, counts, as it were, accordingly; but visitings or tea-drinkings interchanged among Titbullians do not score. (*UT* 294).

scrape 'remove the dirt from the soles of (one's boots or shoes) by drawing them over a door-scraper'. − 'I'd scrape my shoes on the scraper of the door' (*MC* 43 663).

[4] **come up to the scratch,** used figuratively. − Pray, as a Member of the Committee, come up to the Scratch. (*Pilgr.* 3 513, 1843).

screw 'a penny packet of tobacco'. − The poisonous voice of envy distinctly asserted that he ... retailed ... tobacco by the screw... (*SB* 335).

screwed 'twisted into a spiral form'. − He held the usual screwed bit of whity-brown paper in his hand, from which he ever and again unscrewed a spare pinch of snuff. (*LD* I 19 221).

screw-power. Not in the *OED*. − taking her veiled nose between his thumb and finger, he appeared to throw the whole screw-power of his person into the wring he gave it. (*LD* II 23 691).

scrunch 'crush' in figurative use. Not in the *OED*. − 'I have found out that you must either scrunch them [*sc.* footmen], or let them scrunch you.' (*OMF* III 5 464).

scrunched. − he had compromised with the parents of three scrunched children, and just 'worked out' his fine, for knocking down an old lady. (*SB* 149).

[1] **searcher.** Not in the *OED*. − See II.17.

sea-sicky. Not in the *OED*. − See II.46.

season-ticket. − The regular passengers, who have season-tickets, go below to breakfast... (*SB* 102).

sedentary-pursuited. Not in the *OED*. − See II.21.

[4] **He will never see sixty-five again.** Not in the *OED*. − See II. 6.

³ **see somebody out** 'outlast somebody' (in a drinking contest). — 'I have heard him say that he could see the Dundee people out, any day, and walk home afterwards without staggering...' (*PP* 49 682).

seedy 'poorly'. First *OED* ex 1858. — Have been at work all day, and am seedy in consequence. (*Pilgr.* 5 165, 1847).

self-abnegating. First *OED* ex 1864. — He shook [hands] in a self-abnegating way, as one who shook for Tellson & Co. (*TC* 2 12 136).

self-committal. First *OED* ex 1862. — I have seen him so terrify a client or a witness by ceremoniously unfolding this pocket-handkerchief as if he were immediately going to blow his nose, and then pausing, as if he knew he should not have time to do it, before such client or witness committed himself, that the self-committal has followed directly, quite as a matter of course. (*GE* 29 227).

self-disrespect. Not in the *OED*. — He had, therefore, no self-disrespect to avenge... (*DS* 58 816).

self-distress. Not in the *OED*. — 'It would be useless self-distress and torment to reckon up such chances and possibilities...' (*BH* 44 608).

self-repressed. First *OED* ex 1870 (*ED*). — To say of a man so severely ... self-repressed that he is triumphant, would be to do him as great an injustice as to suppose him troubled with love or sentiment... (*BH* 41 574).

self-reproachful. First *OED* ex 1869. — I felt so miserable and self-reproachful... (*BH* 3 22).

self-snatchation. — I ... have no power of self-snatchation (forgive me if I coin that phrase) from the yawning gulf before me. (*MH* 48).

² **sell** 'an act of betrayal'. — 'I say, ... what a time this would be for a sell! I've got Phil Barker here: so drunk, that a boy might take him.' (*OT* 26 188).

³ **send round** 'send (a message) to someone in the neighbourhood'. 'I hope, Mr. Pip, you will excuse my sending round...' (*GE* 31 242).

² **serpentine** 'bring into a condition by serpentine behaviour'. — 'If you're an eel, sir, conduct yourself like one ... I am not going to be serpentined and corkscrewed out of my senses!' (*DC* 35 517).

² **set-out** 'a set of people'. — See II.16.

³ **sew up** 'nonplus'. — 'Here's Mr. Vinkle reg'larly sewed up with desperation, miss.' (*PP* 39 551).

shabby-gentility. — See II.45.

³ **shake together** 'muster'. Not in the *OED*. — Sadler's Wells Theatre ... was in the condition of being entirely delivered over to as ruffianly an audience as London could shake together. (*HW* I 344, 1851).

Shakespearianly. Not in the *OED*. — 'Then it was that I began, if I may so Shakespearianly express myself, to dwindle, peak and pine.' (*DC* 52 751).

shaky 'not completely sound in health'. — I am rather shaky just now, but shall pull up. (*Lett.* (1880) I 100, 1844).

shark-headed, shark-header, of a kind of screw. — 'a gross or two of shark-headed screws for general use ... And shark-headers is open to misrepresentations...' (*GE* 15 104).

sheep 'spy'. Not in the *OED*. — 'I wish for your sake Mr. Barsad was not a Sheep of the Prisons.' Sheep was a cant word of the time for a spy, under the gaolers. (*TC* 3 8 282).

shepherd, represented as an official title of the 'pastor' or 'minister' of a sect. — 'The kiss of peace,' says the shepherd; and then he kissed the women all round (*PP* 22 298).

[1] **the shivers** 'an attack of shivering'. — 'I'll beat the shivers so far, *I*'ll bet you.' (*GE* 3 16).

[4] **answer the shop.** First *OED* ex 1862. — 'there was ... only me to answer the shop.' (*BH* 42 585).

short-timer 'a child who is allowed to attend school for less than the full number of hours daily'. First *OED* ex 1883. — ... my visit to the Short-Timers (*UT* 214, 1860).

[4] **give the cold shoulder.** — 'He gives me the cold shoulder on this very matter' (*OCS* 66 498).

shovel-pitcher. Not in the *OED*. — he had been ten years a pickpocket, and as a 'shovel-pitcher', or passer of counterfeit money,

had visited every town in England. (*HW* I 240, 1851).

show 'a portable booth exhibiting strange objects'. — at his heels went Thomas Codlin, bearing the show as usual. (*OCS* 19 150).

show-fight, used attributively. Not in the *OED*. — See III.4.

[3] **shut up** 'be the end of (a matter)'. — 'Now, I'll tell you what it is, and this shuts it up; ... I'll let him off for another five down and a bottle of wine; and if you mean done, say done...' (*LD* I 12 141).

shy 'doubtful in amount or quality'. First *OED* ex 1850. — The accounts are rather shy, after *Dombey* (*Pilgr.* 5 610, 1849).

single-barrelled, of a railway station. Not in the *OED*. — Bang! a single-barrelled Station! (*UT* 477).

six-foot, ironical address to a small boy. Not in the *OED*. — But he [*sc.* a waiter] greatly relieved my mind by putting a chair for me at the table, and saying very affably, 'Now, six-foot! come on! (*DC* 5 66).

six-footer 'a coffin'. — He has received orders to construct 'a six-footer'. (*BH* 33 467).

six-roomer. First *OED* ex 1894. — 'It's a six-roomer, exclusive of kitchens,' said Mr. Guppy... (*BH* 64 861).

skeleton suit. — See II.10.

skirmishingly. — See II.29.

[2] **skylight** 'furnish with a skylight'. — If the Buffs proposed to new sky-light the market-place,

the Blues ... denounced the proceeding. (*PP* 13 158).

slack-bake 'bake insufficiently'. — Men ... who had mismanaged the workhouse, ground the paupers, diluted the beer, slackbaked the bread. (*SB* 22).

slack-baked, in figurative use. — one beaming smile, from his nutbrown face down to the slackbaked buckles in his shoes. (*BR* 41 307).

slangular 'pertaining to slang'. — See II.13.

[1] **slap-bang** 'an eating-house where no credit is given'. — They ... dined at the same slap-bang every day... (*SB* 266).

slashing 'very large'. — ... some fair creature with a slashing fortune at her own disposal (*HT* 2 7 174).

slip-room 'a long and narrow room'. — a baldheaded cobbler who rented a small slip-room in one of the upper galleries (*PP* 44 618).

slow-coach, of a person. — See II. 41.

Smallweedy. Not in the *OED*. — ... all the Smallweedy affairs of life (*BH* 34 478).

smartness, used as a countable in the plural. Not in the *OED*. — See III.7.

smear, intransitive vb. with reflexive function. Not in the *OED*. — Jo ... nods and shambles and shivers, and smears and blinks... (*BH* 46 635).

[3] **smear out** 'rub out with a smear'. — If he did by accident form a letter properly, he immediately smeared it out again with his arm. (*OCS* 3 28).

smifligate (variant of *spiflicate*) 'handle roughly, crush'. — Mr. Pyke threatened with many oaths to 'smifligate' a very old man (*NN* 27 349).

smifligation. — Mrs. Nickleby ... conjecturing ... that smifligation and bloodshed must be in the main one and the same thing (*NN* 27 349).

smoothingly. First *OED* ex 1854. — 'You are to reflect, Mr. Woodcourt,' observed Mr. Kenge, using his silver trowel, persuasively and smoothingly, 'that this has been a great cause' (*BH* 65 866).

sneezy (of things) 'dusty, causing one to sneeze'. — They ... have signed their names in one of the old sneezy registers... (*DS* 57 807f.).

within sniff of 'sniffing distance'. First *OED* ex 1878. — ... until he was brought at length within sniff of the sea. (*CS* 708, 1857).

up to snuff 'knowing, sharp', in attributive use. — an up-to-snuff old vagabond (*DS* 31 441).

[2] **soap-and-water** 'treat with soap and water'. — and Mrs. Miff says, by the bye she'll soap-and-water that 'ere tablet presently. (*DS* 31 437).

sofane, adj. — a sofa, of incomprehensible form regarded from any sofane point of view... (*UT* 56).

solitary 'solitary confinement'. — A.B. ..., committed for eighteen months' solitary, had himself said... (*HT* 1 5 24).

something else, in suggestive use. — See II.39.

something short 'undiluted spirits'. — 'If you'll order the waiter to deliver him anything short, he won't drink it off at once, won't he! — only try him!' (*PP* 46 653).

something-ean, of a category that is not or cannot be specified. — ... four something-ean singers in the costume of their country (*PP* 15 201).

soupy 'like soup'. First *OED* ex 1872. — I had been taking note of the crumbs on all the tables, the dirty table-cloths, the stuffy, soupy, airless atmosphere... (*UT* 333).

speak 'communicate with (a passing vessel) at sea', in transferred use. — Two or three stragglers ... 'spoke him' — so the captain entered it — on the subject of spectacles (*DS* 39 544).

speciality 'a thing or article specially characteristic of, produced or manufactured by, a particular place, business firm, etc.'. — The romantic drama ... is the speciality of your theatre. (*Lett.* (1880) II 191, 1863).

[1] **specimen,** used derogatorily of a person. — See II.41.

[4] **as broad awake as spectacles,** intensifying idiom. Not in the *OED*. — 'when you was as broad awake as spectacles' (*DS* 43 606).

spiter 'one who spites others'. Not in the *OED*. — He was hanged at the yard-arm ..., after having it impressively pointed out to him ... that this was what spiters came to. (*UT* 715, 1868).

[1] **spoffish** 'bustling, fussy, officious'. — a little spoffish man ... entered the room. (*SB* 361).

spoken, used elliptically of words which are spoken in connexion with a song. — 'I ... often giv' Mrs. Higden and Johnny a comic song myself, with "Spoken" in it ...' (*OMF* IV 16 810).

spongeless. — my sponge being left behind at the last Hotel... I went, spongeless, to pass the evening with the Family P. Salcy. (*UT* 271).

[1] **spot** 'inform against' (cant). — this man had 'spotted' the other, to save himself and get the money. (*OMF* I 12 159).

spout 'a lift formerly in use in pawnbrokers' shops, up which the articles pawned were taken for storage; a pawnshop'. — 'Eh?' said Jingle. 'Spout — dear relation — uncle Tom — couldn't help it — must eat, you know' (*PP* 42 597).

spumous 'foaming'. — some Coketown boys ... rowed a crazy boat, which made a spumous track upon the water (*HT* 2 1 112).

[1] **square** 'put (a matter) straight'. — 'I have squared it with the lad,' says Mr. Bucket, returning, 'and it's all right.' (*BH* 22 314).

[1] **squeaker** 'a (young) pig'. — 'If you'd been born a Squeaker —' (*GE* 4 24).

stablewards. — the helpers ... then lounged admiringly stablewards (*NN* 5 50).

stage-stricken. — The stage-stricken young gentlemen who ... long to embrace the theatrical profession (1838 *Mem. Grimaldi* i).

staggery 'liable to stagger'. — 'Why if I felt less like a walking brandy-bottle, I shouldn't be quite so staggery this mornin',' replied Sam. (*PP* 16 212).

[1] **stand** 'pay for (a treat)'. — See II.28.

stand 'place, leave standing'. — See II.28. For the verb used reflexively see III.37.

[1] **stand up** 'take shelter from rain'. First *OED* ex 1887. — nobody thought of 'standing up' under doorways or arches; they were painfully convinced it was a hopeless case (*SB* 472).

stand-up 'standing up boldly'. — 'he was ... one of the finest, stand-up men, you ever see.' (*BR* 39 298).

start 'an incident that causes surprise'. — 'what with your mother-in-law a-worrying me to go, and what with my looking for'ard to seein' some queer starts if I did, I put my name down for a ticket' (*PP* 22 298).

station-house 'the lock-up attached to a police-station'. — Tell them of hunger and the streets, ... the station-house, and the pawnbroker's, and they will understand you. (*SB* 205).

stay-at-home, noun. — a vast number both of travellers and stay-at-homes were in this condition... (*BR* 1 1).

steady-goer. — 'Always the vay vith these here old 'uns hows'ever, as is such steady goers to look at' (*PP* 18 246).

[2] **steam-rattle**, vb. — ... until I ... was being steam-rattled through the mists ... towards the lights of London. (*CS* 94).

[4] **stick it into** 'make extortionate charges from'. — 'in short, my dear fellow, we stick it into B. ... and make a devilish comfortable little property out of him' (*MC* 27 445).

sticker 'bill-sticker'. — I would introduce that something into a Posting-Bill, and place a large impression in the hands of an active sticker. (*UT* 413).

stony-toed. — And a breezy, goose-skinned, blue-nosed, red-eyed, stony-toed, tooth-chattering place it was... (*CB* 83).

[2] **strait-waistcoat**, vb. — 'Ve thought ve should ha' been obliged to strait-veskit him last night...' (*PP* 39 551).

street-breakfast. — At the corner of a by-street, near Temple Bar, was stationed a 'street-breakfast'. (*SB* 389f.).

streety 'characteristic of the streets'. — His son began ... to be of the prison prisonous and of the streets streety. (*LD* I 6 64; cf. **prisonous**).

[3] **strike upon** 'reach (the ear)'. — 'The words which cut me off from Miss Dombey for ever, will strike upon my ears like a knell...' (*DS* 56 791).

string box 'a box containing string'. — Mr. Snagsby has dealt ... in string boxes, rulers, inkstands ... ever since he was out of his time... (*BH* 10 127).

[4] **be a quick study** 'be a good memorizer'. — See II.35.

[3] **stump up** 'fork out'. — 'Why don't you ask your old governor to stump up?' (*SB* 449).

Sundays 'Sunday papers'. Not in the *OED*. — See II.14.

supernumerary. — See II.35.

suppose, used intransitively. — See II.28.

swarmer 'one of a swarm of insects'. — 'Oh, vermin!' said Mr. Pecksniff. 'Oh, bloodsuckers! ... vermin and swarmers...' (*MC* 52 802).

the Sweeps, a nickname for the Rifle Brigade. First *OED* ex 1879. — 'when I put up the window, and see them [*sc.* apprentices] standing on the door-step with their little pumps under their arms, I am actually reminded of the Sweeps.' (*BH* 38 538).

[1] **swipey** 'tipsy'. — See II.44.

swivel eye 'a squinting eye'. — she found herself possessed of what is colloquially termed a swivel eye (*OMF* II 12 351).

[3] **take down** 'get above (another scholar) in class'. — 'I took him down once, six boys in the arithmetic class' (*MC* 19 318).

take oneself off 'go away'. — he ... took himself off on tip-toe. (*OT* 24 173).

taker-out: see **putter-in.**

[3] **talk over** 'win over'. First *OED* ex 1862. — 'I am not to be talked over. *You* wouldn't be talked over, if you were used so' (*BH* 14 185).

[1] **tall,** of time: 'long'. — We were a pretty tall time coming that last fifteen mile. (*AN* 14 190).

teak-built, used figuratively. — the lovely Peg, that teak-built and trim ballad, that had gone ashore upon a rock, and split into mere planks and beams of rhyme. (*DS* 32 469).

[1] **tease** 'a person addicted to teasing'. — See II.40.

[2] **temporary** 'a person employed temporarily'. — 'Being only a permanency I couldn't be expected to show it like a temporary' (*DS* 3 31).

[4] **be on terms** 'be friends'. First *OED* ex 1864. — See II.38.

theatreless. *OED* ex 1853. — a tremendous storm of hail, rain, sleet, and thunder would burst out ..., and send us, theatreless, to bed. (*HW* II 415, 1852).

[4] **I don't think,** used after an ironical statement, to indicate that the reverse is intended. — See II.12.

three-out, noun, 'a glass holding a third of some measure of liquor'. — A couple of ladies ... having imbibed the contents of various 'three-outs' of gin and bitters ... (*SB* 70).

throwing-off, used attributively. — The throwing-off young gentleman ..., a bragging, vaunting, puffing young gentleman (*SB* 538).

[3] **tick off** 'mark with a tick'. First *OED* ex 1861 (*GE*). — there was something in this girl which could hardly be set forth in a tabular form ... he was not sure

that if he had been required ... to tick her off into columns in a parliamentary return, he would have quite known how to divide her. (*HT* I 14 92).

tickler 'something that tickles'. Not in the *OED* in this sense. − I want to know more about the promised 'tickler' (*Pilgr.* 2 237, 1841; an editorial comment informs us that Dickens's correspondent had told him that he was 'engaged in a new work, some parts of which will tickle you').

tidal train 'a train running in connexion with a tidal steamer'. First *OED* ex 1866. − The South-Eastern Company have brought Pavilionstone into such vogue, with their tidal trains, ... that a new Pavilionstone is rising up. (*UT* 447, 1855).

³**tide out** 'cause to flow as a tide or stream'. − See II.15.

tidy, adj., (1) 'pretty good'. − Which I thought for a coast-guardman was rather a tidy question. (Lett. 1844 (ed. 2) I 116). − (2) 'considerable'. − 'you came along at a tidy pace too' (*NN* 32 408).

¹**timber doodle** 'spirituous liquor'. First *OED* ex 1873. − See II.34.

time 'the duration of a term of imprisonment'. − he excused himself to the company by stating that his 'time' was only out an hour before (*OT* 18 133).

against time 'with the utmost speed'. First *OED* ex 1854. − the kennels seem to be doing matches against time ... (*SB* 135).

time-taking 'slow'. − Mr. Nickleby, who was a slow and time-taking speaker ... (*NN* 1 5).

tinderous 'tinder-like'. The quotation below antedates the *OED* example by a few months. − ... even old tinderous and touch-woody P.J.T. Possibly Jabbered Thus, at some odd times ... (*ED* 11 126).

⁴**miss one's tip** 'be unsuccessful'. − 'Jupe [a circus clown] has misssed his tip very often, lately ... Was short in his leaps and bad in his tumbling ... In a general way that's missing his tip' (*HT* I 6 31).

tip-cheese, the name of a game. − at tip-cheese, or odd and even, his hand is out. (*PP* 34 474).

title 'a titled person'. First *OED* ex 1900. − See II.40.

toady 'toadyish'. Not in the *OED*. − Mr. and Mrs. Pocket had a toady neighbour; a widow lady of that highly sympathetic nature that she agreed with everybody ... (*GE* 23 180).

⁴**Tom Tiddler's ground** 'a place where money can be easily made'. − See II.36.

³**tone down**. First *OED* ex 1860. − See II.15.

²**t'other** 'damn'. Not in the *OED*. − See II.39.

¹**touch** 'attain equality with'. − See II.43.

³**touch up** 'remind, jog the memory of'. − 'old Bounderby has been keeping me at it rather. But I touch him up with you when he comes it too strong ...' (*HT* I 14 93).

touch-me-not-ishness. — there was a dignity in the air, a touch-me-not-ishness in the walk ... of the spinster aunt ... (*PP* 8 96).

touchwoody. Not in the *OED*. See tinderous.

[1] town-mader 'townsman'. Not in the *OED*. — 'Regular town-maders?' asked Mr. Claypole. (*OT* 42 324).

[3] trade on 'take advantage of'. First *OED* ex 1884. — 'I saw how ... you were traded on in my name ...' (*DC* 45 660).

[3] trail off 'tail off'. — The soft-hearted Slowboy trailed off at this juncture into such a deplorable howl ... (*CB* 220).

[2] train 'go by train'. First *OED* ex 1888. — Again — who, coming and going, pitching and tossing, boating and training ..., could ever have calculated the fees to be paid at an old-fashioned house? (*UT* 449).

transcendental, applied to the movement of thought in New England of which Emerson was the principal figure (*OED* 3.d.). — 'Two literary ladies present their compliments to the mother of the modern Gracchi ... It may be another bond of union ... to observe, that the two L.L.'s are Transcendental' (*MC* 34 542).

[2] treacle 'dose with treacle'. — a long row of boys waiting ... to be treacled ... (*NN* 8 89).

[2] Treasury, vb., in the passive: 'to be honoured by the Treasury'. — he ... was Treasuried, Barred, and Bishoped, as much as he would (*LD* I 33 399).

trembly. — 'it's very weak and silly of me ... to be so trembly and shaky' (*DS* 1 6).

Trinculize. Not in the *OED*. — See II.46.

[3] tuck into 'feed heartily on'. — 'if you'll just let little Wackford tuck into something fat' (*NN* 39 505).

tumbling boy 'acrobat'. — he sent an express to the wharf for the tumbling boy ... (*OCS* 11 84).

tumbling girl. First *OED* ex 1896. — 'I am thinking about Tom Gradgrind's whim ..., ma'am, of bringing up the tumbling-girl' (*HT* I 7 44).

turfy 'suggestive of horse-racing'. — it was an easy, horse-fleshy, turfy sort of thing to do. (*MC* 26 421).

turn 'a momentary shock'. — 'What a hard-hearted monster you must be, John, not to have said so, at once, and saved me such a turn!' (*CB* 192).

[4] on the turn 'growing angry'. Not in the *OED*. — My dog knew as well when she was on the turn as I did. (*CS* 442).

[3] turn out of 'get out of'. — My last special feat was turning out of bed at two, after a hard day ... (*UT* 94, 1860).

[1] turnip, humorously applied to a person. — 'But now,' continued Sam, 'now I find what a reg'lar soft-headed, inkred'lous turnip I must ha' been.' (*PP* 33 453).

twigsome 'twiggy'. — the twigsome trees by the wayside ... (*UT* 62, 1860).

twist (1) 'a contortion'. — Another dry twist in place of a smile, made his face crooked here. (*OMF* III 1 432). — (2) 'a strain of a limb or joint'. — 'You have got a twist in that bone ...' (*OMF* I 7 80).

unapproachable 'that cannot be approached in confidence or intimacy'. — 'Mr. Dombey is unapproachable by any one' (*DS* 53 750).

unbear 'free (a horse) from the bearing-rein'. — 'Unbear him half a moment to freshen him up, and I'll be back.' (*BH* 56 765).

unboy 'unman'. Not in the *OED* in this sense. — the small fifer ... seemed for the moment quite unboyed, though he speedily recovered his presence of mind. (*UT* 213, 1860).

²**unchangeable**, converted into a noun. Not in the *OED*. — See II. 14.

²**uncommercial**, noun. — I have as much experience of French railways as most uncommercials. (*UT* 188, 1860).

under-idea. Not in the *OED*. — But my soul sinks before the commencement of the second part ... and the introduction of the under-idea. (*Pilgr.* 4 625, 1846).

undersawyer 'a subordinate or inferior person'. — See III.26.

undiscussible. — See II.27.

undistinctive. — See II.27.

¹**unholy** 'awful'. — An unholy glare ... shone in the eyes of Mr. Wegg (*OMF* IV 3 652).

unpensioning. — See II.27.

unpost. Not in the *OED*. — See III.24.

unpostponably. Not in the *OED*. — I am so deeply and unpostponably engaged ... (*Pilgr.* 5 193, 1847).

unprisoned 'released from prison'. — Perhaps not one of the unprisoned souls had been able quite to separate itself in living thought from its old companion. (*OCS* 52 389).

unproducible. Not in the *OED*. — See II.5.

unravenlike. Not in the *OED*. — Nothing can be more unravenlike than that. (*Pilgr.* 3 296, 1842).

unruffable. — Sam ... obeyed all his master's behests with ... unruffable composure ... (*PP* 33 447).

unruffianly. Not in the *OED*. — the Ruffian is tolerated among us to an extent that goes beyond all unruffianly endurance. (*UT* 301).

unscratchable. Not in the *OED*. — We had in my time ... fourteen hours' firing to fix the glaze and to make it 'run' all over us equally, so as to put a good shiny and unscratchable surface upon us. (*UT* 558).

unshiplike. — a sullen, cumbrous, ungraceful, unshiplike leviathan ... (*AN* 5 78).

unsnap 'undo the action of snapping'. — See II.27.

unweighable. — ... mysterious things ... are not settled to have been weighed and measured — or to have been unweighable and unmeasurable ... (*UT* 632, 1852).

[1] **up in** 'well versed in'. — 'Intrigue, and Ways and Means, you're all up in, so we shall only want one rehearsal...' (*NN* 23 295).

[1] **up to** 'engaged in'. — 'What's the old 'un up to now?' (*PP* 27 368).

up-all-night, used attributively. — See III.4.

up-towning 'going uptown'. Not in the *OED*. — 'Two can go uptown. Tain't only one wot can go uptown.' — 'Don't lose your temper,' said Joe. — 'Shall if I like,' growled Orlick. 'Some and their up-towning!' (*GE* 15 106).

used-up 'worn out, debilitated'. — 'a smoke-dried, sunburnt, used-up, invalided old dog of a Major' (*DS* 10 125).

uvularly. — Number Two laughed (very uvularly), and the skirmishers followed suit. (*UT* 24, 1860).

veinous 'having prominent veins'. — ... crouched on the veinous root of an old tree. (*DS* 27 381).

velveteeny. — He wore a fur cap, and shorts, and was of the velveteen race, velveteeny. (*UT* 96, 1860; cf. **prisonous**).

ventriloquial. — See II.32.

vestrylization 'decentralization'. Not in the *OED* (which, however, has the form *vestralization*, 1886). — you had an excellent opportunity of judging between this Centralization on the one hand, and what I may be permitted to call Vestrylization [laughter] on the other. (Fielding, p. 130, 1851).

vinegaring 'applying vinegar to'. — much damping of foreheads, and vinegaring of temples (*BR* 19 147).

vinegary, used figuratively. — A vinegary face has Mrs. Miff. (*DS* 31 436).

visit, in intransitive use. — See II. 28.

vixenish 'characteristic of a vixen'. — See II.23.

vociferate 'drive by means of clamour'. First *OED* ex 1880. — See II.28.

vocular. — See II.32.

vote of thanks. — Then a vote of thanks was moved to the mayor for his able conduct in the chair. (*PP* 13 174).

[1] **wag** 'play truant'. — See I.7.

wait 'the time of an audience's waiting between the acts'. — The waits between the acts being very much longer than the acts themselves. (letter quoted in Forster's *Life of Charles Dickens*, Vol. Two, p. 163 (1855)).

waiterhood. — There was an innocent young waiter ... as yet unversed in the wiles of waiterhood (*OMF* IV 4 669).

waitering 'the job of a waiter'. *OED* ex 1866. — What is the inference to be drawn respecting true Waitering? You must be bred to it. (*CS* 318, 1862).

[3] **walk into** 'devour greedily'. — See II.15.

walking-matching. — 'ever since I took to bird-catching and walking-matching ...' (*DS* 22 305).

wall-eyed 'squinting' or 'having eyes of different colour'. — a little, pale, wall-eyed, woe-be-gone inn (*BH* 39 547).

walnut-shelly, adj. – See II.26.

²**water-cart** 'sprinkle with water'. Not in the *OED*. – when the great metropolis is so much hotter, so much noisier, so much more dusty or so much more water-carted (*UT* 391).

¹**water-cart**, used attributively to refer to crying. – 'Come, come ... blow this 'ere water-cart bis'ness' (*PP* 16 215).

¹**waxy** 'angry'. – 'It would cheer him up more than anything, if I could make him a little waxy with me' (*BH* 24 353).

way 'progress, speed (of a ship)'. First *OED* ex 1857 (*LD*). – he came out of his corner with such way on him, that Rob retreated before him... (*DS* 25 354).

in this way 'thus', when not the manner of an action but the action itself is in question. – 'Come, come, ma'am,' said Mr. Pickwick, 'I can't let you cut an old friend in this way...' (*PP* 28 382).

beg one's way. – 'to-morrow we will beg our way to some quiet part of the country' (*OCS* 44 327).

Weggery 'behaviour typical of Silas Wegg'. Not in the *OED*. – ... the paths of Weggery (*OMF* III 14 578).

well, noun. (1) *a well of a (place),* i.e. damp, cold, and dark. – He then conveyed him ... into the veriest old well of a shivering best-parlour that ever was seen (*CB* 29). – (2) 'the space on the floor of a law-court where the solicitors sit'. – ... the various solicitors in the cause ... ranged in a line, in a long matted well ... between the registrar's red table and the silk gowns (*BH* 1 2). – (3) 'a deep narrow space formed by the surrounding walls of a building, or buildings'. – Climbing to a high chamber in a well of houses, he threw himself down in his clothes on a neglected bed. (*TC* II 5 85).

well-conducted 'displaying exemplary conduct, well-behaved'. – '... whether you consider me a highly virtuous ... and well-conducted man in private life' (*NN* 4 35).

wender. Not in the *OED*. – The few late wenders of their way... (*CS* 746).

West-ender. – a pleasant fiction, invented by jealous West-enders (*NN* 37 469).

⁴**fetch up/come up with a wet sail** 'make swift progress'. First *OED* ex 1876. – See II.12.

wet-feeted. – It was in vain for me to ... tell him he'd be ... wet-feeted to death by the slop and mess (*CS* 413, 1864).

whip, noun. (1) 'an appeal to a number of persons for contributions to a sum'. First *OED* ex 1861. – a whip of £ 3..10..0 each will handsomely and generously pay the wine charges on the late trip. (*Pilgr.* 5 137, 1847). – (2) 'organizing secretary of a political party'. – ... the Whip for his party hands it about ... to keep men together who want to be off. (*BH* 68 787).

whitewasher 'one who frees from blame'. First *OED* ex 1862. — The landlady's lively speech was received with greater favour at the Break of Day, than it would have elicited from certain amiable whitewashers of the class she so unreasonably objected to, nearer Great Britain. (*LD* I 11 127).

²**wholesale** 'sell wholesale'. First *OED* ex 1885. — we have been prevailed upon to allow this number of our Miscellany to be retailed to the public, or wholesaled to the trade, without any advance upon our usual price. (*SB* 644).

²**wide-awake** 'a wide-awake person'. *OED* ex 1890. — 'You have been told that he might pull through it..., Wide-Awake; have you?' said Fledgeby. (*OMF* III 12 564).

wiglomeration 'ceremonious fuss in legal proceedings'. — See II.45.

wind, noun, 'a symbolical representation of the wind'. — a cherub on a monument, with cheeks like a young Wind. (*DS* 31 442).

windmilly. — A windmilly country this (*UT* 271, 1863).

wine-vaults 'public house'. — The old tottering public-house is converted into a spacious and lofty 'wine-vaults'. (*SB* 67).

winter 'hibernate', in figurative use. — The Miss Willises ... seemed to have no separate existence, but to have made up their minds just to winter through life together. (*SB* 14).

¹**with** 'mixed with sugar'. — two glasses of rum-and-water 'warm with—' (*SB* 232).

¹**without** 'not mixed with sugar'. — glasses of brandy-and-water cold without ... (*SB* 103).

¹**work (somebody) off** 'hang (somebody)'. — 'wouldn't it be better for all parties if we was to work him off?' ... Hugh, inferring what his companion meant rather from his gestures than his technical mode of expressing himself ... rejected this proposition (*BR* 54 416).

workful 'full of hard work'. — You saw nothing in Coketown but what was severely workful. (*HT* I 5 22).

³**wrap up,** used absolutely with reflexive import. — 'She never wrapped up enough. If a man don't wrap up ... he has nothing to fall back upon' (*DS* 40 573).

wrapped-up 'muffled up in a wrap'. — the shining figure of a wrapped-up man (*BH* 2 9).

wrapper 'a sheet put over furniture for protection'. — the tarnished paws of gilded lions, stealthily put out from beneath their wrappers (*DS* 23 319).

wrench 'pain caused by separation'. First *OED* ex 1849. — I succeeded in detaching myself from it [*sc.* the *Daily News*], very early in its existence, by a great wrench (*Pilgr.* 5 74, 1847).

wrong 'keel over'. — See II.44.

yaw-yaw 'talk affectedly'. — See II.14.

yellow-boy 'guinea'. — 'the bright, shining yellow-boys' (*OCS* 42 316).

[2] **yellow-soap** 'wash with yellow soap'. — the children were yellow-soaped and flannelled, and towelled, till their faces shone again ... (*SB* 38).

APPENDIX B: ARCHAISMS

This is a list of words that were or became obsolete in Dickens's day.

admire 'wonder'. The last *OED* ex is from *DS*. – See II.8.

aggravator 'a greased lock of hair'. First ex: 'his hair carefully twisted into the outer corner of each eye, till it formed a variety of that description of semi-curls, usually known as "aggerawators".' (*SB* 230). Last ex 1861.

in bank 'in a bank, in store'. Last *OED* ex 1753. – ... with a handsome sum in bank (*BR* 82 631).

beglared 'glared at'. – a bystander, without beholding Mrs. Wilfer at all, must have known at whom she was glaring, by seeing her refracted from the countenance of the beglared one. (*OMF* III 16 613).

bend 'pervert'. – See II.7.

brown George, a kind of wig. First ex 1840, last ex 1882. – ... a theatrical wig, of a style and pattern known as a brown George (*NN* 25 326).

carry it 'behave, conduct oneself'. – See II.7.

clearness 'innocence'. Last *OED* ex 1701. – Clissold, being questioned, stood upon his perfect clearness in the matter (*CS* 280, 1860).

comportable 'consistent'. The only *OED* ex is from 1624. – the fine mask looked at him sideways with a stronger concentration of keenness, closeness, and dislike, than was comportable with its wearer's assumption of indifference. (*TC* 2 9 116).

correspondent 'a person who holds (secret) communication with another'. – See II.7.

crown-witness, presumably obsolete, though not labelled as such by the *OED*. – 'You were very sound, Sydney, in the matter of those crown-witnesses today.' (*TC* 2 5 83).

delivery 'communication, statement'. Last *OED* ex 1653. – 'one of the prophetic deliveries of M.R.F. must for ever remain unfulfilled.' (*OMF* I 12 147).

develop 'reveal'. – Nathaniel Pipkin determined that, come what might, he would develop the state of his feelings. (*PP* 17 230).

fortune 'a woman of fortune'. Last ex 1823. – she had *some* reason to believe the ladies were fortunes (*SB* 280).

godfatherly 'befitting a godfather'. – See II.7.

hard-favoured 'ugly'. Last ex: 'You have got it at last, sir,' says Mrs. Chadband, with another hard-favoured smile. (*BH* 19 268).

impression 'attack'. Last ex 1799. — See II.7.

kettle-drum 'kettle-drummer'. Last ex 1755. — a marine painter's Reading of the sea, the kettle-drum's Reading of an instrumental passage... (*OMF* III 10 542).

mark 'a badge worn by a pupil who has committed a fault'. — See II.8.

middle-aged 'mediaeval'. — See II.8.

rapine 'carry away by rapine'. — See II.7.

repressal 'repression'. The *OED* has only one example, dating from 1593. — It is clear that he [*sc.* the Ruffian] is, of all others, *the* offender for whose repressal we maintain a costly system of Police. (*UT* 308).

ridicule 'reticule'. Last *OED* ex: 'Pockets, women's ridicules...', said Mr. Claypole. (*OT* 42 321).

scratcher 'a toy producing a sound of tearing cloth when rubbed upon a person's back'. The only *OED* example is: 'The noise of these various instruments..., the 'scratchers', and the dancing, is perfectly bewildering. (*SB* 118).

shampoo, used figuratively, = 'brush'. — the other shampoo'd Mr. Winkle with a heavy clothes-brush. (*PP* 5 65).

spike park 'the grounds of a prison'. The only *OED* example is: 'Can't step far — no danger of overwalking yourself here — spike park.' (*PP* 42 597).

thin, of the members of a group: 'not numerous'. Last ex 1725. — But the number of workhouse inmates got thin as well as the paupers; and the board were in ecstasies. (*OT* 2 11; Dickens may have put the adjective to this use for the sake of the pun).

timber fiction. — See II.7.

toss up 'cook a meal hastily'. Last *OED* ex 1818. — the nice little hot dinner which the widow tossed up for him (*PP* 14 181).

trader 'a prostitute'. Last *OED* ex 1760. — 'Ha,ha! The liars that these traders are!' (*DC* 50 721).

BIBLIOGRAPHY

Editions

The Letters of Charles Dickens. The Pilgrim Edition:
Vol. One. 1820-1839. Edited by Madeline House and Graham Storey. Oxford 1965.
Vol. Two. 1840-1841. Edited by Madeline House and Graham Storey. Oxford 1969.
Vol. Three. 1842-1843. Edited by Madeline House, Graham Storey, and Kathleen Tillotson. Oxford 1974.
Vol. Four. 1844-1846. Edited by Kathleen Tillotson. Oxford 1977.
Vol. Five. 1847-1849. Edited by Graham Storey and K.J. Fielding. Oxford 1981.

Letters from Charles Dickens to Angela Burdett-Coutts 1841-1865. Selected and edited from the collection in the Pierpont-Morgan Library, with a critical and biographical introduction by Edgar Johnson. London 1955.

The Speeches of Charles Dickens. Edited by K.J. Fielding. Oxford 1960.

The Uncollected Writings of CHARLES DICKENS. Household Words 1850-1859. 2 vols. Edited by Harry Stone. Allen Lane, The Penguin Press 1969.

Memoirs of Joseph Grimaldi by Charles Dickens, edited by Richard Findlater, New York 1968.

Grammars and dictionaries

J. S. Farmer and W. E. Henley, *Slang and its Analogues.* Reprint edition 1970 by Arno Press, Inc. (originally published 1890-1904).

O. Jespersen, *A Modern English Grammar* I - VII, 1909-1949.

Lindley Murray, *English Grammar,* 1795. Reprinted by The Scolar Press, Menston 1968.

The Oxford English Dictionary with Supplement.

H. Poutsma, *A Grammar of Late Modern English* I – IV, Groningen 1904-1928.

F. Th. Visser, *An Historical Syntax of the English Language* I - III, 1963-1973.

J. Redding Ware, *Passing English of the Victorian Era:* A Dictionary of Heterodox English, Slang, and Phrase. London 1909.

Books and articles

Hans Aarsleff, *The Study of Language in England, 1780-1860.* Princeton University Press 1967.

Hans Aarsleff, *From Locke to Saussure.* Essays on the Study of Language and Intellectual History. University of Minnesota Press 1982.

Valerie Adams, *An Introduction to Modern English Word-Formation,* Longman 1973.

L. Borinsky, 'Dickens' Spätstil', *Die Neueren Sprachen,* vol. 6 (1957), 405-428.

G. L. Brook, *The Language of Dickens,* London 1970.

John Carey, *The Violent Effigy.* A Study of Dickens' Imagination. London 1973.

Seymour Chatman, *The Later Style of Henry James.* New York 1972.

A. O. Cockshut, *The Imagination of Charles Dickens.* London 1961.

Philip Collins (ed), *DICKENS. The Critical Heritage.* London 1971.

George H. Ford, *Dickens and His Readers,* Princeton University Press 1955.

George H. Ford and Lauriat Lane (eds), *The Dickens Critics,* Cornell University Press 1963.

Stanley Gerson, 'Dickens's Use of Malapropisms', *The Dickensian,* vol. 61 (1965), 40-45.

Stanley Gerson, *Sound and Symbol in the Dialogue of the Works of Charles Dickens.* Stockholm Studies in English XIX, Stockholm 1967.

Stephen C. Gill, '"Pickwick Papers" and the 'Chroniclers by the Line': A Note on Style'. *Modern Language Review* 1968, 33-36.

Edgar Johnson, *Charles Dickens. His Tragedy and Triumph,* 1 – 2. Little, Brown & Co. 1952.

Jean Mc Clure Kelty, 'The Modern Tone of Charles Dickens', *The Dickensian,* vol. 57 (1961), 160-165.

Mark Lambert, *Dickens and the Suspended Quotation.* Yale University Press 1981.

Inge Leimberg and Lothar Černy, *CHARLES DICKENS. Methoden und Begriffe der Kritik.* (Erträge der Forschung, Band 39, Darmstadt 1978).

Sylvère Monod, *Dickens the Novelist.* University of Oklahoma Press 1968.

Sylvère Monod, 'L'expression dans *Our Mutual Friend:* Manière ou maniérisme?' *Etudes anglaises* X (1957), 37-48.

Sylvère Monod, '"When the Battle's Lost and Won..." Dickens v. the Compositors of *Bleak House'. The Dickensian,* vol. 69 (1973), 3-12.

K. M. Elisabeth Murray, *Caught in the Web of Words.* James Murray and the Oxford English Dictionary. Yale University Press. New Haven and New York 1978.

Norman Page, '"A Language fit for Heroes". Speech in *Oliver Twist* and *Our Mutual Friend'. The Dickensian,* vol. 65 (1969), 100-107.

Norman Page, 'Forms of Address in Dickens'. *The Dickensian,* vol. 67 (1971), 16-20.

David Parker, 'Dickens's Archness'. *The Dickensian,* vol. 67 (1971), 149-158.

Louise Pound, 'The American Dialect of Charles Dickens'. *American Speech* 22 (1947), 124-130.

Randolph Quirk, 'Charles Dickens, Linguist', in *The Linguist and the English Language,* London 1974, 1-36.

J. C. Reid, *DICKENS: Little Dorrit.* Studies in English Literature No. 29, 1967.

Knud Sørensen, 'Subjective Narration in *Bleak House'. English Studies* vol. 40 (1959), 431-439.

Garrett Stewart, *Dickens and the Trials of Imagination.* Harvard University Press 1974.

Harry Stone, 'Dickens and Interior Monologue'. *PQ* 38 (1959), 52-65.

J. H. Stonehouse (ed), *Catalogue of the Library of Charles Dickens from Gadshill.* London 1935.

Kathleen Tillotson, *Novels of the Eighteen-Forties.* Oxford 1954.

Dorothy Van Ghent, 'The Dickens World: A View from Todger's', in M. Price (ed), *Dickens. A Collection of Critical Essays,* 1967.

Stephen Wall (ed), *Charles Dickens. A Critical Anthology.* Penguin Books 1970.

Tadao Yamamoto, *Growth and System of the Language of Charles Dickens.* An Introduction to a Dickens Lexicon. Revised edition, Kansai University Press 1952.

INDEX